Lecture Notes in Economics and Mathematical Systems

Managing Editors: M. Beckmann and W. Krelle

266

Multi-Stage Production Planning and Inventory Control

Edited by S. Axsäter, Ch. Schneeweiss and E. Silver

Springer-Verlag
Berlin Heidelberg New York Tokyo

ISBN 3-540-16436-7 Springer-Verlag Berlin Heidelberg New York Tokyo
ISBN 0-387-16436-7 Springer-Verlag New York Heidelberg Berlin Tokyo

Printing and binding: Beltz Offsetdruck, Hemsbach/Bergstr.
2142/3140-543210

P R E F A C E

Multi-Stage production planning and inventory control is one of the most challenging problem areas in the field of management. Quite generally, in any realistic multi-stage and stochastic situation it is concerned with how to lower the total of holding, set-up and shortage costs.

In particular three problems have to be solved. The first deals with stochastics, or more specifically with the sizing and location of safety stocks within a multi-stage (production or distribution) system. The second problem is concerned with multi-stage lot-sizing within an MRP-system and the third deals with coordination of decisions at different hierarchical planning levels. All three problems are interrelated and it is only recently that considerable progress has been made in each of the three areas.

Hence it was only natural to discuss the state of the art of these rapidly growing problem areas in production and inventory control and to organize a workshop which in October 1985 was held at the University of Mannheim, Germany. During two days about 40 specialists from 14 nations discussed 11 papers which were presented by research workers from many of the most active centers of production planning and inventory control all over the world. From the North American Continent, for instance, production groups from Cornell University (J. Muckstadt), MIT (S. Graves), and the University of Calgary (E. Silver) were represented whereas from Europe the groups at the Universities of Eindhoven (J. Wijngaard and K. v. Donselaar), Leuven (L. Gelders, v. Wassenhove, R. Luyten), Linköping (L. Rosling, H. Jönsson), Lulea (S. Axsäter), Hamburg (H. Stadtler) and Mannheim (H.O. Günther, C. Heinrich, Ch. Schneeweiss) presented their work.

Besides the working seminar in Igls and the International Symposium on Inventories of ISIR in Budapest the workshop represented one of the main activities in the production field in Europe. It continued the developments of two earlier workshops in Eindhoven and Gent, all three being, in part, activities of the European Working Group of Production and Inventory Control.

It is a great pleasure for us to present all the papers of the workshop in this proceedings volume. We arranged the papers according to the main themes mentioned above:
- Safety stocks and lot-sizing in inventory production and distribution systems,
- multi-stage lot-sizing,
- practical applications and integration problems.

A first paper "Some Modelling Theoretic Remarks on Multi-Stage Production Planning" which served as a short summary at the closing session, has been placed at the beginning of the proceedings as it may be useful as an orientation for the reader.

The workshop and hence the proceedings would not have been possible without the financial support of the German Research Foundation to which we would like to express our deep gratitude. Also we very much appreciate the hospitality of the University of Mannheim.

We wish to thank all attendents for their active participation in the many discussions. Special thanks, however, are due to the two discussants of each paper, who greatly contributed to the success of the workshop.

Finally we should like to express our gratitude to Mrs. G. Eberhard and Mrs. U. Wünsche-Preuss for their assistance during the workshop and in preparing the drafts, and to H.O. Günther and C. Heinrich who not only helped in the local organization but also contributed in arranging the scientific programme and in the publishing of these proceedings.

Sven Axsäter, Lulea, Sweden
Christoph Schneeweiss, Mannheim, Germany (FR)
Edward Silver, Calgary, Canada

December 1985

TABLE OF CONTENTS

SOME MODELLING THEORETIC REMARKS
ON MULTI-STAGE PRODUCTION PLANNING

Ch. Schneeweiss
University of Mannheim, Germany
D-6800 Mannheim 1, Schloss

Preliminary Remarks

The papers of these proceedings are grouped according to the areas
"Inventory and Distribution Problems", "Multi-Stage Lot-Sizing", and
"Practical Applications and Hierarchical Integration Problems". This
grouping represents only one possible way of showing the relationships
between the different contributions. In fact, there are many other
alternative aspects which could lead to different groupings.
Therefore, the following remarks may serve to exhibit some further
relations. Of course, an exhaustive discussion and appreciation of
all the different aspects the papers deal with is not intended.

Instead let us adopt the fairly general view of modelling theory. This
view might help to categorize the different approaches and to relate
them to the larger framework of production planning problems. It will
also show the different types of validations used in the papers and
will reveal areas which deserve still further research efforts.

1. Some Modelling Theoretic Aspects

Problem solving is often described as follows: given a problem at hand,
construct a model, solve the model, and implement the solution. Most
research workers, of course, would agree that this description is an
extremely simplified formulation of a rather complex process. In
contrast, however, we are all tempted to forget the complexity of this
process. This would not be too serious if we could in fact concentrate
on certain isolated aspects. If, however, such an isolation is not
possible, a broader view has to be adopted.

One of the most portentous observations seems to be that constructing
a model is not simply just a one stage process. In most cases one has
to costruct at least two models (see Fig. 1). The first model describes
the problem at hand with all its details as comprehensive as possible.
It will be called "Empirical Model" (EM) (or "Master Model" in [4]).
It is obtained from the problem at hand by an abstraction

process which may be called <u>pre-analysis</u> [4]. Usually the empirical model is far too complicated to allow for a calculation of decisions. However, if decisions are obtained by a heuristic or some kind of submodel, this permits the evaluation and ranking of the decision alternatives. Therefore a further reduction is necessary to obtain a "Formal Model" (FM) from which decisions may be derived. This reduction or <u>relaxation</u> process may be called <u>main-analysis</u> (see Fig. 1).

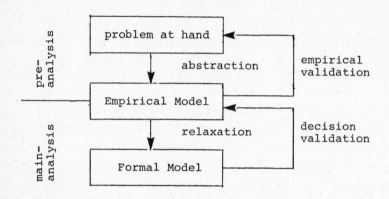

Fig. 1   Two-stage modelling process

The main idea of considering a two stage process can be seen in its conceptual ability of splitting the difficult task of validation. The Empirical Model has to be validated in quite a different way than the formal model. In fact, the Empirical Model has to be validated empirically with respect to its different hypotheses whereas the Formal Model is validated with respect to the decisions generated by this model. Hence one obtains considerable freedom for constructing a Formal Model, and this freedom will increase the better the Empirical Model is validated.

In principal, the two stage character of the modelling process is well known to all those who construct heuristics (often as special solutions to Formal Models) and test these heuristics at least with respect to a more realistic setting. Often, however, this relationship is not fully recognized. As an example let us consider the treatment

of costs. Costs are an empirical concept and belong to the EM-level.
Considering "costs" or "cost parameters" on the FM-level is only
correct if these values are not meant to be empirical quantities but
control variables which on the EM-level may influence empirically
measurable costs. This implies that on the FM-level costs should not
be "measured" but they should be adapted to the EM-level and thus
should be used as additional control parameters.

In order to gain a deeper insight into this so-called parameter
adaptation let us add some remarks concerning the main-analysis
(see also [2]). Usually a reduction from the empirical to the formal
model cannot be performed in one step. This is particularly true for
the complicated models of multi-stage production planning. Instead
a whole hierarchy of different reductions is considered consisting
of different lower model levels. The construction of this tree down
to the FM-level and the calculation of possible solutions is called
the construction phase of the main-analysis. In a second phase the
obtained solution has to be validated with respect to the Empirical
Model. This validation, however, is often only performed with respect
to an intermediate model, i.e. to a model within the reduction tree.
Sometimes this will suffice to select a suitable decision or at
least to outrank certain alternatives. This might be of considerable
help. Ultimately, however, a selection has of course,to be made with
resp. to the Empirical Model. (See Fig. 2).

In the next Section we shall try to construct such a model tree in
order to capture at least some aspects of the papers published in
this volume.

2. A Modellogramm for Some Important Multi-Stage Production Planning Models

The contributions of this proceedings volume concentrate on three
main problems
- integration of hierarchical planning models
- determination of safety stocks
- multi-stage lot-sizing
Only for the last topic shall we try (in Section 2.3) to construct a
detailed "modellogramm".

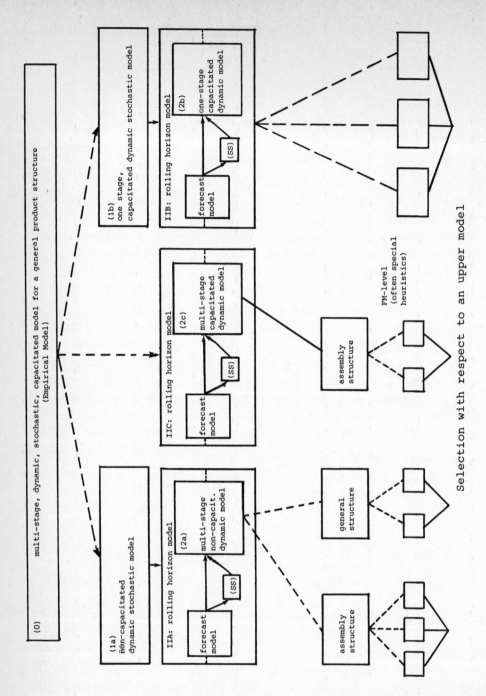

Fig. 2 Modellogramm for production lot-sizing problems

2.1 Integration of Hierarchical Planning Levels

Production models usually have a hierarchical structure consisting of many levels. Two of these levels are of particular interest. These are well known as medium and short term planning levels with the Master Production Schedules (MPS) as their interface. In most cases this two level structure is not just an abstract conceptual invention but is given by the structure of the organization being considered. Hence one of the main planning problems is the integration of these two levels, i.e. how decisions on the two levels can be adapted to each other.

At the medium level not only the aggregation of products and production facilities is of importance but also of planning intervals. It is this problem of a suitable aggregation-disaggregation of time which is the main concern of the paper of Stadtler. Problems of hierarchical integration are also discussed in the paper of Guenther within a special case study. In this paper, besides other problems of hierarchical integration, the problem of time-aggregation-disaggregation is also discussed, for which, however, due to the special case, a different solution is proposed. Furthermore, the paper of Graves et al. is also concerned with disaggregation problems. They allocate an aggregated safety stock, determined by medium term production smoothing to single items.

2.2 Coping with Stochastics

The most ambituous way of dealing with uncercainty within a multi-stage production or distribution system would be the application of stochastic dynamic programming or markovian decision processes (see the paper of van Luyten). This leads (at least for simpler production structures) to policies with implicitly defined safety stocks. For more complex structures, however, one treats stochastics within a rolling horizon procedure by updating forecasts and calculating safety stocks (see model IIa in the modellogramm of Fig. 2). This can be done on an aggregated (Graves et al.) or a disaggregated level (Jönsson/Silver, Donselaar/Wijngaard) for production systems (Graves et al., Donselaar/Wijngaard) or for inventory distribution systems (Jönsson/Silver). All three papers discuss a two-stage system for which the question arises at which stage safety stocks should be located and how large they should be. Graves et al. use decision rules

for a highly aggregated problem whereas the paper of Donselaar/
Wijngaard applies (S,S)-policies for a disaggregated single item
problem. Since (S,S)-policies may be approximately considered as
special linear policies [3] both papers reveal an interesting
relationship at least as far as the determination of safety stocks
is concerned and which may be exploited in order to gain further
insight into some difficult mathematical problems both papers have
to deal with.

All three papers compare different possibilites of locating and
sizing safety stocks. For a distribution system (Jönsson/Silver)
the question arises how much inventory should be stocked at the
lowest level of the system whereas in the papers of Donselaar/
Wijngaard and Graves et al. the question of locating and sizing
safety stocks between two main production levels is considered.
In the paper of Jönsson/Silver three different policies are
compared:
(1) a simple policy which ships the total amount to the lowest level
    and which does not allow redistribution,
(2) a complete redistribution policy, and
(3) a policy which retains a certain amount at the higher level for
    later redistribution.

2.3 Multi-Stage and Multi-Item Lot-Sizing

The remaining five papers (Axsäter/Nuttle, Rosling, Heinrich/
Schneeweiss, Gelders, van Wassenhove, Muckstadt) are concerned
with deterministic models. For this type of problem the modellogramm
of Fig. 2 has been constructed. As a starting point let us take as an
Empirical Model (0) in Fig. 2) a multi-stage multi-item capacitated
stochastic dynamic production planning model (for which a lot-sizing
decision is not known). As a first reduction (relaxation) we may
drop the capacity constraints and consider only the "pure" multi-stage
case (model (1a)). On the other hand (model (1b)) we may disregard the
multi-stage character but take into account capacity constraints. The
next reduction step concerns stochastics. Models (IIa) and (IIb)
represent rolling horizon models adjoined to (1a) and (1b)
respectively. We are left with the (deterministic) "windows" (2a) and
(2b) which are starting points for the 5 remaining papers, that is,
considering (2a) we are in the usual deterministic MRP-setting and
concerning (2b) we have the deterministic capacitated lot-sizing
problem.

For the capacitated lot-sizing problem (model (2b)) many heuristics have been developed, for instance the well known Dixon/Silver heuristic or the more recently proposed heuristic of Günther [1]. Gelders et al. present in their paper a straight forward branch and bound solution which may effectively be used as a heuristic.

The remaining 4 papers are concernced with the multi-stage situation. Assembly structures are investigated in the papers of Axsäter, Rosling and Muckstadt whereas general production structures are considered in Heinrich/Schneeweiss. The solution of the deterministic lot-sizing problem for assembly structures has been considerably advanced by the papers of Axsäter/Nuttle and Rosling. By a basically rather simple idea Axsäter and Nuttle demonstrate that on the average approximately 50% of the stages of an assembly structure can be shown to collapse. This leaves a much simpler problem for the application of heuristics or even to solve optimally the basic integer programming problem. Such an optimal solution, which is also achievable for larger problems is given in the paper of Rosling. His algorithm is based on a highly effective branch and bound procedure. For general structures Heinrich/Schneeweiss present an algorithm which is mainly based on the observation that the multi-stage character of a system should be incorporated into a model considering only constant demand. Time varying demand can then be taken into account on a one-stage basis. Compared to the rather extensive nearly optimal multi-pass heuristic of Graves the authors obtain promising results.

The four papers just mentioned only investigate the multi-stage non capacitated or the one stage capacitated relaxation. The remaining paper of Muckstadt considers, at least for an assembly structure, the more realistic situation of a capacitated multi-stage problem. Muckstadt develops an algorithm that can be used to establish the time between external procurements and between movement of stock from stage to stage recognizing handling and storage constraints.

Considering the modellogram of Fig. 2 all four papers (except for Axsäter/Nuttle, which gives structural results) have to be validated with resp. to an upper level model. This is often done only with respect to window (2a), (2b) or (2c). All comparisons with respect to the rolling horizon models IIa, IIb or IIc would of course be very reasonable, showing further properties of the developed solution prodecures. Finally, however, a comparison with respect to (1a) or (1b) or even to (0) should be done which then of course is superimposed by the

difficult problem of determining safety stocks. (Whether
one can use an intermediate model or an ultimate reference model
depends of course on the problem at hand. In fact, sometimes
stochastics may be neglected which would then leave us with (2a),
(2b) or (2c) as an Empirical Model. Since, however, a heuristic should
be able to take into account a fairly wide class of empirical problems
a validation with respect to "higher Empirical Models" would increase
its appicability.)

As already mentioned safety stocks have been dealt with in the four
papers described in Section 2.2. This have been done mostly for
special structures. The determination of the Safety Stock (SS) in
IIA is in general, a very difficult problem. Often it is necessary
to restrict oneself to rather specialized situations.

Summarizing, for most of the papers in this volume the modellogram
not only shows which type of models has been constructed. It also
shows with respect to which models they have been validated. Hence the
range of application can clearly be seen. Furthermore it plainly shows
the fields which still need further investigations. This includes
further research for problems with general production structures.
Furthermore far more efforts should be devoted to the realistic
capacitated multi-stage problem and to the optimal calculation of
safety stocks and safety times within a general MRP situation.

References

[1] Günther, H.O.: Planning Lot Sizes and Capacity Requirements in a
    Single Stage Production System, Mannheim 1985 (to be published
    in EJOR)

[2] Schneeweiss, Ch.: Construction and Selection of Quantitative
    Planning Models - A General Procedure Illustrated with Models
    for Stock Control, in: EJOR 6 (1981), pp. 372-379

[3] Schneeweiss, Ch.: Inventory-Production Theory, in: Lectures Notes
    in Economics and Mathematical Systems 151, Berlin-Heidelberg-New
    York 1977

[4] Schneeweiss, Ch.: On a Formalisation of the Process of Quantitative
    Model Building, Mannheim 1985 (to be published in EJOR)

TWO-STAGE PRODUCTION PLANNING IN A DYNAMIC ENVIRONMENT

Stephen C. Graves, Harlan C. Meal, Sriram Dasu, Yuping Qui

Alfred P. Sloan School of Management
Massachusetts Institute of Technology
Cambridge, MA 02139

INTRODUCTION AND OVERVIEW

In this document we report on research to develop and study
mathematical models for production smoothing in a dynamic production
environment. This effort was part of a larger study whose goal was
to investigate the production planning practices for an electronic
equipment manufacturing firm, and in particular to explore possible
mechanisms for improvement. To motivate the presentation of our
research, we indicate the nature of this production environment.

We were concerned with a component production facility. As is
typical for most classes of components, the facility is very capital
intensive, and it is expensive and/or difficult to change the
production level. Thus, the facility attempts to operate at an even
level with high utilization of the key resources. Furthermore, the
production lead time for the components is long relative to the
assembly lead time for the equipment which require these components.
Since component demand is derived from the equipment assembly
schedules, the predictability and stability of component demand
depends on the scheduling activity at the equipment facilities. In
our case, the equipment facilities were unable to freeze their
schedules, but revised them frequently to changes in their demand
forecasts. Hence, component demand had significant uncertainty and
variability within its manufacturing lead time. Nevertheless,
component production needed to provide a high level of service to
its customers, the equipment facilities. Finally, the manufacturing
process for the components is not totally reliable, but has
significant uncertainty in yield.

As a consequence of this characterization, the planning and
scheduling of component production needs to permit production

smoothing, while providing reliable service to its customers. In light of the uncertainty in the component manufacturing and demand processes, we examined a make-to-stock system. We considered a hierarchical planning system (Hax and Meal, 1975) with two levels: one to set the aggregate production level (e.g 400 lots/month) and one to schedule the daily lot starts (e.g. one lot of item j, two lots of item k ...). Our study then focused on the design of such a make-to-stock system.

Key questions in the design of a make-to-stock system are what items should be stocked, at what point(s) in the production process should stock be accumulated, and what stock level is needed to provide satisfactory service and permit adequate production smoothing. To address these questions, we must specify the rules or algorithms that will set the aggregate output rate and determine the daily production starts. We develop mathematical models, termed production smoothing models, to set the aggregate output rate. (For a review of production smoothing models, see Silver 1967.) We then give a mechanism for "disaggregating" the aggregate output into production starts for individual items. The analysis of these models determines the stock level(s) necessary for a desired service level. In addition, from these models one can quantify the tradeoff between the smoothness of aggregate production and the stock level.

In the next section we describe the production smoothing models and give their analyses. We first present a model for a one-stage production system. We then give two extensions to this model to treat a two-stage production system. To compare the models and evaluate their performance, we report in section 3 on a computational study based on data gathered from the electronic equipment manufacturer. In particular, we simulate the models over a wide range of parameter settings to assess their accuracy and to generate insight into their behavior.

DEVELOPMENT AND ANALYSIS OF PRODUCTION SMOOTHING MODELS

We develop here a set of production smoothing models that can be used to look at the tradeoffs between production smoothing and inventory requirements. We assume that production smoothing is done at an aggregate level for families of products that have similar processing requirements. For now, we will make the following simplifications:

we ignore lot-sizing considerations;

we assume no uncertainty in the build time for the
  products;

we assume no constraint on production capacity;

other simplifications will be introduced as needed.

The models focus on the production smoothing/inventory
considerations in the light of forecast uncertainty, demand
variability, and yield uncertainty. We will use a simulation to
examine the consequences of the simplifying assumptions.

We model the production activity in a very gross way. We are
not concerned with detailed scheduling issues, but rather with the
planning issues. We assume that the production system can be
decomposed into a series of stages where we may maintain an
inventory between successive stages and in finished goods (see
Figure 1). Then we assume a known and fixed lead time for each
stage: all production started at a stage at time t finishes that
stage at time $t+\ell$, for ℓ being the lead time of the stage. We are
concerned both with setting the aggregate production level for each
stage, and with deciding how to disaggregate it into a production
level for individual items. Furthermore, we want to understand how
much inventory is needed as safety stock, and where it is needed.
We desire to keep the aggregate production levels as smooth as
possible at each stage, and to keep the safety stocks as low as
possible, while providing satisfactory customer service. We have
developed a production smoothing model to illuminate these
tradeoffs.

To present the production smoothing models, we first describe
the aggregate forecast process that drives the production smoothing
models. We then consider production smoothing for one production
stage. We use the production smoothing model for one stage as the
building block for developing two distinct models for smoothing two
production stages.

Forecast Process

A key input to the production smoothing process is the forecast
of aggregate demand. We assume that this forecast is by month for
up to the next 12 months, and that it is revised monthly. To model
the process of forecast revision, we define $F_t(s)$ as the forecast
made at month t of aggregate demand in month s (s>t). Then, we
define $\delta_t(s)$ by

(1) $F_t(s) = F_{t-1}(s) + \delta_t(s)$

so that $\delta_t(s)$ denotes the change at time t in the aggregate forecast for time s. We assume that $\delta_t(s)$ is a random variable with the following characteristics:

$$E[\delta_t(s)] = 0 ,$$
$$Var[\delta_t(s)] = \sigma^2(s-t) ,$$

and $\delta_t(s)$ and $\delta_{t'}(s)$ are independent for all $t \neq t'$.

We denote the aggregate demand in month t as $F_t(t)$: the 'forecast' of demand in t made at time t. From (1), we can express the aggregate demand as

$$(2) \quad F_t(t) = F_{t-k}(t) + \sum_{i=1}^{k} \delta_{t-k+i}(t)$$

where $F_{t-k}(t)$ is the initial forecast for demand in t made k months ago. The k-month forecast error is given by

$$F_t(t) - F_{t-k}(t) = \sum_{i=1}^{k} \delta_{t-k+i}(t) ,$$

and has zero mean and variance equal to $\sum_{i=1}^{k} \sigma^2(k-i) = \sum_{j=0}^{k-1} \sigma^2(j)$.

Thus, the forecast not only is unbiased, but also improves over time.

We assume that the demand process, $D(t) = F_t(t)$, is stationary with $E[D(t)] = \bar{D}$, and $Var[D(t)] = \sigma_D^2$ for all t. (We will use D(t) and $F_t(t)$ interchangeably to denote aggregate demand in month t.) From (2) we now can compute the variance of $F_{t-k}(t)$:

$$Var[F_{t-k}(t)] = \sigma_D^2 - \sum_{j=0}^{k-1} \sigma^2(j) .$$

Thus, the variance of the initial forecast depends upon the forecast horizon length k. The longer is the forecast horizon, the smaller is the forecast variance; presumably, for a longer forecast horizon, there is less information available on aggregate demand and there is more likelihood to use $\bar{D}$ as the forecast.

Production Smoothing for One Stage

We now develop a production smoothing model for one production stage. We assume that the production stage produces one family and produces it to stock, i.e., a finished goods inventory. We use a

production smoothing model to set an aggregate production rate (e.g.
aggregate starts per month) for the family for each month. To set
the actual production starts we must disaggregate the aggregate
production plan according to the net requirements for individual
items.

To smooth production, we must maintain an inventory stock since
the aggregate production rate, being a smoothed average of the
aggregate demand rate, will deviate from the aggregate demand rate
over short time intervals. To determine the aggregate inventory
requirements we need to analyze the behavior of the production
smoothing model. In particular, we expect that the more we smooth
production, the greater will be the stock requirements. But since
customer service is determined by the stocks for individual items,
we also need to understand how the aggregate plan is to be
disaggregated.

The production smoothing model is given by

$$(3) \quad P(t+\ell) = \frac{1}{n+1} [F_t(t+1, t+\ell+n) - P(t+1, t+\ell-1) - \hat{I}(t) + SS]$$

where t denotes the current time period, and

$P(t+i)$ = the planned aggregate production started at time $t+i-\ell$ to be completed by time $t + i$;

ℓ = the lead time for production;

$F_t(t+1, t+\ell+n) = F_t(t+1) + \ldots + F_t(t+\ell+n)$;

$P (t+1, t+\ell-1) = P (t+1) + \ldots + P (t+\ell-1)$;

$\hat{I}(t)$ = aggregate inventory on-hand at start of time period t;

SS = target safety stock level;

n = window length.

Thus, in period t we set $P(t+\ell)$, the planned production to be
completed ℓ periods later. We assume that the lead time is
deterministic, but that there is uncertainty in the production yield
so that actual production completed at time $t+\ell$ will deviate from
$P(t+\ell)$. In (3), the term within the brackets represents the
forecast over the time interval $t+1, \ldots t+\ell+n$ minus the cumulative
production planned for completion by time $t+\ell-1$ and minus an
inventory adjustment (the difference between the actual and target
inventory). We term the quantity within the brackets to be the net
requirements over the time interval $t+\ell, t+\ell+1, \ldots t+\ell+n$. Thus, we
set $P(t+\ell)$ to be the average of the net requirements over this time

window $t+\ell$, ... $t+\ell+n$ where n is an integer decision variable equal to the length of the time window. The value of n will determine the level of production smoothing. The safety stock target, SS, is also a decision variable that is set to provide acceptable customer service on all items in the family.

We note that this production smoothing model is a linear rule. In this respect it is similar to the linear-decision-rule model developed by Holt et al. (1955,1956). However, our decision rule differs from that of Holt et al. in that it is not a consequence of minimizing some cost function. Rather, we just pose this decision rule in terms of its control parameters, n and SS, and will try to show that it is both an interesting and reasonable rule to consider. In this respect, it is very similar to the study by Cruickshanks et al (1984). It is simple and does permit analysis of its behavior. In particular, we will see that under suitable assumptions we obtain the disaggregation implications from this rule. Also, there is evidence that linear rules of this form are optimal or near optimal not only for quadratic cost functions but also for more general cost functions (Schneeweiss 1971, 1974). And, while the rule may not be the optimal form, we nevertheless can find the optimal parameter choice for this form.

We need to be careful to express all variables in (3) in common units. In particular, the units need be aggregate measures of production capacity. For instance, for the manufacture of integrated circuits it might be natural to express planned production in wafer starts. However, the actual inventory is likely to be known in terms of chips for individual items. Thus, we need translate, using yield factors, this actual inventory into the equivalent wafer starts for the items and then aggregate over all items in the family. Similarly, for the assembly of electronic equipment, we might express planned production in terms of required assembly hours; for a parts fabrication facility, the units might be machine hours required on the bottleneck facility.

To analyze (3) we use the inventory balance equation,

$$(4) \quad \hat{I}(t) = \hat{I}(t-1) + \hat{P}(t) - D(t)$$

where $\hat{P}(t)$ is the actual family production completed at time t and $D(t)$ is the family demand at time t. We assume that

$$(5) \quad \hat{P}(t) = P(t) - \varepsilon(t)$$

where $\varepsilon(t)$ is a random variable that reflects the yield uncertainty. We assume that $\varepsilon(t)$ is independent and identically distributed over time, has zero mean and has variance σ_P^2 .

Now we use (3) to consider the difference $P(t+\ell) - P(t+\ell-1)$:

$$(6) \quad P(t+\ell) - P(t+\ell-1) = \frac{1}{n+1} \{F_t(t+\ell+n) + \delta_t(t+1,t+\ell+n-1)$$
$$- F_{t-1}(t) - P(t+\ell-1)$$
$$+ P(t) - \hat{I}(t) + \hat{I}(t-1)\}$$

where $\delta_t(t+1,t+\ell+n-1) = \delta_t(t+1) + \ldots + \delta_t(t+\ell+n-1)$.
We use (4), (5) and the substitution $F_t(t) = D(t)$ to simplify (6) to

$$P(t+\ell) - P(t+\ell-1) = \frac{1}{n+1} \{F_t(t+\ell+n) + \delta_t(t,t+\ell+n-1)$$
$$- P(t+\ell-1) + \varepsilon(t)\} \ ,$$

from which we obtain

$$(7) \quad P(t+\ell) = \frac{1}{n+1} \{F_t(t+\ell+n) + \delta_t(t,t+\ell+n-1) + \varepsilon(t)\}$$
$$+ \frac{n}{n+1} \{P(t+\ell-1)\} \quad .$$

Thus, we see that the production smoothing model (3) is equivalent to (7), which is a simple smoothing equation. Planned production for time period $t+\ell$ is a weighted average of the planned production for the previous time period $t+\ell-1$, and the initial forecast for $t+\ell+n$, modified by the change in the cumulative forecast over the interval $(t,t+\ell+n-1)$ and by the realized yield deviation for the production completed in t. The window length n determines the weights so that $1/(n+1)$ is the smoothing parameter.

The significance of (7) is not only its interpretation as a simple smoothing equation, but also its usefulness for characterizing the long-term behavior of this production smoothing model. From (7), we can show that in steady-state

$$(8) \quad E[P(t+\ell)] = \bar{D}$$

and

$$(9) \quad Var[P(t+\ell)] = (\sigma_D^2 + \sigma_P^2) \ / \ (2n + 1) \quad .$$

We defer the details of this derivation to the appendix. We can also use (7) to characterize the production 'step',

$[P(t+\ell) - P(t+\ell-1)]$, as well as study other cases in which the demand process is not stationary (e.g., the demand process has a trend component or a seasonal component).

From (8) and (9) we see that the window length n does not affect the expected aggregate production rate, but does control the variability of the aggregate production rate. As we increase n, the production variance decreases and the aggregate production becomes smoother. Thus, the choice of n dictates the degree of production smoothing given by (3).

Aggregate Inventory Behavior

In addition to the aggregate production level, we also want to understand the behavior of the aggregate inventory level. This is necessary to see the effect of the production smoothing on customer service for individual items. To do this, we focus on $I(t+\ell)$: the planned aggregate inventory level at time $t+\ell$. At time t, $I(t+\ell)$ is defined as the current inventory at time t, plus planned production to be completed over $t+1, \ldots t+\ell$, minus the cumulative demand forecast through $t+\ell$:

$$(10) \qquad I(t+\ell) = \hat{I}(t) + P(t+1, t+\ell) - F_t(t+1, t+\ell).$$

By using (3) to substitute for $P(t+1, t+\ell-1)$ in (10), we obtain

$$(11) \qquad I(t+\ell) = SS + F_t(t+\ell+1, t+\ell+n) - nP(t+\ell).$$

From (11), we see that

$$(12) \qquad E[I(t+\ell)] = SS.$$

In addition, we can show its variance (after substantial algebra) to be

$$(13) \qquad Var[I(t+\ell)] = \frac{n^2}{2n+1} \cdot (\sigma_D^2 + \sigma_P^2)$$

$$+ \sum_{j=0}^{n-1} [1 - 2(\frac{n}{n+1})^{j+1}] [\sigma_D^2 - \sum_{i=0}^{P+j} \sigma^2(i)].$$

This characterization of the planned aggregate inventory level will be useful in determining the customer service level for a specification of the target safety stock SS and of the smoothing parameter n. While the expectation of planned inventory level equals the target safety stock, its variance depends on the window length n. From (13) we argue that the variance of the planned inventory level essentially increases linearly with the window length n, since the second term in (13) is dominated by the first (linear) term.

Disaggregation and Customer Service

To determine the proper choice for the target safety stock SS, we need to know how the aggregate inventory is spread over the individual items or equivalently, how the aggregate production level is disaggregated into item production. We must set the production starts for each item so that the planned production level for the family is achieved; that is,

$$\sum_k P(k,t+\ell) = P(t+\ell)$$

where $P(t+\ell)$ is given by (3) and $P(k,t+\ell)$ is the production level for item k started at time t for completion by time $t+\ell$. This implies that the planned inventory level for item k at time $t+\ell$, call it $I(k,t+\ell)$, must satisfy

$$(14) \qquad \sum_k I(k,t+\ell) = I(t+\ell)$$

where $I(t+\ell)$ is given by (10).

To characterize the service level for item k in period $t+\ell$ for a particular disaggregation, we can express its planned inventory as

$$I(k,t+\ell) = \hat{I}(k,t) + \sum_{i=1}^{\ell} [P(k,t+i) - F_t(k,t+i)]$$

where $\hat{I}(k,t)$ is current inventory and $F_t(k,t+i)$ is the current demand forecast for month $t+i$. The actual inventory at time $t+\ell$ will be

$$\hat{I}(k,t+\ell) = \hat{I}(k,t) + \sum_{i=1}^{\ell} [\hat{P}(k,t+i) - \hat{D}(k,t+i)]$$

where for time $t+i$, $\hat{P}(k,t+i)$ is actual production and $D(k,t+i)$ is demand, and where negative inventory denotes a backorder. We assume that the difference $I(k,t+\ell) - \hat{I}(k,t+\ell)$, which reflects the yield uncertainty and cumulative forecast error for k over the lead time of ℓ time periods, is a normally-distributed random variable with zero mean and a variance σ_k^2. Consequently, we can use $z_k = I(k,t+\ell) / \sigma_k$ to indicate the service level for k at time $t+\ell$ from a particular disaggregation (14). z_k denotes the number of standard deviations of safety stock protection provided by $I(k,t+\ell)$.

Now suppose we set $P(k,t+\ell)$, or equivalently $I(k,t+\ell)$, so that the likelihood of stockout in period $t+\ell$ is the same for all items. Thus, we want $z_k = z$ for all items k, or equivalently

(15) $\qquad I(k,t+\ell) = z \; \sigma_k$

for all k. By substituting (15) into (14), we find that

$$z = I(t+\ell) \; / \; \sum_k \sigma_k \; .$$

Thus, we can use (12) and (13) to characterize the service level (as specified by z) for a choice of SS and n. We see that z is a random variable, and thus the service level will vary from month to month. The expected service level depends only on the safety stock target SS. But the amount of variability in the service level depends on the smoothing parameter n; the more that we smooth production, the greater will be the variability in service from month to month.

We have assumed here that it will always be possible to disaggregate production to satisfy (15). This is not guaranteed. Indeed, if current inventories are 'out-of-balance', the simultaneous satisfaction of (14) and (15) may imply negative production ($P(k,t+\ell) < 0$) for items with large current inventories. Obviously, this is not possible. However, we expect that the assumption of 'balanced' inventories will be appropriate for the family of items that we produce to stock; we will test this assumption with the simulation exercise. We note that a similar assumption of 'balanced' inventories is made by Eppen and Schrage (1981) and by Federgruen and Zipkin (1984) in their studies on centralized ordering policies for multilocation distribution systems.

Two-Stage Models

In this section we extend the one-stage model to a production operation with two stages, e.g. fabrication and assembly. For such an operation we may have not only a finished goods inventory, but also an intermediate inventory between the two stages (see Figure 1). The intermediate inventory permits one to decouple, at least partially, the production of the upstream stage (parts fabrication) from that for the downstream stage (assembly). Thus, the production smoothing model needs to set aggregate production rates for both stages. In addition, we will need to characterize how each stage disaggregates the aggregate production plan.

We mention three approaches for production smoothing for two stages. The first approach is to view the two stages as one stage without an intermediate inventory, and then to use the previous model; we will not discuss this approach any further, but will include it in the simulation study of the various models. The second and third approach use the intermediate inventory to permit some decoupling of the stages. They differ in terms of how the upstream stage smooths its production. In the second model, production smoothing by the upstream stage relies on information about the intermediate inventory, and on forecasts of the production level for the downstream stage. In the third model, production smoothing by the upstream stage is based on the echelon inventory.

The notation will be very similar to that for the one-stage model. We let ℓ_1 and ℓ_2 denote the lead times for the upstream and downstream stage, respectively, and define $\ell=\ell_1+\ell_2$. Then at time t we want to find for the upstream stage $Q(t+\ell_1)$, planned production that starts in t to be completed by $t+\ell_1$, and for the downstream stage $P(t+\ell_2)$, planned production that starts in t to be completed by $t+\ell_2$. We use $J(t+\ell_1)$ to denote the planned intermediate inventory, and $I(t+\ell_2)$ to denote the planned finished-goods inventory, at the times $t+\ell_1$ and $t+\ell_2$, respectively.

We present these models for the simplest two-stage production environment. We assume that there is a one-to-one mapping between items produced in the upstream stage and items produced by the downstream stage. That is, each item from the upstream stage receives further processing at the downstream stage and results in a unique end item. Furthermore, we assume that the production units are defined so that one unit of downstream production starts requires as input one unit of completed upstream production. Although we present the models for this setting, we can extend it to more complex environments, such as when the downstream stage performs assembly of sets of components produced by the upstream stage.

To extend the one-stage model to a two-stage system requires the specification and analysis of a production smoothing rule for each stage. We desire to do this in a way that permits one to see how the planning at one stage impacts the other stage, and how the intermediate inventory can be used to decouple the stages. We discuss first the downstream stage, since it will be simpler.

Downstream Stage

The production smoothing model for the downstream stage is identical to that given for a one-stage system. Namely, we set the planned production level at time t for completion by time $t+\ell_2$ by the rule

$$(16) \qquad P(t+\ell_2) = \frac{1}{n+1} \{F_t(t+1,t+\ell_2+n) - P(t+1,t+\ell_2-1)$$

$$- \hat{I}(t) + SS_2\} \quad ,$$

where n is the window length and SS_2 is the finished-goods safety-stock target. Thus, as in (3) we set the planned production to equal the average of the net requirements over the time window $t+\ell_2$, ... $t+\ell_2+n$. We assume that sufficient component inventory is available to permit the execution of (16). As a consequence, the analyses from the previous section of the planned inventory apply directly to $P(t+\ell_2)$ given by (16) and to $I(t+\ell_2)$ as implied by (16). The extension of (3) to the upstream stage is less clear. This is because the demand on the upstream stage is not independent, but is set by the production by the downstream stage: $P(t+\ell_2)$ is the demand on the intermediate inventory at time t. Consequently, to extend (3) we need an appropriate forecast of the planned production for the downstream stage over the smoothing window for the upstream stage. We suggest below two approaches.

Upstream Stage: Production to Intermediate Inventory

The first approach is to smooth the upstream production using an explicit forecast of the downstream production over the smoothing window. The production smoothing rule is

$$(17) \qquad Q(t+\ell_1) = \frac{1}{m+1} \{P_t(t+\ell_2+1,t+\ell+m) - Q(t+1,t+\ell_1-1)$$

$$- \hat{J}(t) + SS_1\}$$

where m is the window length, $P_t(t+\ell_2+1,t+\ell+m) = P_t(t+\ell_2+1) + ... + P_t(t+\ell+m)$ and $P_t(t+\ell_2+i)$ is a forecast made at time t of $P(t+\ell_2+i)$ for $i=1, ... \ell_1+m$. $\hat{J}(t)$ denotes the actual intermediate inventory at time t, net of the downstream production started at time t; that is,

$$(18) \qquad \hat{J}(t) = \hat{J}(t-1) + \hat{Q}(t) - P(t+\ell_2) \quad ,$$

and SS_1 is the target safety stock for the intermediate inventory.

We note here that $P(t+\ell_2+i)$ will be the demand on the upstream stage at time $t+i$. Hence, $P_t(t+\ell_2+1, t+\ell+m)$ denotes the demand forecast for the upstream stage over the time interval $t+1, \ldots t+\ell_1+m$.

Using (18) we can rewrite (17) as a simple smoothing equation that is analogous to (7):

$$(19) \quad Q(t+\ell_1) = \frac{1}{m+1} \{P_t(t+\ell+m) + [P_t(t+\ell_2, t+\ell+m-1)$$

$$- P_{t-1}(t+\ell_2, t+\ell+m-1)] + \varepsilon_1(t)\} +$$

$$\frac{m}{m+1} \{Q(t+\ell_1-1)\}$$

where $\varepsilon_1(t) = Q(t) - \hat{Q}(t)$. Thus, planned production for the upstream stage is a weighted average of the production level from the previous period and the initial forecast of cumulative net requirements in time $t+\ell+m$.

To specify $P_t(t+\ell_2+i)$, we note that (16) is equivalent to a simple smoothing equation

$$(20) \quad P(t+\ell_2) = \frac{1}{n+1} \{F_t(t+\ell_2+n) + \delta_t(t, t+\ell_2+n-1) + \varepsilon_2(t)\}$$

$$+ \frac{n}{n+1} \{P(t+\ell_2-1)\}$$

where $\delta_t(\quad , \quad)$ is the forecast revision as defined before, and $\varepsilon_2(t) = P(t) - \hat{P}(t)$. Now the forecast of $P(t+\ell_2+1)$ made at time t should be

$$(21) \quad P_t(t+\ell_2+1) = (\frac{1}{n+1}) F_t(t+\ell_2+n+1) + (\frac{n}{n+1}) P(t+\ell_2) \quad ,$$

since the expected forecast revision is zero and the expected yield variation is zero. Similarly we can use (21) to forecast $P(t+\ell_2+i)$ for $i=2, \ldots \ell_1+m$:

$$(22) \quad P_t(t+\ell_2+2) = (\frac{1}{n+1}) F_t(t+\ell_2+n+2) + (\frac{n}{n+1}) P_t(t+\ell_2+1)$$

$$\vdots$$

$$P_t(t+\ell+m) = (\frac{1}{n+1}) F_t(t+\ell+m+n) + (\frac{n}{n+1}) P_t(t+\ell+m-1) \quad .$$

In spite of the fact that the smoothing equations for the upstream stage [(17) and (19)] have the same form as those for a single-stage system [(3) and (7)], we have not analyzed fully the random variable for planned production $Q(t+\ell_1)$. This is because the planned

upstream production $Q(t+\ell_1)$ is a smoothed average of the downstream
planned production, which itself is a smoothed average of customer
demand. We have not been able to 'decode' this double smoothing in
a way to find the variance of $Q(t+\ell_1)$, or any other measure of
production smoothing. (However, it is easy to show that $E[Q(t+\ell_1] =$
$\bar{D}$.) We will need to use simulation to see exactly the behavior of
this smoothing model. Despite this lack of an analytic result, we
do expect that the behavior of this smoothing model for the upstream
stage will closely parallel that predicted for a single-stage
system. In particular, due to the double smoothing, we expect that
the variability of the upstream production will depend upon the sum
of the window lengths, m+n.

The planned intermediate inventory at time $t+\ell_1$ is given by

$$J(t+\ell_1) = \hat{J}(t) + Q(t+1,t+\ell_1) - P_t(t+\ell_2+1,t+\ell),$$

which can be rewritten as

$$J(t+\ell_1) = SS_1 + P_t(t+\ell+1,t+\ell+m) - mQ(t+\ell_1)$$

by substituting from (17) for $Q(t+1,t+\ell_1-1)$. Again, although it is
clear that $E[J(t+\ell_1)] = SS_1$, we have not been able to characterize
analytically the variability in the planned intermediate inventory.
Nevertheless, we need the planned intermediate inventory to specify
how the upstream aggregate planned production $Q(t+\ell_1)$ is
disaggregated into planned production for individual items, e.g.
$Q(k,t+\ell_1)$ for item k.

For this model we disaggregate the upstream production to try
to equalize the service levels from the intermediate inventories
across all items. To do this, we set $Q(k,t+\ell_1)$ such that
$\sum_k Q(k,t+\ell_1) = Q(t+\ell_1)$, and such that the planned intermediate
inventory for item k, $J(k,t+\ell_1)$, provides the same level of
protection against stockout for all k. Define $\tilde{\sigma}_{k1}^2$ to be the
variance of the deviation between the planned intermediate inventory
and the actual intermediate inventory at time $t+\ell_1$:

$$\tilde{\sigma}_{k1}^2 = Var[J(k,t+\ell_1) - \hat{J}(k,t+\ell_1)]$$

$$= Var[\sum_{i=1}^{\ell_1} \{Q(k,t+i) - \hat{Q}(k,t+i)$$

$$- P_t(k,t+\ell_2+i) + P(k,t+\ell_2+i)\}]$$

Then, for given $\tilde{\sigma}_{k1}^2$ we disaggregate $Q(t+\ell_1)$ so that the planned intermediate inventory for k is given by

$$J(k,t+\ell_1) = z \ \tilde{\sigma}_{k1},$$

where z is

$$z = J(t+\ell_1) \ / \ \sum_k \tilde{\sigma}_{k1}.$$

Unfortunately, though, we are not able to determine analytically $\hat{\sigma}_{k1}^2$, since we cannot determine the forecast error for downstream production, $Var[P_t(k,t+\ell_2+i) - P(k,t+\ell_2+i)]$. Hence, we would either need to estimate it empirically or substitute the known forecast error for demand, $Var[F_t(k,t+\ell_2+i) - D(k,t+\ell_2+i)]$, for the forecast error for downstream production.

Upstream Stage: Production to Echelon Inventory

The second approach for smoothing the upstream production is based on the notion of echelon inventory. The echelon inventory for a production stage equals all inventory, including work-in-process, that is downstream of the stage. In a two-stage system, the echelon inventory for the upstream stage is the intermediate inventory, plus the work-in-process within the downstream stage, plus the finished-goods inventory. Each period this echelon inventory is increased by the amount of production completed by the upstream stage, and is decreased by the amount of customer demand. We set the planned production level for the upstream stage to be the average of the net requirements on the echelon inventory over the interval $t+\ell, t+\ell+1$, ... $t+\ell+m$, where m is the window length:

$$(23) \qquad Q(t+\ell_1) = \frac{1}{m+1} \ \{F_t(t+1,t+\ell+m) - P(t+1,t+\ell_2)$$

$$- \ Q(t+1,t+\ell_1-1) - \hat{I}(t) + SS_2$$

$$- \ \hat{J}(t) + SS_1\} \qquad .$$

To explain the bracketed term, note that $(\hat{I}(t) - SS_2) + P(t+1,t+\ell_2) + (\hat{J}(t) - SS_1)$ is the current echelon inventory (exclusive of safety stocks), and $Q(t+1,t+\ell_1-1)$ is the planned input to the echelon inventory over $(t+1,t+\ell_1-1)$. The sum of the current echelon inventory and the planned input over $(t+1,t+\ell_1-1)$ should cover customer demand over $(t+1,t+\ell_1+\ell_2-1)$ since ℓ_2 is the lead time for the downstream stage. Production at the upstream stage that is started at t will be input into echelon inventory at time $t+\ell_1$, but will not be available for customer demand until $t+\ell_1+\ell_2 = t+\ell$. Now, since $F_t(t+1,t+\ell+m) = F_t(t+1,t+\ell-1) + F_t(t+\ell,t+\ell+m)$, we see that the bracketed term in (23) corresponds to the net requirements on the echelon inventory over $(t+\ell,t+\ell+m)$. As we have done previously, we set planned production to be the average of the net requirements on the appropriate inventory over the chosen smoothing window.

The analysis of (23) is identical to that for (3) for the one-stage system where we replace n by m, $P(t+\ell)$ by $Q(t+\ell_1)$, SS by (SS_1+SS_2) and $\hat{I}(t)$ by $(\hat{I}(t) + P(t+1,t+\ell_2) + \hat{J}(t))$. In particular, we can rewrite (23) as

$$Q(t+\ell_1) = \frac{1}{m+1} \{F_t(t+\ell+m) + \delta_t(t,t+\ell+m-1)$$

$$+ \varepsilon_1(t) + \varepsilon_2(t)\} + \frac{m}{m+1} \{Q(t+\ell_1-1)\} \quad,$$

from which we can obtain

$$E[Q(t+\ell_1)] = \bar{D}$$

and

$$Var[Q(t+\ell_1)] = (\sigma_D^2 + \sigma_P^2 + \sigma_Q^2) / (2m+1)$$

where $\sigma_P^2 = Var[\varepsilon_2(t)]$ and $\sigma_Q^2 = Var[\varepsilon_1(t)]$.

Thus, as expected, the aggregate upstream production rate equals, on average, the demand rate, while its variance is inversely proportional to the window length for smoothing.

While the characterization of the planned intermediate inventory $J(t+\ell_1)$ is not immediate for this model, it is for the planned echelon inventory at time $t+\ell_1$, $I(t+\ell_1) + P(t+\ell_1+1,t+\ell) + J(t+\ell_1)$. In fact, the analysis for the planned echelon inventory parallels that for the planned inventory for the one-stage system, (10) - (13). To see this, we write the counterpart to (10) to define the planned echelon inventory:

(24) $\quad I(t+\ell_1) + P(t+\ell_1+1,t+\ell) + J(t+\ell_1) = \hat{I}(t) + P(t+1,t+\ell_2) + \hat{J}(t)$

$$+ Q(t+1,t+\ell_1) - F_t(t+1,t+\ell_1)$$

Then, we use (23) to substitute for $Q(t+1,t+\ell_1-1)$ in (24) to obtain

$$I(t+\ell_1) + P(t+\ell_1+1,t+\ell) + J(t+\ell_1) = SS_1 + SS_2 + F_t(t+\ell_1+1,t+\ell+m)$$
$$- m\, Q(t+\ell_1) \quad .$$

From this, we find that the mean echelon inventory equals $SS_1 + SS_2 + \ell_2\bar{D}$, while its variance is given by

$$(25) \qquad \frac{m^2}{2m+1} \cdot (\sigma_D^2 + \sigma_P^2 + \sigma_Q^2)$$

$$+ 2\sum_{j=0}^{\ell_2+m-1} [1 - 2(\frac{m}{m+1})^{j+1}]\, [\sigma_D^2 - \sum_{i=0}^{\ell_1+j} \sigma^2(i)] \quad .$$

To disaggregate $Q(t+\ell_1)$ we need to find the planned production for each item k, $Q(k,t+\ell_1)$ such that

$$\sum_k Q(k,t+\ell_1) = Q(t+\ell_1) \quad .$$

We can do this in a similar manner to that for the one-stage system. Namely, we set $Q(k,t+\ell_1)$ so that the planned echelon safety stock for item k, defined as $I(k,t+\ell_1) + P(k,t+\ell_1+1,t+\ell) + J(k,t+\ell_1) - \ell_2\bar{D}(k)$, equals $z\sigma_{k1}$ where z is given by

$$z = \frac{I(t+\ell_1) + P(t+\ell_1+1,t+\ell) + J(t+\ell_1) - \ell_2\bar{D}}{\sum_k \sigma_{k1}} \quad ,$$

and σ_{k1}^2 equals the variance of

$$\sum_{i=1}^{\ell_1} [Q(k,t+i) - \hat{Q}(k,t+i)] + [F_t(k,t+i) - D(k,t+i)] \quad .$$

In words, σ_{k1}^2 is the variance of the deviation between the planned echelon inventory for time $t+\ell_1$ and the actual echelon inventory for time $t+\ell_1$ for item k. Thus, this disaggregation equalizes the planned echelon safety stocks for all items, where we have normalized by the standard deviation of the cumulative upstream yield uncertainty and forecast error over the lead time ℓ_1. The rationale for this disaggregation scheme is to try to spread the planned echelon safety stock (i.e. either in the intermediate or finished-goods inventory), 'evenly' over the items. By 'evenly', we intend for each item's echelon safety stock to provide the same level of protection against uncertainty from the forecast errors and yield uncertainty in the upstream stage over its lead time ℓ_1.

As before, the measure of the level of protection from the disaggregation, z, is a random variable. Its mean is given by $(SS_1+SS_2) / \Sigma \sigma_{k1}$, while its variance is directly proportional to (25).

It will be convenient to term the first (produce to intermediate inventory) approach as the decoupled model and to term the second (produce to echelon inventory) as the nested model. In the first case, the intermediate inventory decouples the stages. The upstream stage produces to this inventory based on a forecast of downstream usage, while the downstream stage draws its raw materials from this inventory. In the second case, both the upstream and downstream stages produce to the same forecast, namely the demand forecast. But the stages are 'nested' in that the upstream stage produces to the echelon inventory which contains the downstream stage and its inventory.

COMPUTATIONAL STUDY

To examine the proposed production smoothing models, we conducted a computational study based on data gathered on the set of items produced in one manufacturing facility. The purpose of the computational study is threefold: to understand how much inventory is needed in a make-to-stock system and where that inventory should be positioned; to compare the effectiveness of the different production smoothing models for a two-stage system; and to determine, via a comparison to a simulation, the accuracy of the approximate analyses of these smoothing models. We first describe the test data, then the simulation program that we have developed, and finally the computational results.

Test Scenario

To test the production smoothing models we abstracted a test scenario based on data gathered from a manufacturing operation. We have disguised this data to protect the identity of the manufacturing firm. However, the reported results are representative of the results obtained using the actual data.

In Table 1 we give the mean demand rate (units per month) and its standard deviation for the family of items. Of the 38 items in this family, we consider only 25 as candidates for the make-to-stock system. We exclude all items that have a start rate of less than 200 units per month, since it would be too risky to plan to stock these low-demand items.

We assume that there are two production stages and that each
tem requires processing from both stages. The lead time for the
irst stage is three months ($\ell_1=3$) and is one month for the second
tage ($\ell_2=1$). The first stage processes each item in a lot of
xactly 500 units. The second stage can process lots of any size.
e will find it convenient to express the simulation results in
erms of the lots for the upstream stage (500 units/lot).

For the sample of 25 items, the mean monthly demand is 81 lots
er month (500 units/lot) and the standard deviation of aggregate
emand σ_D is 28.5 lots per month ($\sigma_D^2 = 811$).

For the test scenario we assume that the forecast process is
nbiased, and that for each item k, the variance of the forecast
evision step is given by

$$\sigma^2(0) = \sigma^2(1) = .1 \ \sigma_D^2$$

$$\sigma^2(2) \qquad = .13 \ \sigma_D^2$$

$$\sigma^2(3) \qquad = .2 \ \ \sigma_D^2$$

$$\sigma^2(4) = \sigma^2(5) = .23 \ \sigma_D^2$$

$$\sigma^2(j) \qquad = 0 \quad \text{for } j > 5.$$

hus, any forecast for 6 or more months ahead equals the mean
onthly demand, and is not revised until there is 5 or less months
o go.

We assume that there is no uncertainty in the production yield
n each stage. There are two reasons for this. First, we had no
ata from which to estimate the parameters of the yield uncertainty.
econd, we had observed in an earlier study of a comparable
roduction operation that the uncertainty in the forecast errors
ominated that in the yield realization. Hence, we hope that by
ncluding only the uncertainty in the forecast errors we will
apture the primary behavior of the smoothing models. Nevertheless,
iven information on yield uncertainty, we could easily incorporate
his into our study.

We can find σ_k^2 , the variance of the cumulative forecast error
or item k over a given lead time ℓ, from the above specification of
he variance of the forecast revision steps and from the knowledge
f σ_D^2 for item k (Table 1). For instance, if $\ell=3$ then

$$\sigma_k^2 = \sigma^2(0) + (\sigma^2(0) + \sigma^2(1)) + (\sigma^2(0) + \sigma^2(1) + \sigma^2(2)) = .63\sigma_D^2.$$

For later reference, we note that the sum over the 25 make-to-stock items of the standard deviations of the cumulative forecast errors, $\sum_k \sigma_k$, is 25 lots when $\ell=1$ month, 63 lots when $\ell=3$ months, and 86 lots when $\ell=4$ months.

Simulation Program

We have written in PL-1 a program to simulate the production planning process for a two-stage production system. The simulation is a discrete-time simulation where the time unit is one month. Each month the simulation generates customer demand and a demand forecast for the next twelve months for each item. The end inventories for the items are increased by completed downstream production and are depleted by the demand amount. Backorders are created when insufficient inventories exist. The simulation then applies a specified production smoothing model [e.g. (3)] and its disaggregation to determine the production starts for the downstream stage. The intermediate inventories for the items are increased by completed upstream production and are depleted by usage from the production starts by the downstream stage. Note that the intermediate inventory cannot have backorders; rather, if insufficient inventory exists, then the downstream production starts need to be reduced. Finally, the simulation then applies a specified production smoothing model [e.g. (17)] and its disaggregation to determine the production starts for the upstream stage. This process is then repeated each month for the run length of the simulation. Note that, in effect, the simulation acts as if the events, customer demand, production starts, and completed production, occur at the start (or end) of every month.

For our tests the simulation is run for 1000 months where the first 40 months are for initialization and various statistics are collected over the remaining 960 months. The simulation relies on a common demand and forecast time series in order to increase the comparability of simulation runs for different smoothing models. Thus, any differences in performance between two simulation runs will be due to the smoothing models and not due to any differences in the realization of the demand or forecast process. To generate the demand and forecast time series, the forecast revision process obtains $F_t(s)$ as a lognormal random variable with mean $F_{t-1}(s)$ and with variance $\sigma^2(s-t)$ [see (1)].

In the previous section we develop the disaggregation procedure with no restrictions on the sign of the production outcome. Indeed, this procedure may suggest the impossible, namely negative production for an item with an excessively high inventory. The simulation does not permit negative production. Rather, if the disaggregation results in this outcome for a particular item, then the production starts for that item are set to zero and the disaggregation procedure is repeated for the remaining items.

Similarly, the disaggregation procedure assumes that sufficient raw material is available to make the desired production starts. For the upstream stage, the simulation retains this assumption. However, for the downstream stage, the simulation will not start more production of a particular item than is available in its intermediate inventory (i.e. we do not permit backordering on the intermediate inventory). Rather, if the desired production for an item exceeds the available raw material, we set its production equal to the raw material level and then repeat the disaggregation procedure for the remaining items (after we reduce the planned aggregate production by the amount preset for the excluded item).

For the simulation we impose a lot size of 500 units for all items for the upstream stage. Thus, for each item the monthly production starts must be a multiple of 500 units. To reflect this restriction, we modify the disaggregation procedure to compute the desired number of units to start, divide by 500 to convert to lots, and then round to the nearest integer. We assume no such restriction for the downstream stage, although we could impose a fixed lot size, if appropriate.

The simulation also has the capability to limit the aggregate production for each stage. For instance, the upstream stage might not be capable of starting more than 90 lots per month. In this case, we would modify the production smoothing model to set production starts equal to the minimum of the desired start rate from the model and the capacity limit, say 90 lots. However, in the computational work that we report, we do not use this capability, but assume that there are no limits to the production at each stage.

The disaggregation of upstream production for the decoupled (produce to intermediate inventory) approach requires an item forecast of downstream production. We generate this forecast via an item-level version of (21) - (22), with one modification. We replace the actual production starts for item k, $P(k, t+\ell_2)$, in (21)

by the amount that would be started if there were no shortages in
the intermediate inventory. This modification is necessary because
stockouts in the intermediate inventory perturb the actual
production starts from their desired level; hence, the actual
production starts may not be an accurate reflection of future
production by the downstream stage.

Computational Results

In this section we present and discuss our computational work.
We do this in two parts. First, we consider the application of a
one-stage model and study its behavior on the test scenario.
Second, we consider the two versions of the two-stage model and
compare them against each other and versus the one-stage model for
the test scenario.

To apply the one-stage model to the test scenario, we assume a
make-to-stock system with a finished-goods inventory but with no
intermediate inventory. In effect, we combine the two stages in the
test scenario into one stage with a production lead time $\ell = 4$
months. Each month we use (3) to set the aggregate production start
rate, which is disaggregated based on the finished-good inventories
via (14)-(15).

We used the simulation to compare the "actual" behavior (as
found from the simulation) of the one-stage model with the predicted
behavior from our analysis of the one-stage model, e.g. (9), (13).
We report our results in Table 2. We have run the simulation for
window lengths n=0,1,2,...6 and for safety stock targets of SS = 80,
120 and 150 lots (recall that $\Sigma\sigma_k$ = 86 lots for ℓ = 4 months). To
show the consequences from production smoothing, we report the
standard deviations of aggregate production P(t) and of the actual
aggregate inventory position $\hat{I}(t)$. As a measure of service we report
the fill rate, which equals the fraction of demand that is satisfied
by inventory without any delay.

From this table we can see how the two decision parameters, the
window length and the safety stock target, affect the reported
performance measures. Namely, the window length essentially
determines the measures of production smoothing [the standard
deviations of P(t) and $\hat{I}(t)$], while the safety stock target
determines the fill rate. This is consistent with the analysis of
the production smoothing model. Furthermore, the analytic results
(9), (13) are reasonably accurate predictions of the actual
(simulated) values.[1] This indicates that the approximations made by

he analysis (i.e. ignoring lot-sizing, and assuming that
nventories remain balanced so that the proposed disaggregation is
lways feasible) do not give significant errors in this test
cenario.

Finally, from Table 2 we see the implications of a make-to-
tock system for this family of items. The average production
tarts needed for the sample of items in the test scenario is 81
ots per month. We see that maintaining a finished-goods inventory
f 80 lots (about one month of demand), on average, will result in a
0% fill rate. Increasing this safety stock by 50% to 120 lots
mproves service to a 95% fill rate. To get to a 98% fill rate
equires an investment in another 30 lots. The choice of window
ength for the production smoothing model dictates the extent of
roduction smoothing. With no smoothing (n=0), the monthly
roduction start rate, while equal to 81 lots on average, has a
tandard deviation of nearly 30 lots. Thus, we expect production
tarts to exceed 120 lots 16% of the time, and similarly to fall
elow 50 lots 16% of the time. Substantial production smoothing is
ossible by increasing the window length, but with decreasing
eturns. For instance, a window length of $n=2$, which corresponds to
sing a six-month cumulative forecast ($6=n+\ell$), reduces, the standard
eviation of production starts by almost 60% over no smoothing. The
ost from increased production smoothing is a slight degradation in
ill rate, and an increased variability in the actual inventory
osition.

We examined the two-stage models to see what improvement is
ossible by inserting an intermediate inventory between the stages.
o examine the smoothing behavior, we first simulated the two
moothing models for a fixed safety stock but with varying window
engths. As with the one-stage system, the smoothing behavior is
ffectively independent of the safety stock targets for reasonable
tocking levels. Table 3 gives the results for the decoupled
pproach (produce to intermediate inventory) while Table 4 gives the
esults for the nested approach (produce to echelon inventory). In
oth cases the safety stock targets are $SS_1 = 100$ and $SS_2 = 120$.

Table 3 shows that for the decoupled approach the production
moothing behavior for the downstream stage is as predicted and is
ndependent of the upstream stage. The production behavior for the
pstream stage, for which we do not have an analytic prediction,
eflects the effect of double smoothing: the upstream production is

set by smoothing the forecast of downstream production, which itself is a smoothed average of the demand forecast. Consequently, for a fixed window length for the upstream stage there is greater smoothing as the downstream window length grows. In contrast with the one-stage system, the fill rate provided by the safety stocks is very dependent on the level of production smoothing. In particular, the fill rate declines dramatically with longer window lengths (more smoothing) for the downstream stage. This is due to the fact that the item forecasts of downstream production used by the upstream stage become less accurate with longer window lengths for the downstream stage.[2] As a consequence, the intermediate inventory has frequent stockouts, which ultimately results in poor customer service.

In Table 4 we see the comparable production smoothing behavior for the nested approach. Here, the analytic predictions of the production smoothing for both stages are reasonably accurate. Furthermore, the level of smoothing for the upstream stage is totally independent of the downstream stage. And the fill rate is virtually independent of the choice of smoothing parameters, as we saw for the one-stage system.

To explore the impact of the safety stock levels, we contrast in Table 5 the fill rates from the two approaches for a series of safety stock choices. Due to the fact that the fill rate for the decoupled approach is very sensitive to the level of production smoothing, we simulated a set of cases with substantial smoothing ($m=3$, $n=2$) and another set with limited smoothing ($m=1$, $n=0$). We chose the safety stock levels to provide insight into the proper positioning of these stocks and to allow comparison with the one-stage model (Table 2). We did not permit the downstream safety stock target to be set below 40 lots, since below that we have no hope of providing reasonable service (recall that $\Sigma\sigma_k = 25$ lots when $\ell = 1$). Based on the results in Table 5, we make the following observations:

a) For the nested approach (produce to echelon inventory), for a fixed total safety stock ($SS_1 + SS_2$), the fill rate is relatively insensitive with slight improvement as more safety stock is placed downstream.

b) For the coupled approach (produce to intermediate inventory) the fill rate is very sensitive to both the amount of smoothing and the positioning of the safety stock. As seen in Table 3, service again deteriorates with increased smoothing. For a fixed total safety stock, fill rate improves as more stock is placed in the intermediate inventory as long as a minimal level ($SS_2=40$) is kept downstream; beyond this minimum, service will be degraded.

c) In comparing the two approaches, we see that the nested approach dominates the decoupled approach for the case with substantial smoothing. When there is limited smoothing, however, the decoupled approach is slightly better, provided the appropriate inventory positioning.

In comparing either of the approaches for the two-stage model with the one-stage model, we need more inventory with a two-stage model than with a one-stage model for a given fill rate. For instance, a safety stock of 120 lots with the one-stage model, gives a 95-96% fill rate. The nested approach for the two-stage model provides a 90%-92% fill rate for the same total safety stock; the decoupled approach can provide a 94% fill rate but with limited smoothing. However, it typically will cost less to hold stock in the intermediate inventory than in the finished-goods inventory. Thus, a two-stage model can be preferable to the one-stage model if the holding cost for the intermediate inventory is low enough relative to the cost for the finished-goods inventory. For instance, suppose a 90% fill rate is desired. We can achieve this with the one-stage model with a finished-goods safety stock of 80 lots for window lengths $n=2$ and $n=3$. For comparable smoothing with the two-stage model, we would need the nested approach with smoothing windows $m=3$, $n=2$ and with intermediate safety stock of 80 lots and a finished-goods safety stock of 40 lots. Thus, the two-stage model would be preferable if the holding cost for 80 lots of intermediate inventory is less than that for 40 lots of finished-goods inventory.

FOOTNOTES

1
Note that we report the standard deviation of actual inventory,
rather than that of planned inventory as given by (13). Since the
actual inventory is given by

$$\hat{I}(t+\ell) = I(t+\ell) + \sum_{i=1}^{\ell} \{P(t+i) - \hat{P}(t+i)\}$$

$$+ \sum_{i=1}^{\ell} \{F_t(t+i) - D(t+i)\} \quad ,$$

we can express its variance in terms of the variance of $I(t+\ell)$ given
by (13).

2
To disaggregate upstream production for the decoupled approach, we
need an item forecast of downstream production. We obtained this
forecast via an item-level version of (21) - (22). By using an
alternate forecasting method, namely proportioning the aggregate
forecast by the expected demand level, we could avoid the
degradation in fill rate seen in Table 3. However, this alternate
forecast method resulted in system performance that was strictly
dominated by the nested model (Table 4).

APPENDIX

Derivation of (8) and (9)

By recursive substitution for $P(t)$ in (7) we obtain

$$P(t+\ell) = \sum_{i=0}^{\infty} (\frac{1}{n+1})(\frac{n}{n+1})^i \{F_{t-1}(t-1+\ell+n) +$$

$$\delta_{t-i}(t-i, \ t-i+\ell+n-1) + \varepsilon(t-i)\} \quad ,$$

where we assume that an infinite time history exists. By assumption
we have that for all i

$$E[F_{t-i}(t-i+\ell+n) + \delta_{t-i}(t-i, \ t-i+\ell+n-1) + \varepsilon(t-i)] = \bar{D} \quad ,$$

and

$$Var[F_{t-i}(t-i+\ell+n) + \delta_{t-i}(t-i, \ t-i+\ell+n-1) + \varepsilon(t-i)] = \sigma_D^2 + \sigma_P^2 \quad ,$$

Furthermore, we have assumed that these bracketed terms are
independent across time. Thus, we obtain

$$E[P(t+\ell)] = \sum_{i=0}^{\infty} (\frac{1}{n+1})(\frac{n}{n+1})^i \ \bar{D}$$

$$= \bar{D} \quad ,$$

$$Var[P(t+\ell)] = \sum_{i=0}^{\infty} (\frac{1}{n+1})^2 \ (\frac{n}{n+1})^{2i} \ (\sigma_D^2 + \sigma_P^2)$$

$$= (\sigma_D^2 + \sigma_P^2) \ / \ (2n+1) \quad .$$

Figure 1: Two-Stage System

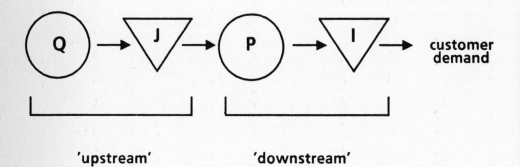

TABLE 1: DEMAND FOR TEST SAMPLE.
500 demand units equals one lot.
Starred items(*) are excluded from Make-to-Stock System.

ITEM CODE	DEMAND	
	MEAN	STD. DEV
*1	2	2
*2	1	1
*3	18	21
*4	8	16
5	651	961
6	214	362
*7	137	298
*8	11	15
9	325	238
10	237	293
11	483	569
*12	2	6
13	1315	1121
14	1953	1685
15	6729	4793
*16	1	3
17	554	722
*18	48	49
*19	20	30
20	1887	1951

TABLE 1 CONTINUED ON NEXT PAGE.

TABLE 1 (continued)

ITEM CODE	DEMAND	
	MEAN	STD. DEV
21	2193	1908
22	587	604
23	615	728
24	833	665
*25	47	151
*26	8	11
27	1206	1603
28	15691	12278
29	1142	2286
30	336	677
*31	81	242
32	246	660
33	749	890
34	817	1199
35	232	636
36	360	822
37	279	634
38	819	1336

Safety Stock

Window Length	SS = 80	SS = 120	SS = 150	Predicted Std. Deviations
n = 0	29.8, 30.1* .92	29.8, 30.2 .96	29.1, 30.1, .98	28.5, 30.8
n = 1	17.4, 34.0 .91	17.3, 34.3 .96	17.2, 34.1, .98	16.4, 34.9
n = 2	13.1, 37.5 .90	13.1, 37.9 .96	13.0, 37.6, .97	12.8, 39.4
n = 3	10.8, 40.8 .90	10.8, 41.3 .95	10.8, 41.0, .97	10.8, 43.6
n = 4	9.3, 44.0 .89	9.4, 44.4 .95	9.3, 44.0, .97	9.5, 47.4
n = 5	8.3, 46.8 .89	8.4, 46.9 .95	8.2, 46.7, .97	8.6, 51.0
n = 6	7.6, 49.0 .89	7.6, 49.4 .94	7.4, 49.3, .97	7.9, 54.4
Predicted fill rate	.90	.96	.98	

Table 2: Results from One-Stage Model

x,y / z : x = standard deviation of P_t; y = standard deviation of $\hat{I}_t$; z = fill rate.

downstream window length / upstream window length	n = 0	n = 1	n = 2	n = 3	upstream stage prediction
m = 0	29.2, 27.4,* .99	24.1, 15.9, . 98	22.0, 12.4, .93	19.9, 10.6, .88	**
m = 1	17.2, 27.4, .99	15.9, 15.9, .98	14.7, 12.4, .93	13.6, 10.5, .88	
m = 2	13.0, 27.4, .99	12.6, 15.9, :97	11.9, 12.4, .92	11.2, 10.5, .87	
m = 3	10.7, 27.2, .99	10.7, 15.9, .97	10.2, 12.4, .92	9.8, 10.5, .87	
downstream stage prediction	28.5	16.5	12.8	10.8	

Table 3: Production Standard Deviations for Two-Stage Model: Production to Intermediate Inventory ($SS_1 = 100$, $SS_2 = 120$)

* $\boxed{x,y, z}$: x = standard deviation of Q_t ; y = standard deviation of P_t ; z = customer fill rate.

** No analytic prediction is currently available.

upstream window length \ downstream window length	$n=0$	$n=1$	$n=2$	$n=3$	upstream stage prediction
$m=0$	29.2, 27.4*	29.2, 15.9	29.2, 12.4	29.2, 10.6	28.5
$m=1$	17.2, 27.4	17.2, 15.9	17.2, 12.4	17.2, 10.6	16.5
$m=2$	13.1, 27.3	13.1, 15.9	13.1, 12.4	13.1, 10.6	12.8
$m=3$	10.9, 27.2	10.9, 15.9	10.9, 12.4	10.9, 10.6	10.8
downstream stage prediction	28.5	16.5	12.8	10.8	

Table 4: Production Standard Deviations for Two-Stage Model: Production to Echelon Inventory ($SS_1 = 100$, $SS_2 = 120$)

* $\boxed{x,y}$: x = standard deviation of Q_t; y = standard deviation of P_t.

Note, the fill rate is .98 for all instances.

		FILL RATE (m = 3, n = 2)		FILL RATE (m = 1, n = 0)	
SS_1	SS_2	PRODUCE TO ECHELON INVENTORY	PRODUCE TO INTERMEDIATE INVENTORY	PRODUCE TO ECHELON INVENTORY	PRODUCE TO INTERMEDIATE INVENTORY
40	40	.83	.69	.84	.81
0	80	.83	.66	.85	.39
80	40	.90	.78	.91	.94
40	80	.91	.77	.92	.88
0	120	.91	.74	.92	.43
110	40	.93	.84	.94	.97
70	80	.94	.84	.95	.96
30	120	.94	.82	.95	.87
140	40	.95	.88	.96	.98
100	80	.96	.88	.97	.98
60	120	.96	.87	.97	.97

Table 5 : Comparison of Fill Rates for Two-Stage Models

References

Cruickshanks, A. B., R. D. Drescher and S. C. Graves, "A Study of Production Smoothing in a Job Shop Environment," Management Science 30, 3 (March 1984, 168-380.

Eppen, G. and L. Schrage, "Centralized Ordering Policies in a Multiwarehouse System with Lead Times and Random Demand," in Schwarz, L. (ed.), Multi-Level Production/Inventory Control Systems: Theory and Practice, North-Holland Amsterdam, 1981.

Federgruen A. and P. Zipkin, "Approximations of Dynamic, Multilocation Production and Inventory Problems," Management Science, 30, 1, (January 1984), 69-84.

Hax, A. C., and H. C. Meal, "Hierarchical Integration of Production Planning and Scheduling," In Studies in Management Sciences, Vol. I, Logistics, M. A. Geisler (ed.). North Holland-American Elsevier, New York, 1975.

C. Holt, F. Modigliani, and H. Simon, "A Linear Decision Rule for Production and Employment Scheduling," Management Science 2, 1-30 (1955).

_____, _____, and J. Muth, "Derivation of a Linear Decision Rule for Production and Employment," Management Science 2, 159-177 (1956).

Schneeweiss, C.A., "Smoothing Production by Inventory - An Application of the Wiener Filtering Theory," Management Science 17, 7 (March 1971), 472-483.

_____ "Optimal Production Smoothing and Safety Inventory," Management Science, 20, 7 (March 1974), 1122-1130.

Silver, E. A., "A Tutorial on Production Smoothing and Work Force Balancing," Operations Research, 15, 6 (November-December 1967), 985-1010.

OVERVIEW OF A STOCK ALLOCATION MODEL FOR A TWO-ECHELON
PUSH SYSTEM HAVING IDENTICAL UNITS AT THE LOWER ECHELON

Henrik Jönsson
Linköping Institute of Technology
Linköping, Sweden

and

Edward A. Silver
The University of Calgary
Calgary, Alberta, Canada

ABSTRACT

A two-echelon inventory system with one central warehouse and n identical regional warehouses is considered. Customer demand occurs only at the regional warehouses. A PUSH control system is used, implying that the allocation of stock is
coordinated centrally. Given an initial system stock, a fixed planning horizon, and
two shipping possibilities from the central warehouse until the next system replenishment (at the end of the planning horizon), the problem of deciding how much to
ship initially to each warehouse is addressed. The stock retained at the central
warehouse will be allocated to the branches at the second shipping opportunity so as
to, if possible, balance the inventory levels, thus maximizing the customer service
until the time of the next replenishment.

Given a desired customer service level, the appropriate initial system stock
and the associated allocation are derived. The performance is compared with a simple ship-all policy and with an extreme policy allowing a complete redistribution of
the inventory among the regional warehouses at the second shipping opportunity. The
results show that significant benefits can be achieved by the retention of a portion
of the system stock at the central warehouse.

INTRODUCTION

In this paper, we consider the allocation of inventories for a single item in a
two-echelon inventory system with one central warehouse (CW) and n identical regional warehouses (RW's). A PUSH control system is used whereby the CW coordinates
all shipments to the RW's. See Brown (1982) and Silver and Peterson (1985) for more
details on PUSH systems. It is assumed that the system is replenished once every
order cycle. The cycle is a predetermined fixed number of periods (presumably
chosen to minimize the expected setup and inventory holding costs). At the start of
each order cycle the CW ships out most of the available system inventory, but retains a central safety stock which is shipped later in the cycle so as to balance
the inventories. The objective is to minimize the expected number of backorders for

a given initial system stock level or, equivalently, to minimize the system stock required to achieve a desired service level.

We assume that the demands at the warehouses are independent and normally distributed (with the same mean and variance at each RW). Backorders are allowed and the lead times are negligible. The policy considered is to send out two shipments from the CW during each order cycle (of duration H periods). After the initial allocation in the order cycle, only a small system safety stock is retained at the CW. This stock is distributed to the RW's at the beginning of the last period of the cycle so as to balance the inventory, because that is when the risk of incurring backorders is largest. This policy produced very good results for the special case of just two RW's studied in Jönsson and Silver (1984).

In the rest of this paper we discuss the service measure utilized, then provide an overview of the approach used in selecting the system stock level and the quantity retained centrally so as to achieve the desired service level with the lowest amount of system stock. Some results are presented including comparison with two simpler policies which are used as benchmarks. A much more detailed presentation of the material, including a number of references on PUSH system research, can be found in Jönsson and Silver (1985).

SERVICE MEASURE USED

Let H represent the horizon length, i.e., the time between system replenishments. Then the initial allocation in a cycle is made at time 0 and the second occurs at the end of period H-1. Also let D represent the average total demand at all of the regional warehouses in a cycle (time H). The system customer service measure used is then given by

$$P = 1 - \frac{E[\text{number of units short in periods H-1 and H}]}{D} = 1 - \frac{ES}{D} \tag{1}$$

The reason for only including the expected shortages in the last two periods of the cycle is that the shortages in earlier periods tend to be very small.

APPROACH

In this section we first discuss the appropriate allocation to the regional warehouses at time 0 and the associated expected units short at time H-1 given values of I_0 (the system stock at the start of the cycle) and I_c (the amount of stock held centrally, i.e., not allocated to the regional warehouses at time 0). Then we consider the allocation of I_c at time H-1 and the resulting inventory levels at the regional warehouses. For a given pair (I_0, I_c) the distributions of these inventory levels imply expected shortage levels at time H. Finally we outline the choice of the minimum I_0 (and associated best I_c value) to achieve a desired service level, P.

a). Initial Allocation (at Time 0) and the Associated Expected Units Short at Time H-1

For given values of I_0 and I_c we have a quantity I_0-I_c to allocate among the n identical warehouses at time 0. To minimize the expected number of backorders at time H-1 it follows that each regional warehouse should be initially allocated $(I_0-I_c)/n$. Moreover, knowing the mean and variance of the normally distributed demand at each warehouse, the expected total units short at time H-1 can be expressed analytically in terms of the unit normal loss function; see, for example, Silver and Peterson (1985).

b). Allocation of I_c at Time H-1

Where the next system replenishment will arrive at time H it follows that all of the central stock I_c should be allocated out to the regional warehouses at time H-1. Moreover, because the regional warehouses have identical demand distributions the appropriate allocation of I_c is evident given current (at time H-1) inventory levels at the n regional warehouses. Specifically, if we let RW_1 denote the regional warehouse with the lowest inventory level prior to the allocation, RW_2 that one with the second lowest level, etc., then we first use the central stock to raise the level at RW_1 up to that at RW_2, then we raise RW_1 and RW_2 up to the level of RW_3, etc. In other words, we use the I_c so as to maximize the lowest resulting inventory level at any of the RW's. A key quantity is n_b, the number of lowest inventory levels that we are able to balance in this fashion.

For any given set of resulting inventory levels (after the allocation) one can write an analytic expression for the expected total units short at time H. The difficulty is that, because demands are not known with certainty, the inventory levels, prior to the allocation at time H-1, are random variables, hence the inventory levels after the allocation are also random variables. Because of the aforementioned method of allocating I_c we are interested in the ranked values of the inventory levels prior to the allocation at time H-1. Where all the RW's start at the same level at time 0 and have identical normal demand distributions, then the inventory levels at time H-1 have a ranked-order multivariate normal distribution whose parameters can be numerically evaluated for any number of warehouses. The quantity n_b, defined in the previous paragraph, is a random variable. However, as discussed in Jönsson and Silver (1985) one can approximate the distributions of the resulting (after allocation) ranked inventory levels by normal distributions whose means and variances depend upon the parameters of the ranked-order distribution (prior to the allocation) and the value of I_c. The approximation involves n_b only through its expected value. With normal distributions of the stocks after allocation one is again able to express the expected units short at time H in terms of the unit normal loss function.

c). Selection of I_c and I_0

The procedures outlined in the two previous subsections permit us to compute, ES, the E(number of units short in periods H-1 and H) term in Eqn. (1), for a given pair (I_0, I_c). For any given value of I_0 we use the procedures to search on I_c to minimize the expected units short. Let the resulting value be denoted by ES'. Now from Eqn. (1) we know that we want a value of ES^* where

$$ES^* = D(1-P) \qquad (2)$$

The idea is to search on I_0, using the above method for each I_0, until $ES' \simeq ES^*$. In particular, if $ES' < ES^*$, then I_0 is made smaller than the current value, whereas, if $ES' > ES^*$, then I_0 is increased from the current level.

ALTERNATIVE INVENTORY CONTROL POLICIES

To estimate the effectiveness of our policy of retaining some central safety stock we compared its performance with that of
   i). a ship-all policy
   ii). an extreme PUSH policy.
For both of these policies it is straightforward to analytically determine the service level for a given value of the initial system stock.

In the ship-all policy all of the system stock, I_S, is allocated at the start of a system cycle to the RW's and then no further shipments of units between locations are carried out until the next system replenishment arrives. Obviously the inventory required (I_S) to obtain the service level P must be greater than or equal to I_0 since the inventory levels cannot be balanced at all at the end of period H-1.

In the extreme PUSH policy, the system stock, I_E, is allocated initially as in the ship-all policy. However, at the end of period H-1 the inventories at the RW's are completely balanced by carrying out transshipments between the RW's. Naturally, this policy requires lower inventory holding costs than does our central safety stock policy because a complete balancing of the inventories is accomplished at the end of period H-1. However, higher handling and transportation costs are incurred.

RESULTS

The performance of the basic policy (i.e., the policy of retaining a safety stock at the central warehouse) was studied through some 48 numerical examples (n = 2, 5, 10, 20; P = 98%, 99%; H = 4, 8, 12; and CV = 0.2, 0.4 where CV is the coefficient of variation of demand per unit time period at a regional warehouse). Corresponding results, I_S and I_E, were computed for the alternative policies enabling a comparison of differences in average inventory levels. Table 1 shows the averages and ranges observed in some of the key characteristics which are defined are follows:

I_0/D - the system inventory, expressed as a multiple of the average system demand, required to achieve the desired P value.

I_c/I_0 - the fraction of the inventory retained as safety stock at the central warehouse (CW).

$100(I_S-I_0)/(I_S-I_E)$ - the percentage inventory reduction for the basic policy as a fraction of the difference between the alternative policies.

$100(I_S-I_0)/(I_S-D/2)$ - the percentage reduction in the average system inventory during an order cycle through the use of CW safety stock instead of a ship-all policy.

MEASURE	AVERAGE VALUE	RANGE
I_0/D	1.061	.997 to 1.193
I_c/I_0	.054	.23 to .102
$100(I_S-I_0)/(I_S-I_E)$	64.0	13.6 to 98.8
$100(I_S-I_0)/(I_S-D/2)$	5.7	0.7 to 13.9

TABLE 1 - Summary of Results

Looking at the I_c/I_0 ratio it is seen that, on the average, approximately 5% of the stock is held centrally. From the third measure in Table 1 it is evident that a major portion of the inventory benefits of the extreme PUSH system can be achieved by the policy of the current paper. The last line of Table 1 indicates that approximately a 6% reduction in the average required inventory level can be achieved in comparison with the ship-all policy. Additional results are presented in Jönsson and Silver (1985).

CONCLUSIONS

In this paper, we have discussed a control policy appropriate for a system involving a central warehouse and n identical regional warehouses. Two opportunities for allocation existed, one at the start of the system cycle (of duration H), the other after H-1 periods. A procedure was outlined for determining the required system stock I_0 (and associated best quantity I_c to be held centrally after the first allocation) so as to achieve a desired system service level.

Possible extensions of the work include:

i). letting the time of the second allocation (redistribution) be a decision variable as opposed to being set at time H-1.

ii). treating the case of warehouses with differing demand distributions.

ACKNOWLEDGEMENT

The research leading to this paper was partly supported by the Natural Sciences and Engineering Research Council of Canada under Grant A1485.

REFERENCES

Brown, R. G., 1982, Advanced Service Parts Inventory Control (Norwich, Vermont, Materials Management Systems Inc.).

Jönsson, H. and Silver, E. A., 1984, "Stock Allocation from a Central Warehouse in a Two-Location PUSH Type Inventory Control System", WP-21-84 (Faculty of Management, The University of Calgary, Calgary, Canada) - also to appear in the Proceedings of the Third International Symposium on Inventories.

Jönsson, H. and Silver, E. A., 1985, "Stock Allocation Among a Central Warehouse and Identical Regional Warehouses in a Particular PUSH Inventory Control System", WP-07-85 (Faculty of Management, The University of Calgary, Calgary, Canada) - also submitted to the International Journal of Production Research.

E. A. Silver and R. Peterson, 1985, Decision Systems for Inventory Management and Production Planning, Second Edition, Chapter 12 and Appendix B (New York, John Wiley & Sons).

SYSTEM - BASED HEURISTICS FOR MULTI-ECHELON DISTRIBUTION SYSTEMS

R. LUYTEN

ABSTRACT

A two-echelon distribution system is investigated. We determine the form and nature of the optimal ordering policy which is determined by means of Markovian Decision Process - analysis. Several heuristic procedures, all based on the echelon stock concept, are proposed and tested against the optimal solution in a simulation experiment.

Katholieke Universiteit Leuven, Division of Industrial Management, Celestijnenlaan 300A, B-3030 Leuven, Belgium

I. INTRODUCTION

This paper treats a two-echelon inventory system. The higher echelon is a single location reffered to as the depot, which places orders for supply of a single commodity. The lower echelon consists of several points, called the retailers, which are supplied by shipments from the depot, and at which random demands for the item occur. Stocks are reviewed and decisions are made periodically. Orders and/or shipments may each require a fixed lead time before reaching their respective destinations.

Section II gives a short literature review of distribution research. Section III introduces the multi-echelon distribution system together with the underlying assumptions and gives a description of how this problem can be viewed as a Markovian Decision Process. Section IV discusses the concept of cost modifications in a distribution context. Section V presents the test-examples together with their optimal solutions and also gives the characteristic properties of these optimal solutions. These properties then will be used in section VI to give adapted versions of various heuristics which were used in assembly experiments previously and which will be tested against the test-examples.

II. LITERATURE REVIEW

Clark and Scarf [9,10] were among the first to discuss the multi-echelon distribution system under continuous review in a stochastic environment for a finite horizon. Their papers derive the form of an optimal policy for a serial system, which can be seen as a two-echelon distribution system with one retailer, when there is no setup cost at the retailer and of an approximate policy when there is a setup cost at the retailer. They show how this policy can be obtained by decomposing the problem into two seperate single-location problems : The problem for the retail outlet includes its "own" costs, ignoring all others; a critical-number policy solves this problem when there is no setup cost at the retailer, otherwise an (s,S) policy is optimal. The optimal policy and the expected cost function for each period are then used to define a convex "induced penalty cost" function for each period. This function is added to the depot's holding costs and ordering costs to form the second problem. An (s,S) policy solves this problem and constitutes an optimal (or near-optimal in case theire is a setup cost at the retailer) ordering policy for the system as a whole. A (near-) optimal shipment policy results from a slight modification of the retailer's policy : in each period, ship when your stock is not greater than the order point; ship up to S if the depot has that much stock, otherwise, ship as much as possible. At the end of their paper, they extend this policy to the multi-retailer case and suggest a decomposition which works on echelon stock at the depot, but which is appropriate only when the retailers are in balance, i.e. no retailer has more than its fair share. They expect the retailers to be in balance in most of the cases; we believe this to be true only in specific configurations when you do not restrict the ordering policy at the retailer level.

Schwarz [32] considers the 1 depot, n retailers, problem in a continuous review, stationary demand rates, deterministic environment without lead times; he also assumes identical costs at all retailers in most of his analysis. He provides some properties of the optimal solution :
1. Deliveries are made to the depot only when :
   a. the depot has zero inventory and
   b. at least one retailers has zero inventory.
2. Deliveries are made to any given retailer only when that retailer has zero inventory.
3. All deliveries to any given retailer between successive deliveries to the depot are of equal size.

Defining a single cycle policy as a policy in which all retailers have zero inventory at the moment the depot is ordering, he proves that the optimal policy for a 1 retailer problem and for a n identical retailers problem is a single cycle policy. Because the basic properties of an optimal solution are not sufficiently strong to know the form of an optimal policy in a multi-retailer problem, he determines optimal policies within certain classes of policies. More specifically, he considers single cycle policies, seperate retailing, where the n-retailer problem is simply divided into n one-retailer problems, and sequential subset partitions of the retailers with each subset following a single cycle policy, where a sequential subset partition of the retailers is a partition of the retailers where each subset only contains consecutive retailers when the retailers are sorted in ascending demand rate. Note that the sorting of the retailers before the sequential subset partitions are determined is in ascending demand rate because the retailers are assumed to have identical costs; in case the retailers have different costs, the sorting should be based on the ratio of the setup cost and the holding cost multiplied with the demand rate, i.e. the relative order quantity expressed in periods. Schwarz also gives several lower bounds for the cost of the optimal policy in the multi-retailer case . These bounds are based on relaxations of the original problem.

Schwarz, in co-operation with Graves, discusses the same problem further in [21] and extends it to the general multi-echelon distribution system. They show that the optimal stationary, a stationary policy is a policy in which each facility orders the same lot size every time it orders, policy is a single cycle policy. They also extend the system myopic concept, which was developed by Schwarz and Schrage [33] for an assembly environment, to distribution systems. A system myopic policy is defined as a policy which optimizes a given objective function with respect to any two stages and ignores multistage interaction effects; translated to a two-echelon distribution context, the system is seen as n subsystems each with 1 retailer, the retailer has its own costs whereas the depot has its own holding cost and a prorated order cost. Each subsystem defines that specific retailer's number of orders for each depot order; using fixed values for the number of orders at each retailer for every depot order, an optimal depot order quantity can be computed; the order quantity for the retailers then is a simple mathematical expression of the respective demand rates, costs and the number of orders for every depot order. This system myopic policy still can be improved using an iteration scheme for the depot's order quantity and the retailers' number of orders for every order of the depot.

Eppen and Schrage [16] consider a 1 depot, n identical cost retailers, problem in which the depot does not hold stock. Demand at the retailers is assumed to be stationary, normally distributed with no correlation between the demands at the different retailers. The depot might make it possible to obtain quantity discounts from the supplier and to exploit the "portfolio efficiencies" or "statistical economies of scale" made possible by carrying a single inventory during the depot's lead time. Provided the allocation assumption holds, i.e. when the incoming order at the depot is great relative to the retailers' inventories what allows the depot to allocate to the retailers such that the retailers become balanced, they come up with approximately optimal policies for the case in which there is no setup cost at the depot and for the case in which there is one. In case the depot has no setup cost, the depot orders every period; in case the depot has a setup cost, the depot orders every m periods. When the depot orders, it always uses a base stock policy, i.e. it brings the total system stock (on hand and on order) up to a certain number. The base stock level and m are calculated using analytical approximations.

Gross, Soland and Pinkus [22] give an explicit procedure for the extension of the Clark and Scarf approach to distribution systems. Their analysis is based on a finite horizon problem in which there is only a setup cost for the depot. Their basic approach is that the "imputed shortage cost" function at higher echelons is constructed on a marginal basis, i.e. when the depot cannot fulfill the optimal policy of all retailers, the imputed shortage cost will be the minimum additional cost at the different retailers. Note that this approach still is based on the balance assumption; they claim however that the balance assumption will in most cases be fulfilled provided the holding, shortage, and transportation costs per unit at each of the lower level installations are of the same order of magnitude.

Williams [36] examines several heuristics for an infinite horizon, deterministic, constant demand rate problem setting. He studies assembly, distribution and conjoined assembly/distribution problems. All his heuristics are stationary single cycle policies, the difference between the heuristics being the way in which the relationships between the different stages are considered. Williams is to our knowledge the first to warn against the use of single cycle policies in certain problem settings :

> "Imagine, for example, a distribution system in which one retailer has a setup cost which is ten times greater than that of any other stage, combined with an echelon holding cost which is much smaller than that of any other stage. Then it might be advantageous for the lot sizes to be nonstationary and for this particular retailer to be supplied by, say, only every third batch processed at the depot".

Jackson [24] studies a 1 depot, n retailers problem. This paper is an extension of the Eppen and Schrage paper where the depot did not hold stock to a situation in which a more general allocation policy is used. The policy considered is a simple one : in each period after receiving a shipment at the depot allocate in each period sufficient stock to each retailer to raise its inventory position up to its order up to level until either the depot runs out of stock or until the next shipment at the depot arrives. The periods between successive shipments to the depot can be subdivided in three kinds : ample stock periods, one allocation period and empty periods. Compared to the Eppen and Schrage allocation, this allocation policy uses the depot as a pooling risk facility and defers echelon retailer costs. Jackson admits his allocation policy need not be optimal because it ignores the distribution of total system stock over the different facilities and the evolution of this distribution during the order cycle; the ship up to policy only is appropriate when the retailer order costs are relatively small; else an (s,S) type shipping policy would be more appropriate.

Jackson and Muckstadt [25,26] examine the 1 depot, n retailers problem in a two periods context (where the two periods might be unequal length). This implies that the retailers have to make two allocation decisions towards the retailers, one at the moment an order is coming in at the depot, this is called the beginning of period 1, and one in the beginning of period 2 for every decision at the depot. One function of the centrally hold stock in period 1 is to ensure a more balanced distribution of stock in period 2. The risk of imbalance is pooled over period 1, thus reducing the expected level of backorders in the system without requiring additional system stock. They characterize the solution to the period 2 allocation problem and derive necessary and sufficient optimality conditions for the period 1 decision variables for the identical retailers case with no correlation between the demands at the different retailers and give approximate solution methods for the problems in which either there is correlation between the demands at the different retailers or there are nonidentical retailers.

Federguen and Zipkin [17, 18, 19] extend the Clark and Scarf results to the infinite horizon case, address computational issues, and propose approximation techniques. Zipkin [37] uses an additional state variable, the imbalance vector which is a measure of imbalance in the system, to get approximately optimal policies. Most of the papers by Federgruen and Zipkin assume no setup costs at the retailers, are based on infinite horizon results, use decomposition techniques and assume a constant penalty cost/holding cost ratio over all retailers; some papers allow correlation between the different retailers and/or allow the depot to hold stock while others do not. They prove that myopic allocation, allocation which tries to get the system in balance over $(\tau+1)$ periods, the first period affected by the current allocation decision, is not appropriate in some problem settings, e.g. when there is a setup cost at the depot and the coefficients of variation of the demand are different at the different retailers.

Timmer, Monhemius and Betrand in a recent article [34] advocate the use of a base stock system in lieu of an MRP-system to cope with dependent demand. They define a base stock system as a system in which the production decisions in all production stages are based on the same demand information. A base stock system can be seen as a compromise between statistical inventory control in which ordering decisions at the different production facilities are made independently and materials requirements planning in which the master schedule is exploded to calculate time phased gross requirements which can be translated to net requirements by subtracting stocks on hand and scheduled receipts at the various tocking points. Safety measures, essentially safety stock and safety time, then can be calculated in echelon terms; this avoids the unnecessary accumulation of slack and the huge amount of expediting messages found so often both in statistical inventory control systems and in material requirements planning systems. Lot-sizing decisions are only partly discussed. They state :

1. The lot size at the output side should be a multiple of the lot size at the input side and in case of branching, i.e. when there is commonality or when there is a distribution problem, at least equal to the largest lot size the output side; there is however no methodology given to calculate the lot sizes.
2. If the actual content of a stockpoint is not entirely sufficient to allow to release the quantity ordered to replenish the next stockpoint, adapt the order to be released to the quantity now available; this is the same policy as was proposed by Clark and Scarf.

We believe that this paper provides a new look on the discussion on the appropriateness of statistical inventory control vs. material requirements planning; the base stock system should be considered as a viable alternative though we admit that there should be some more research on the practical problems of lot sizing and imbalances in such a system.

Wijngaard and Wortmann [35] discuss the use of inventories in MRP-systems. They remark that most previous research on MRP and safety stocks is not totally consistent with current MRP-II methodology because it assumes there is no rescheduling possible and that the master production schedule is identical to the demand forecast; our previous research [28] also falls in this category. The base stock control system of Timmer et al. then is used to calculate echelon-based norms on safety measures such as safety stock, safety time and overestimation of the requirements, under the assumption of lot for lot lot-sizing. It is noted that when we do allow rescheduling, the protective stocks resulting from the above mentioned safety measures become dead stock because the rescheduling messages make that this stock is never used. The paper concludes with a short discussion on the proper use of the master production schedule under a base stock control system.

III. MODEL FORMULATION

In this section we introduce the multi-echelon production/inventory system and its underlying assumptions. We also describe how this system can be modelled as a Markovian Decision Process. Attention is restricted to the situation where the demand process is stationary and the planning horizon is infinite. The product structure we investigate is depicted in figure II.1. It is a two-echelon structure in which echelon 2 can be seen as a depot and echelon 1 are the independent retailers. Another interpretation is that echelon 2 is the raw material, e.g. crude oil, and echelon 1 are the different end products, e.g. the derivates. Yet another interpretation is that echelon 2 is a common product which is used in the different products at echelon 1. We will always refer to such a product structure as to a distribution system.

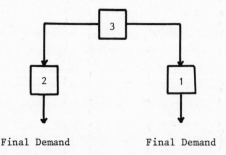

Figure II.1 : A two-echelon distribution system.

The model we present is based on the following assumptions :
1. A periodic review policy is followed;
2. The procurement and production lead times, which are measured in periods, are known constants;
3. The demand distributions are known, demand is independent from period to period and there is no correlation between the different end products;
4. All excess demand is backordered.

We also assume that the relevant costs consist of
1. production costs at each stage, which are composed of a fixed setup cost per production run and a constant cost per unit produced;
2. holding costs which are charged proportional to the installation stock at the end of the period;
3. linear shortage costs which are charged proportional to the number of final products backordered at the end of each period.

Note that the constant cost per unit can be ignored in our analysis as we assume that costs remain stationary over time and we have an infinite planning horizon.

The multi-echelon stochastic production/inventory problem introduced above can be modelled as a Markovian Decision Process. It is assumed that the system is observed at time t = 0,1, ..., T and classified into one of a finite number of states labeled 1,2, ..., N. For every state 1, a number of decision alternatives are possible, labeled 1,2, ..., K(i). (The number of possible policies might differ from state to state.) Whenever the system is in state i and decision alternative k is chosen the system moves to state j with known transition probability $p_{i,j,k}$ for all i,j=1,2,...K(i). The cost structure is introduced through $q_{i,k}$, the expected one-period cost when the system is in state i and decision alternative k is chosen.

In terms of the multi-echelon stochastic production planning problem described above the states i, i=1,2, ..., N, represent the echelon inventory position at each stage (which might be positive, negative or zero). The total number of states equals the product of all possible echelon inventory positions at all stages. (This is an upper bound as it includes 'impossible' states, e.g. a state with an echelon inventory position of 0 at the depot and an echelon inventory position of 3 and 4 at the retailers). The decision alternatives k, k=1,2, ..., K(i), represent the production alternatives at each stage. In case there are capacity constraints, some of these production decisions might be impossible which implies that the number of decision alternatives for state 1 in the capacitated case is less than (or equal to) the number of decision alternatives in the uncapacitated case. Applied to the two-echelon distribution problem of figure II.1, this means that state 25 might correspond to an echelon inventory position of product 3 (the depot) which is +2 units and an echelon inventory position of 2 and -3 at echelon 1 (the two retailers) while decision alternative 8 in state 25 might correspond to producing 5 of product 3, 1 of product 1 and 0 of product 2. The transition probabilities $p_{i,j,k}$ depend on the current state, i, the decision made, k, and the demand distribution which, together with i and k, determines j.

The solution method used is based on the value iteration or successive approximation method developed by Howard [23]. The recursive relation is given by :

$$V_{i,t} = \text{Min } \{q_{i,k} + \alpha * \sum_j p_{i,j,k} \, V_{j,t-1}\}$$

where $V_{i,0} = 0, \; \forall i$

$V_{i,t}$ stands for the expected total (discounted) cost of a system starting in state i and evolving for t periods when an optimal policy is followed, α denotes the discount factor and $q_{i,k}$ and $p_{i,j,k}$ are elements of the cost matrix Q and the transition matrix P^k. For large values of t, a stationary cost structure and stationary transition probabilities, the system will reach its steady state. This means that the decision to be taken in a certain state i is unaffected by the time period in which the decision has to be taken. After stabilisation, only a limited number of states will be possible; these are the recurrent states.

IV. COST MODIFICATIONS IN A DISTRIBUTION CONTEXT

In a previous paper [27] we discussed when and how it can be advantageous to modify the cost structure of a problem such that it better reflects the relation between the natural order sizes of the different stages in an assembly context. Here we will discuss the same problem in a distribution context.

We found that the cost structure in an assembly problem should be changed whenever the natural order size of one or more components is smaller than the natural order size of the end product. When we define the natural order period as the ratio between the natural order size and the average echelon demand per period, i.e. as the natural order size expressed in periods, we also can say that the costs should be changed whenever the natural order period of one or more components is smaller than the natural order period of the end product. Translated to a distribution context we then can say that the costs should be changed whenever the natural order period of the depot is smaller than the natural order period of one or more components. The appropriateness of this statement will be discussed next.

We propose to test the following in an experimental design :

We consider four problems for which the data and the natural order periods are given in table II.1. Problem 1 is the 'easy" problem; the natural order periods of all retailers are smaller than the natural order period of the depot. This implies that all facilities can follow their locally optimal policy without being constrained, at least in most periods, by the next higher echelon. Problem 2 is a more difficult problem; the natural order period of the depot lies between the natural order periods of the two retailers. This implies that the depot and the retailer with the greater natural order period should be on the same cycle while the retailer with the smaller natural order period can follow its own, locally optimal, policy. Problem 3 again is a rather easy problem; the natural order period of the depot is smaller than the natural order period of the two identical retailers. This makes that all products will be on the same cycle. Problem 4 probably is the most difficult problem; the natural order period of the depot is smaller than the natural order period of the two different retailers. It is at this point not clear how one should order in such a situation.

Facility	Shortage cost	Lead Time	Average Ech. Dem.
Depot 3	-----	1	2
Retailer 2	49	1	1
Retailer 1	49	1	1

Facility	Problem 1			Problem 2			Problem 3			Problem 4		
	K	HC	NOP	K	HC	NOP	K	HC	NOP	K	HC	NOP
Depot	32	1	5.7	16	1	4	9	1	3	5	1	2.2
Retailer 2	2	1	2	2	1	2	8	1	4	10	1	4.5
Retailer 1	2	1	2	18	1	6	8	1	4	45	1	9.5

Legend : K   : setup cost
HC : echelon Holding Cost
NOP : Natural Order Period

Table II.1 : Example Data for the Distribution Experiment.

V. PROBLEM STATEMENT AND OPTIMAL SOLUTION

This section gives the data we used in a two-echelon distribution experiment along with the optimal solution of these problems. We also give some properties of the optimal solutions for these problems that will be used in finding appropriate heuristics for distribution problems.

A. The Experiment

This experiment consists of 21 problems, subdivided in 6, 6, 5 and 5 problems for 4 cost structure combinations. The echelon holding cost at each stage of each problem is 1, the lead time at each stage of each problem is 1 and the shortage cost at each retailer of each problem is 49. The demand distribution used in each experiment is given in table II.2. The setup costs for the problems with cost structure 1 are given in table II.3, those for cost structure 2 are in table II.4, those for cost structure 3 are in table II.5 and those for cost structure 4 are in table II.6. Note that the four cost structures used are analogeous to the problems discussed in the previous section.

Demand	Probability of Demand	
	at Retailer 1	at Retailer 2
0	0.25	0.25
1	0.50	0.50
2	0.25	0.25

Table II.2 : Demand Distributions used in the Distribution Experiment

Subproblem	Setup Costs at 3	Setup Costs at 2	Setup Costs at 1
1	8	2	2
2	16	2	2
3	24	2	2
4	32	2	2
5	48	2	2
6	64	2	2

Table II.3 : Setup Data for Problems with Cost Structure 1

Subproblem	Setup Costs at 3	Setup Costs at 2	Setup Costs at 1
1	9	2	18
2	12	2	18
3	16	2	18
4	20	2	18
5	25	2	18

Table II.4 : Setup Data for Problems with Cost Structure 2

Subproblem	Setup Costs at 3	Setup Costs at 2	Setup Costs at 1
1	1	8	8
2	4	8	8
3	6	8	8
4	9	8	8
5	16	8	8

Table II.5 : Setup Data for Problems with Cost Structure 3

Subproblem	Setup Costs at 3	Setup Costs at 2	Setup Costs at 1
1	1	10	45
2	2	10	45
3	5	10	45
4	10	10	45
5	15	10	45

Table II.6 : Setup Data for Problems with Cost Structure 4

B. Optimal Solutions

The optimal solutions for the 21 problems of our experimental design are given by cost structure in tables II.7 - II.10.

Cost structure 1 is a cost structure in which the natural order period of the depot is greater than the natural order period of the two identical retailers. Our hypothesis was that the different ordering decisions would be independent. The results in table II.7 confirm this hypothesis, the only exceptions being the fact the order point at the depot is increased when one of the retailers has more than its fair share and that the retailers order one unit more when there is ample inventory at the depot in those cases where the setup cost at the depot is high.

Cost structure 2 is a cost structure in which the natural order period of the depot
lies between the natural order period of the two retailers. Our hypothesis was
that the depot and the retailer with the greater natural order period, retailer 1
in this cost structure, would be on the same cycle while the retailer with the
smaller natural order period, retailer 2 in this cost structure, would follow its
own policy. The optimal policy, presented in table II.8 at first sight does not
confirm this hypothesis. It looks like a much more complicated policy. We will
however try to relate this strange-looking policy to our hypothesis. The order
point at the depot is 7 but retailer 2, the retailer with the smaller natural order
period which always has a low inventory position, should always have the opportunity to order up to 3 and the order point at the depot is increased when retailer 2
has a high inventory position and retailer 1 is only just above its order point
and thus probably will order next period (and this order will be small as there
will only be a little available at the depot when we do not order at the depot this
period). The order points at the retailers are independent of the inventory positions at the different locations. The order up to level at the depot is dependent
on the inventory position at retailer 1, the retailer with the greater natural
order period. Whenever the inventory position at retailer 1 is small, which implies that this retailer probably will issue an order in the near future, the order
up to level at the depot is set to a high level which makes it possible that retailer 1 orders a lot. Whenever the inventory position at retailer 1 is high, and
what this means depends on the setup cost at the depot (it varies from 5 or more in
subproblem 1, the subproblem with the smallest setup cost at the depot, to 7 or more
in subproblem 5, the problem with the highest setup cost at the depot), the order
up to level at the depot is defined such that the current inventory position at retailer 1 is equal to, or somewhat less than (one could see this as some kind of
safety measure) the fair share of the new echelon inventory position at the depot.
In other words, one then issues an order which probably will be used only by the
second retailer. The explanation for this bizarre behavior is not that difficult :
the order quantity at the depot was increased because retailer 1 otherwise would be
far from its optimal behavior. If retailer 1 has plenty of stock, the depot can
follow its locally optimal policy which leads to a smaller order quantity. The
order up to levels at the retailers are dependent on the echelon inventory position
at the depot. The order up to level at retailer 1 always is very near to the fair
share of the echelon inventory position at the depot while the order up to level at
retailer 2 is 4 or 5. Summarising, and roughly speaking, one could say that the depot and the retailer with the greater natural order period are on the same cycle
while the retailer with the smaller natural order period follows its own policy.
If however the inventory position at retailer 2 becomes small while the inventory
position at retailer 1 still is high, the depot launches a, rather small, additional
order which in most cases will be used only by the second retailer.

Cost structure 3 is a cost structure in which the natural order period of the depot is smaller than the natural order period of the two identical retailers. Our hypothesis was that all should be on the same cycle. The optimal policies of these problems roughly confirm this view. These optimal policies can be explained as follows. The order point at the depot is such that the depot always orders when one of the retailers cannot order up to 3 units (which is the average demand during the echelon lead time at the depot plus the review period) or up to 4 if there is only one unit left at the depot. The order point at the retailers is 2 (the average demand during the lead time plus the review period) in most cases but 3 if the other retailer has plenty of stock and already has its fair share of the echelon inventory position at the depot. The order up to level at the depot varies only a little, except for subproblem 1, the subproblem with the very low setup cost at the depot. The order up to level at the retailers is such that they try to produce up to 7 (6 in subproblem 1) but constrain themselves to their fair share if there would be stock left at the depot if they produced up to 7.

Cost structure 4 is a cost structure in which the natural order period of the depot is smaller than the natural order period of the two different retailers. We did not state an hypothesis for this situation. Table II.10 which shows the optimal solutions for these problems clearly indicates that the optimal policy at a certain facility is not an easily expressed function of the echelon inventory position at that facility but is a complex function of the situation at all facilities. We will first discuss the ordering policy at the retailer level and then say something about the ordering policy at the depot.

We first give the order up to levels, S_1^u and S_2^u, for the subproblems which consist of the depot and one of the retailers, i.e. of seperate retailing, as these will prove to be very important in the interpretation of the optimal policy, both at the retailer and at the depot level. The retailer with the smaller natural order period, retailer 2 in this experiment, orders whenever its inventory position is not greater than two, the average demand during the retailer lead time plus the review period, and when its inventory position is three in some specific situations, i.e. when the echelon inventory position at the depot is relatively high and when the on hand position at the depot is that low that production of retailer 2 can use all this on-hand stock. The retailer with the greater natural order period, retailer 1 in this experiment, orders whenever its inventory position is not greater than one and when its inventory position is two and the depot's echelon inventory position is high which implies that retailer 1 can place a relatively great order. In case both retailers order, they both try to order up to their own unconstrained, seperate retailing, order up to level. In case this is not possible, i.e. almost always, both order less according to the results in table II.10; retailer 1 always gets more than retailer 2, but the difference becomes smaller for greater values of the depot setup cost as the savings in the number of setups at the depot become more important relative to the additional costs of more setups at retailer 1. In case only one retailer produces, he produces up to an order up to level which is equal to the order up to level of the seperate retailing problem minus the average demand during the depot echelon lead time; if however this would mean that he would leave 1 unit at the depot or if the depot echelon stock is equal to the summation of the seperate retailing order up to levels of all retailers, he produces up to the seperate retailing order up to level. This explanation holds for low values of the depot setup cost but the policy is less straightforward for high values of the depot setup cost.

The depot's ordering policy closely approaches the summation of the ordering policies of the depots of two independent serial systems consisting of the depot and one of the retailers, i.e. as if seperate retailing were optimal. The depot orders whenever one of the retailers' inventory positions after production at the retailer level is not greater than the average demand during the retailer lead time and the review period and when the inventory position is slightly higher and this retailer cannot order up to a position which approaches its seperate retailing order up to level. In case both retailers are low in stock after the production decisions at the retailer level the depot order up to level is the summation of the seperate retailing order up to levels; in case only one of the retailers has a low inventory position the depot order up to level is equal to the summation of the inventory position of the retailer with a high inventory position and the seperate retailing order up to level of the retailer with a low inventory position, the rationale being that in this case the depot order will be used only for that retailer because the additional depot holding costs which would be incurred by including provision for an order of the other retailer in the depot order are greater than the savings from a setup at the depot. As was the case for the retailer level this explanation holds for the cases in which the depot setup cost is relatively low. The optimal policy for the cases in which the depot setup cost becomes greater has more exceptions to this behavior.

Subproblem	Policy at Depot		Policy at Retailer 2		Policy at Retailer 1		Cost per period
1	(8,13)		(3,4)		(3,4)		17.76
2	(7,16)		(3,4)		(3,4)		19.74
3	(7,17)		(3,4)		(3,4)		21.27
4	(8,19)		(3,4)		(3,4)		23.05
5	Balance		ECH3A		ECH3A		25.11
	Y	N	<20	>=	<20	>=	
	(7,21)	(8,21)	(3,4)	(3,5)	(3,4)	(3,5)	
6	Balance		ECH3A		ECH3A		27.06
	Y	N	<22	>=	<22	>=	
	(7,23)	(8,23)	(3,4)	(3,5)	(3,4)	(3,5)	

Legend : Balance : balanced inventories at retailer level
                    (no retailer has more than its fair share)

        ECH3A : echelon inventory position at 3 (the depot)
                    after production decision at the depot

Table II.7 : Optimal Policies for Problems with Cost Structure 1.

Subproblem	s_1	s_2	s_3	ECH1	S_3	ECH3A	S_2	S_1	Costs
1	2	3	7	≤ 4	16	≤ 8	4	4	22.48
			Ech1+3	5	11	9	4	5	
			if Ech1 > 4	6	13	10	5	5	
			10	7	14	11	5	6	
			if Ech2 > 4	8	16	12	4	6	
			and Ech1 = 3			13,14	4	7	
						15,16	4	8	
2	2	3	7	≤ 3	16	≤ 8	4	4	23.32
			Ech1+3	4	17	9	4	5	
			if Ech1 > 4	5	12	10	5	5	
			9	6	13	11	5	6	
			if Ech2 > 4	7	15	12	4	6	
			and Ech1 = 3	8	16	13,14	4	7	
						15	5	7	
						16,17	5	8	
3	2	3	7	≤ 4	17	≤ 8	4	4	24.23
			Ech1+3	5	18	9	4	5	
			if Ech1 > 4	6	13	10	5	5	
			9	7	15	11	5	6	
			if Ech2 > 4	8	16	12	4	6	
			and Ech1 = 3			13,14	4	7	
						15	5	7	
						16	5	8	
						17,18	4	8	
4	2	3	7	≤ 3	17	≤ 8	4	4	25.21
			Ech1+3	4,5,6	18	9	4	5	
			if Ech1 > 4	7	15	10	5	5	
			9	8	17	11	5	6	
			if Ech1 > 4			12	4	6	
			and Ech1 = 3			13,14	4	7	
						15	5	7	
						16	5	8	
						17,18	4	8	
5	2	3	7	≤ 3	18	≤ 8	4	4	25.99
			Ech1+3	4,5,6	19	9	4	5	
			if Ech1 > 4	7	16	10	5	5	
			8	8	17	11	5	6	
			if Ech2 > 4			12	4	6	
			and Ech1 = 3			13,14	4	7	
						15	5	7	
						16	5	8	
						17,18,19	4	8	

Legend : ECH3A : echelon inventory position at 3 (the depot)
after production decision at the depot
Ech2 : echelon inventory position at 2 (retailer 2)
before production decision at retailer 2
Ech1 : echelon inventory position at 1 (retailer 1)
before production decision at retailer 1

Table II.8 : Optimal Policies for Problems with Cost Structure 2.

Subproblem	Policy at Depot				Policy at Retailers	Cost per period
	MxAP	MnAP	s_3	S_3		
1	≤ 3	---	8	13	if conc has FS	19.53
	4	= 2	8	12	then s = 3	
		<>2	8	11	else s = 2	
	5	= 3	8	12	if both produce	
		<>3	9	12	then produce everything	
	6	= 3	11	13	available at depot	
		= 4	10	13	else if one produces	
		else	8	13	then if OH3<=6-ech	
					then z=OH3	
					else z=6-ech	
					else	
2	≤ 3	= 3	10	14	if conc has FS	20.81
		<>3	7	14	and FS>=5	
	4	= 3	8	14	then s=3	
		<>3	7	14	else s=2	
	5	= 3	9	12	if both produce	
		<>3	8	12	then produce everything	
	6	= 3	10	13	available at depot	
		<>3	9	13	else if one produces	
	7	---	10	14	then if OH3<=7-ech	
					then z=OH3	
					else z=7-ech	
					else	
3	≤ 3	= 3	8	14	if conc has FS	21.26
		<>3	7	14	and FS>=5	
	4	= 3	8	15	then s=3	
		<>3	7	14	else s=2	
	5	= 3	9	14	if both produce	
		<>3	8	14	then produce everything	
	6	= 3	10	13	available at depot	
		<>3	9	13	else if one produces	
	7	= 3	11	14	then if OH3<=7-ech	
		<>3	10	14	then z=OH3	
					else z=7-ech	
					else	
4	≤ 3	= 3	8	15	if conc has FS	22.15
		<>3	7	14	and FS>=5	
	4	= 3	8	15	then s=3	
		<>3	7	15	else s=2	
	5	= 3	9	15	if both produce	
		<>3	8	15	then produce everything	
	6	= 3	10	13	available at depot	
		<>3	9	13	else if one produces	
	7	= 3	11	14	then if OH3<=7-ech	
		<>3	10	14	then z=OH3	
					else z=7-ech	
					else	

```
--------------------------------------------------------------------------------
5        <= 3   = 3    8    16    if conc has FS                        23.71
                <>3    7    15     and FS>=5
         4     = 3    8    16    then s=3
                <>3    7    16    else s=2
         5     = 3    9    16
                <>3    8    16    if both produce
         6     = 3   10    16    then produce everything
                <>3    9    16        available at depot
         7     = 3   11    15    else if one produces
                <>3   10    15        then if OH3<=7-ech
                                          then z=OH3
                                          else z=7-ech
                                      else
```

Legend : MxAP : maximum echelon inventory position at the retailers
                after production
         MnAP : minimum echelon inventory position at the retailers
                after production
         Conc : concurrent (= other retailer)
         FS   : fair share of echelon inventory position at depot before
                production decision
         OH3 : on hand inventory at depot
         z   : production decision at sole retailer which is producing
         ech : echelon inventory position at sole retailer which is
                producing

Table II.9 : Optimal Policies for Problems with Cost Structure 3.

Sub-pro-blem	Ordering policy – Optimal Solution	Cost per period
1	$S_1^u = 10$; $S_2^U = 7$	26.59

1

$S_1^u = 10$; $S_2^U = 7$ 26.59

<u>Ordering Policy for the retailers</u> :

Retailer 1 order point : if ech3 > 9 then $s_1 = 2$
                                                 else $s_1 = 1$
Retailer 2 order point : $s_2 = 2$

If both retailers order :

Ech3	S_2	S_1
10	3	7
11	3	8
12	5	7
13	5	8
14	5	9
15	6	9
16	7	9
17	7	10

If retailer 1 is the only retailer producing :

if ech3 = $(S_1^u + ech2)$ or ech3 = $(S_1^u + S_2^u)$

then $S_1 = 10$
else $S_1 = 9$

If retailer 2 is the only retailer producing :

if (ech3 = $(S_1^u + ech1)$ and ech3 $\geq$ 15) or ech3 = $(S_1^u + S_2^u)$

then $S_2 = 7$
else $S_2 = 6$

<u>Ordering policy for the depot</u>

Order if ech1a $\leq$ 2 or (ech1a = 3 and ech3 < $(S_1^u + ech2a)$) or
            ech2a $\leq$ 2 or (ech2a = 3 and ech3 < $(S_2^u + ech1a)$) or
            (ech1a = 3 and ech2a = 3 and ech3 $\leq$ 14)

Order up to :

ech1a	ech2a	S_3
2,3	2,3	$S_1^u + S_2^u$
	4	15
	5,6,7	ech2a + S_1^u
4,5,6,7,8,9,10	----	ech1a + S_2^u

| 2 | $S_1^u = 10$; $S_2^u = 7$ | 26.95 |

2

$S_1^u = 10$; $S_2^u = 7$ 26.95

<u>Ordering Policy for the retailers</u> :

Retailer 1 order point : if ech3 > 10 then $s_1 = 2$
                                                  else $s_1 = 1$
Ret. 2 O.P. : if (ech3 = (ech1+6) and ech3 > 10) or ech3 = 15
                    then $s_2 = 3$ else $s_2 = 2$

If both retailers order :

Ech3	S_2	S_1
10	3	7
11	3	8
12	5	7
13	5	8
14	5	9
15	6	9
16	7	9
17	7	10

If retailer 1 is the only retailer producing :

if ech3 = $(S_1^u + ech2)$ or ech3 = $(S_1^u + S_2^u)$ then $S_1 = 10$
                                                     else $S_1^1 = 9$

If retailer 2 is the only retailer producing :

if ech3 = $(S_2^u + ech1)$ or ech3 = $(S_1^u + S_2^u)$ then $S_2 = 7$
                                                     else $S_2^2 = 6$

Ordering policy for the depot

Order if ech1a $\leq$ 2 or (ech1a = 3 and ech3 < $(S_1^u + ech2a - 1)$) or
         ech2a $\leq$ 2 or (ech2a = 3 and ech3 < $(S_2^u + ech1a - 1)$) or
         (ech1a = 3 and ech2a = 3 and ech3 $\leq$ 14)

Order up to :	ech1a	ech2a	S_3
	2	2,3,4	$S_1^u + S_2^u$
		5,6,7	$ech2a + S_1^u$
	3	2,3	$S_1^u + S_2^u$
		4	15
		5,6,7	$ech2a + S_1^u$
	4,5,6,7,8,9,10 ----		$ech1a + S_2^u$

---

3    $S_1^u = 10$; $S_2^u = 7$ or 8 (always produce 5)   27.73

Ordering Policy for the retailers :

Ret. 1 O.P. : if ech3 > 10 or (ech3 = 10 and ech2 = 3)
              then $s_1 = 2$
              else $s_1^1 = 1$

Ret. 2 O.P. : if ech3 = (ech1+6) and ech3 > 10 and ech3 $\leq$ 17
              then $s_2 = 3$
              else $s_2^2 = 2$

If both retailers order :

Ech3	S_2	S_1
10	3	7
11	4	7
12	5	7
13	5	8
14	6	8
15	6	9
16	7	9
17	7	10
18	8	10

If retailer 1 is the only retailer producing :
if ech3 = 15 and ech2 < 5
then S_1 = 8
else if ech3 = 18 or (ech3 > 14 and ech3 = ech2 + 10)
     then S_1 = 10
     else S_1 = 9

If retailer 2 is the only retailer producing :
if ech3 = (7 + ech1) or ech3 $\geq$ 17 then S_2 = 7
                                else S_2 = 6

Ordering policy for the depot

Order if (ech1a $\leq$ 3 and ech3 < (ech2a + 9)) or
         (ech2a $\leq$ 3 and ech3 < (ech1a + 7)) or
         (ech1a = 3 and ech2a = 3 and ech3 < 16)

Order up to :	ech1a	ech2a	S_3
	2,3	2,3,4	S_1^u+8
		5,6,7	ech2a+S_1^u
	4,5,6,7	---	ech1a+7
	8,9,10	---	ech1a+8

---

4   S_1^u = 11 ; S_2^u = 8   29.14

Ordering Policy for the retailers :

Ret. 1 O.P. : if ech3 > 11 or
                 ((ech3 = 10 or ech3 = 11) and ech3 $\geq$ (ech2 + 7))
              then s_1 = 2
              else s_1 = 1

Ret. 2 O.P. : if ((ech3 = 8) and (ech1 = 4)) or
                 ((ech3 > 9) and (ech3 = ech1 + 5)) or
                 ((ech3 $\geq$ 10) and (ech3 = ech1 + 6))
              then s_2 = 3
              else s_2 = 2

If both retailers order :	Ech3	S_2	S_1
	10	3	7
	11	5	6
	12	5	7
	13	6	7
	14	6	8
	15	7	8
	16	7	9
	17	7	10
	18	8	10

If retailer 1 is the only retailer producing :
if ech3 = 15 and ech2 = 3
then S_1 = 8
else if ech3 $\geq$ 18 or ech3 = (ech2 + 10)
     then S_1 = 10
     else if ech3 = 17 and ech2 = 6
          then S_1 = 11
          else S_1 = 9

If retailer 2 is the only retailer producing :
 if (ech3 = 18 and ech1 = 3) or
    (ech3 = 19 and ech1 = 4) or
    (ech3 > 13 and ech3 = ech1 + 8)
 then S_2 = 8
 else S_2 = 7

<u>Ordering policy for the depot</u>

Order if ech1a $\leq$ 2 or ech2a $\leq$ 2 or
         (ech1a = 3 and ech2a > 3 and ech3 < (ech2a + 9)) or
         (ech2a = 3 and ech1a > 3 and ech3 < (ech1a + 7)) or
         (ech1a = 3 and ech2a = 3 and ech3 < 14)

Order up to :	ech1a	ech2a	S_3
	2,3,4	2,3	18
		4,5	19
		6,7	17
		8	19
	5,6	---	ech1a+7
	7,8,9,10	---	ech1a+8

---

5   S_1^u = 11 ; S_2^u = 8 or 9 (always produce 6)   30.28

<u>Ordering Policy for the retailers :</u>

Ret. 1 O.P. : if ech3 > 10 or (ech3 = 10 and ech2 = 3)
              then s_1 = 2
              else s_1 = 1

Ret. 2 O.P. : if (ech3 = 13 and ech1 = 2) or
                 (ech3 > 8 and ech3 = ech1 + 4) or
                 (ech3 $\geq$ 9 and ech3 = ech1 + 5) or
                 (ech3 $\geq$ 10 and ech3 = ech1 + 6)
              then s_2 = 3
              else s_2 = 2

If both retailers order :	Ech3	S_2	S_1
	9	4	5
	10	5	5
	11	5	6
	12	6	6
	13	6	7
	14	6	8
	15	7	8
	16	7	9
	17	8	9
	18	8	10
	19	8	11

If retailer 1 is the only retailer producing :
 if (ech3 $\geq$ 19 and ech2 $\leq$ 6) or (ech3 $\geq$ 15 and ech3 = (ech2 + 10))
 then S_1 = 10
 else if (ech3 = 15 and ech2 = 3) or
         (ech3 = 16 and (ech2 = 4 or ech2 = 5))
      then S_1 = 8
      else if (ech3 = 14 and ech2 = 4)
           then S_1 = 7
           else S_1 = 9

If retailer 2 is the only retailer producing :
 if (ech3 = 9 and ech1 = 2) or
    ((ech3 = 11 or ech3 = 12 or ech3 = 18 or ech3 = 19) and ech1 = 3)
 then S_2 = 6
 else if (ech3 = 10 and ech1 = 2) or
          (ech3 $\geq$ 14 and ech1 $\geq$ 4 and ech3 = (ech1 + 8))
      then S_2 = 8
      else S_2^2 = 7

Ordering policy for the depot

Order if ech1a $\leq$ 2 or ech2a $\leq$ 2 or
          (ech1a = 3 and ech2a > 3 and
          (ech3 < (ech2a + 7) or ech3 < 13)) or
          (ech2a = 3 and ech1a > 3 and ech3 < (ech1a + 7)) or
          (ech1a = 3 and ech2a = 3 and ech3 < 13)

Order up to :	ech1a	ech2a	S_3
	2,3,4	2,3,4	19
		5,6	20
		7,8	18
	5,6	----	ech1a+8
	7,8,9	----	ech1a+7
	10,11	2	ech1a+8
		3	ech1a+9

Legend : echx : echelon inventory position at facility x before production
         echxa : echelon inventory position at facility x after production
         S_x^u : unconstrained order up to level at retailer x
                 (serial problem of depot and retailer x)

Tabel II.10 : Optimal Policies for Problems with Cost Structure 4.

VI. HEURISTIC SOLUTIONS

In this section we first discuss the general principles we used to come up with heuristic solutions. We then discuss modified versions of the three heuristics we used in the assembly experiments [29] and apply these modified heuristics on the 21 problems of the distribution experiment.

A. General Principles

The optimal solutions to the test problems indicate that the optimal policy at any facility is dependent on the inventory positions at all facilities. In a practical context it would be very difficult to implement, control and administer such a complex policy. We therefore tested some simple heuristic policies in which the ordering decision at a given facility is only dependent on the echelon inventory position of that facility, both because the echelon inventory position proved to be a very important variable in the interpretation of the optimal policies in the distribution experiment and because we found that echelon-based policies perform very good in assembly systems; note that the actual allocation policy is not entirely a level by level approach as we restrict the allocation to a facility to its fair share (see general principle 2, infra). Our goal was not that these policies would be optimal but we were interested in policies which are easy to understand and to control and wanted to see the cost influence of such a policy.

The general principles used in the heuristic solutions are derived from the properties of the optimal solutions to the distribution problems. A first principle is that we always work on the cost-modified version of the problems. A second one is that no retailer ever gets more than its fair share and a third one is that there will never be one unit on hand at the depot level as the optimal solutions proved that this was almost never useful. A last principle we use, which is not derived from the properties of the optimal solution but just is common sense, is that we order at the depot level, even when the echelon inventory position at the depot is greater than the depot - order point, whenever one of the retailers has such a low level of inventory, and there is that little on hand and on order at the depot, that it cannot even reach its order point at the moment the order we're deciding on now at the depot level is coming in, assuming the actual demand during the lead time at the depot is equal to the expected demand during the lead time at the depot; this is a dangerous situation, from a service level viewpoint, which should be avoided. The last principle departs from our goal of basing decisions only on information about that facility but we thought this to be essential to avoid too great imbalances.

B. The Modified Clark and Scarf Heuristic

Gross, Soland and Pinkus [22] first used the Clark and Scarf approach in a distribution context. Their reasoning is as follows :
1. Assume the different retailers are independent;
2. Determine the inventory policy for the retailers assuming plenty of stock is available at the depot and calculate an artificial shortage cost for the case the retailer is not able to order up to its locally optimal order up to level.
3. Construct the artificial shortage penalty function at the depot from the marginal artificial shortage cost functions at the different retailers.
4. Determine the inventory policy at the depot using the holding cost function at the depot and the artificial shortage cost function at the depot found in step 3.

Gross et al. developed this reasoning in a very 'friendly' environment : no setup costs at the retailers, no lead times and the retailers are in balance, i.e. the ratio between stock on hand (or echelon inventory position minus expected demand during the echelon lead time at the reatailer when there is an echelon lead time) and expected demand per period is approximately the same at all retailers. Our problems however do have lead times and setup costs and we therefore cannot use this heuristic as such. We will however use its logic to define an analogeous heuristic.

An important difference is that, where Gross et al. worked on the original problem, we always work on the cost-modified problem. This implies that we will never have great imbalances because an imbalance occurs because one of the retailers obtains too much. This is avoided through the cost modification process and through the fact that we never allow a retailer to get more than its fair share (except when there otherwise would be left exactly one unit left at the depot). We will discuss the proposed modified Clark and Scarf heuristic for the four cost structures presented in section IV.

Cost structure 1 is the cost structure in which the natural order period of the depot is greater than the natural order period of all retailers. This implies we can use the original Clark and Scarf heuristic at echelon 1, the retailer level, and the Gross-modification at echelon 2, the depot level. The Gross-modification is adapted to cope with lead times but the idea remains the same; whereas the artificial shortage cost at echelon 2 in the original Clark and Scarf heuristic was based on the cost function of one and only one product at echelon 1, it now is based on the minimum marginal cost at all retailers of echelon 1.

Cost structure 3 is the cost structure in which the natural order period of the depot is smaller than the natural order period of the two identical retailers. This

implies we have to collapse all products and consider them as one product in determining a reasonable policy. Care should be taken to use the correct parameters.
The setup cost is the summation of the setup costs of all facilities considered
(the depot and all retailers), the holding cost is the sum of the holding cost at
the depot and a weighted average holding cost at the retailers, i.e. a weighted installation holding cost, the echelon demand is the sum of the demands at the retailers and the echelon lead time is the lead time at the depot plus the lead time
at the retailers, assuming the lead time is the same at all retailers. We then
can use the original Clark and Scarf procedure for echelon 1 to solve this problem.

Cost structure 2 is a cost structure in which the natural order period of the depot
lies between the natural order period of the different retailers. This implies that
the depot and the retailer with the greater natural order period will be on the same
cycle while the retailer with the smaller natural order period will be able, in most
cases, to follow its locally optimal policy. The policy of the retailer with the
smaller natural order period, and the associated g-function, can be found using the
original Clark and Scarf procedure for echelon 1. The way we find the policy for the
depot and the retailer with the greater natural order period then goes as follows.

Step 1 : Define $K_{3'}$, the setup cost used in this procedure, as the sum of the setup
cost at the depot and the setup cost at the retailer with the greater natural order period (we will have a setup both at the depot and at the retailer with the greater natural order period in every cycle at the depot).
Define $h_{3'}$, the holding cost used in this procedure, as the echelon holding
cost of the depot; we will incorporate the holding cost of the retailer with
the greater natural order period in the calculation of the f-function.

Step 2 : Calculate $\bar{L}_{3'}$, the holding cost function :

$$\bar{L}_{3',n}(y) = \sum_q P^3_{n,n-\tau_3,q} \; [h_3 * (y-q)^+ + \Lambda_{n-\tau_3} (FS(y-q)) \,]$$

The holding cost function consists of 2 parts :
* The holding costs at the moment the order is coming in at the depot
* An artificial shortage cost which is only positive if the fair share of
  the echelon inventory position at the depot the moment the order is coming
  in at the depot is not enough for the retailer with the smaller natural
  order period to reach its locally optimal order up to level. This artificial shortage cost is defined as in the original Clark and Scarf heuristic (see [29], section IV.A.a).

Step 3 : Calculate $\bar{g}_{3',n}$ for all y and let $S_{3',n}$ be the value of y for which

$$\min(\bar{g}_{3',n,y}) = \min(C_{3',n} * y + \bar{L}_{3',n,y} + \sum_q f_{3',n-1,y-q} * P_{n,q})$$

Step 4 : Let $s_{3',n}$ be the greatest value, not exceeding $S_{3',n}$, for which

$$\bar{g}_{3',n,s_{3',n}} \geq \bar{g}_{3',n,S_{3',n}} + K_{3',n}$$

Step 5 : Calculate $f_{3',n,x_{3',n}}$ for all $x_{3',n}$ where $x_{3',n}$ is the echelon stock position at the depot at the beginning of period n.

$$f_{3',n,x_{3',n}} = \begin{cases} \bar{L}_{3',n,x_{3',n}} + \\[6pt] \sum\limits_{dd\tau_3} \sum\limits_{dd(\tau_1+1)} P_{n,n-\tau_3,dd\tau_3} * P_{n-\tau_3,n-(\tau_3+(\tau_1+1)),dd(\tau_1+1)} * \\[6pt] [h_1 * [FS(x_{3',n} - dd\tau_3) - dd(\tau_1+1)]^+ + \\[6pt] P_1 * [- \{FS(x_{3',n} - dd\tau_3) - dd(\tau_1+1)\}]^+] + \\[6pt] \sum\limits_q P_{n,n-1,q} * f_{3',n-1,x_{3',n}-q} \qquad \text{if } x_{3',n} > s_{3',n} \\[10pt] K_{3',n} + \bar{L}_{3',n,s_{3',n}} + \\[6pt] \sum\limits_{dd\tau_3} \sum\limits_{dd(\tau_1+1)} P_{n,n-\tau_3,dd\tau_3} * P_{n-\tau_3,n-(\tau_3+(\tau_1\pm1)),dd(\tau_1+1)} * \\[6pt] [h_1 * [FS(s_{3',n} - dd\tau_3) - dd(\tau_1+1)]^+ + \\[6pt] P_1 * [- \{FS(s_{3',n} - dd\tau_3) - dd(\tau_1+1)\}]^+] + \\[6pt] \sum\limits_q P_{n,n-1,q} * f_{3',n-1,s_{3',n}-q} \qquad \text{if } x_{3',n} \leq s_{3',n} \end{cases}$$

where $dd\tau_3$: demand during lead time at depot;

$dd(\tau_{1+1})$: demand during lead time at retailer with greater natural order period plus review period;

$FS(x)$: fair share for retailer with greater natural period if echelon inventory position at the depot (after ordering) equals x units;

$P_{n,n-t,q}$: probability that the echelon demand at the depot from period n to period n-t equals q.

As was already mentioned in step 1, the f-function not only consists of its usual parts, the holding cost function of the product itself and the recursive part but also of the inventory-based costs of the retailer with the greater natural order period. The first time we can influence the inventory-based costs at this retailer, assuming we only send an order to this retailer the moment an order is coming in at the depot, is within τ_3 (the lead time at the depot) + τ_1 (the lead time between the depot and the retailer under consideration) + 1 period (the review period because we assume the order is coming in at the beginning of the period but we incur inventory-based costs at the end of the period). In case we order at the depot, we can legitimately assume that we will be able to order up to the fair share of the retailer the moment the order is coming in at the depot. In case we do not order at the depot we still assume that this retailer will incur the inventory-based costs of a fair share allocation.

Cost structure 4 is a cost structure in which the natural order period of the depot is smaller than the natural order period of the different retailers. We will try to reduce this cost structure to one of the other cost structures, i.e. we will test whether we come to a reasonable policy by assuming all are on the same cycle (this is a reduction to the policy followed for cost structure 3) or by assuming that the depot and the retailer with the greater natural order period are on the same cycle whereas the retailer with the smaller order period follows its own locally optimal policy (this is a reduction to the policy followed for cost structure 2). We will also test the result of a policy in which we do not consider the existence of a depot (in which we do as if the depot is only there for one product), i.e. of seperate retailing.

The Clark and Scarf-heuristic is a first attempt to decompose the multi-echelon production/inventory problem into several single-echelon production/inventory problems. Strictly speaking, it is not a level-by-level approach as the near optimal solution, and its associated cost, are carried over from stage to stage.

C. The Ehrhardt - Heuristic

R. Ehrhardt published several papers [13,14,15] in which he proposed a new way to find the order point and the order up to level for (s,S)-type policies. His method, which was intended for single echelon production-inventory systems, basically is the result of two loglinear regressions. As data for these regressions, Ehrhardt considered 288 problems (all possible cominations of three types of demand distributions, four values for average demand during one period, two setup costs, four shortage costs and one holding cost) for which the optimal difference between the order point and the order up to level and the optimal order point were calculated.

The first regression determines the difference between the order point and the order up to level, its exogenous variables are the average demand (μ), the ratio between setup costs and holding costs (K/h), the lead time (τ) and the standard deviation of demand (σ) and looks as follows.

$$D_p = 1.465 * \mu^{0.364} * (K/h)^{0.498} * \sigma_\tau^{0.138}$$

where $\sigma_t = (\tau + 1)^{0.5} * \sigma$

The second regression determines the order point, and thus implicitly the order up to level as D_p has already been defined. The exogenous variables are the average demand, the standard deviation of demand, the lead time, the inventory holding cost and the shortage cost and also contains the difference between the order point and the order up to level, an endogeneous variable. This regression gives the following result.

$$s_p = \mu_\tau + \sigma_\tau^{0.832} * (\sigma^{0.5}/\mu)^{0.187} * (0.220/z + 1.142 - 2.866 * z)$$

where $\mu_\tau = (\tau+1) * \mu$

and $z = [D_p/\{(1 + p/h) * \sigma_\tau\}]^{0.5}$

In case the setup costs and the shortage costs are relatively small, which implies that D_p is relatively small, Ehrhardt modifies the rules for finding D_p and s_p. He then compares the regression values of s and S with the order up to level which would be found when the setup costs were zero and demand followed a normal distribution. Empirical tests have shown that this approach can be used whenever the ratio between D_p and μ is smaller than 1.5. The order point and the order up to level are thus defined as follows.

a) When $D_p/\mu > 1.5$, then $s = s_p$
$$S = s_p + D_p$$
b) When $D_p/\mu <= 1.5$, then $s = \min \{s_p, S_0\}$
$$S = \min \{s_p + D_p, S_0\}$$
where $S_0 = \mu_\tau + v * \sigma_\tau$
v is the point for which
$$\int_x e^{-x^2/2} * (2 * \pi)^{0.5} \, dx = \frac{p}{p+h}$$

As was mentioned earlier, Ehrhardt developed this heuristic for end products only. We will however use this heuristic for all facilities. The exogeneous variables are always expressed in echelon terms. This implies we use echelon demand, echelon holding costs and echelon lead times (the echelon lead time is the sum of all individual lead times through successive stages required to manufacture this item and make it into a finished product); the shortage cost used however always is the shortage cost of the end product. It is clear that this heuristic also uses the collapsing principle discussed in section IV.

The Ehrhardt heuristic uses these regression lines in the distribution experiment. The only difference is that we consider other costs when the natural order period of the depot lies between the natural order periods of the different retailers (and in one of the alternatives considered in the case where the natural order period of the depot is smaller than the order period of all different retailers).

The logic goes as follows :

Assume we have a depot with two retailers, retailer 2 has a small natural order period and retailer 1 has a great natural order period and thus will be in the same order cycle as the depot. We also assume the lead times to be zero as they have no significant impact on the order cycle, but only on the order point. Retailer 2 will in most cases be able to order up to its locally optimal order up to level and thus will approximately order every natural order period (every n periods). The only unknown parameter then is the order period of the collapsed part, i.e. the depot and retailer 1. We will call this variable x, i.e. order on the average every x periods at the depot (and thus at retailer 1).

* The total costs per cycle of x periods are

$K_3 + K_1 +$

    Setup costs of 'collapsed' part

$\dfrac{x * (x-1)}{2} * (h_1 + h_3) * AD_1 +$

    Holding costs of 'collapsed' part

$\dfrac{x}{n} * \{K_2 + \dfrac{n * (n-1)}{2} * (h_2 + h_3) * AD_2\}$

    Number of cycles at retailer 2 for every cycle of the 'collapsed'

        part *

    costs per cycle at retailer 2

$[(\dfrac{x}{n} - 1) + (\dfrac{x}{n} - 2) + \dots + 1] * n * n * AD_2 * h_3$

    Holding costs at the depot

        number of cycles at retailer 2 that we still have to go in this

        cycle of the 'collapsed' part *

length of cycle at retailer 2 *

(situation remains the same)

length of cycle at 2 * average demand at retailer 2 per period *

(average demand per cycle is length of cycle * average demand per period)

holding cost per unit at the depot

* The total costs per period thus are

$$TCP = \frac{K_3 + K_1}{x} + \frac{x-1}{2} * (h_1 + h_3) * AD_1 +$$

$$\frac{1}{n} * \left[K_2 + \frac{n*(n-1)}{2} * (h_2 + h_3) * AD_1 \right] + \frac{1}{2} * (\frac{x}{n} - 1) * n * h_3 * AD_2$$

* This is optimized through

$$\frac{\delta TCP}{\delta X} = \frac{-(K_3 + K_1)}{x^2} + \frac{1}{2} (h_1 + h_3) AD_1 + \frac{1}{2} * \frac{n}{n} h_3 * AD_2 = 0$$

$$\frac{-(K_3 + K_1)}{x^2} = - \frac{(h_1 + h_3) AD_1 + h_3 * AD_2}{2}$$

$$X = \left[\frac{2 * (K_3 + K_1)}{h_3 * AD_2 + (h_1 + h_3) * AD_1} \right]^{0.5}$$

* The normal formula for the natural order period is

$$NOP = \left[\frac{2 * K}{h * AD} \right]^{0.5}$$

The relevant setup costs thus are the summation of the setup costs at the depot and at retailer 1 whereas the relevant holding costs are the sum of the holding costs at the depot (h_3) and the weighted holding cost at the retailer (AD_1/ ($AD_1 + AD_2$) * h_1). The relevant average demand of course is the summation of the average demands at the two retailers.

D. The Inventory Holding Costs vs. Shortage Costs - Heuristics

A third heuristic defines the difference between the order point and the order up level as the economic order quantity. The order point is determined by means of a trade-off between additional safety stock holding costs and shortage costs.

The definition of D, the difference between the order point and the order up to level, is to a high degree based on the book by Magee [30, p. 83]. The logic goes as follows.

1. In an (s,S) system the minimal order quantity is equal to the difference between the order point and the order up to level, D. The average order quantity in an (s,S) system thus can be approximated by the minimal order quantity, D, augmented with half of the average demand during one period (only half of the average demand as you reached the order point on the average in the middle of the period).

2. In a deterministic, continuous review system with a constant demand rate, costs are minimised by setting total holding costs equal to the total setup costs without allowing shortages (see the familiar Wilson lot size formula). When the review becomes periodic, the optimal lot size becomes the demand of an integer number of periods. When we express the Wilson lot size in number of periods (let us call this x), we notice that in most cases the optimal number of periods which are in a lot in a periodic review system is the integer greater than x, the reason being that the total cost curve of the EOQ-model is less sensitive at the right hand than at the left hand.

From 1. and 2. it follows that

$$D + \frac{\mu}{2} = EOQ + \delta$$

or $\qquad D = EOQ + \delta - \frac{\mu}{2}$

or $\qquad D \simeq EOQ$

The determination of the order point is based on a trade-off between additional safety stock costs and savings in shortage costs. The procedure goes as follows.

1. Determine the average time between orders, TBO.
2. For all possible order points s, determine
   a. The average shortage costs per period when the order point would be s (and $D = EOQ$), SHP_s.
   b. The additional safety stock holding cost, for the last unit, when the order point would be s, $ASSP_s$.
3. Determine the order point s as the maximum echelon inventory position for which the saving in shortage costs, $SHP_s - SHP_{s-1}$, is greater than the additional safety stock cost, $ASSP_s$.

Most readers should already have noticed that we assumed that D covers an integer number of periods. When D, and thus the economic order quantity, is relatively small, we will follow the same policy as we do in the Ehrhardt-heuristic, i.e. we will use only one critical number, the order up to level. The way we use this heuristic is completely analog to the use of the Ehrhardt-heuristic, i.e. we use the collapsing principle of section IV and when we are dealing with several echelons, we think in a system sense. We will use other costs, the same as those used in the Ehrhardt-heuristic in case the natural order period of the depot lies between the natural order periods of the different retailers (and in one of the alternatives considered in the case where the natural order period of the depot is smaller than the order period of all different retailers).

E. Heuristic Solutions

The heuristic solutions to the test problems are given by cost structure in tables II.12-II.17. We give for each heuristic three solutions for cost structure 4, the cost structure in which the natural order period of the depot is smaller than the natural order period of the two different retailers. The first one behaves as in the case where the natural order period of the depot lies between the natural order periods of the different retailers; the second one behaves as if the central depot works only for one retailer, i.e. it applies the heuristic solutions to the serial subproblems which consist of the depot and each of the different retailers separately to each of the retailers; the last one collapses the problem into a one stage problem as we do in the case where the natural order period of the depot is smaller than the natural order period of the two identical retailers. Each of these heuristics is of course subject to the general principles stated earlier in section A.

A summary of the comparison between the different heuristics against eachother and against the optimal solution with respect to the resulting average costs per period is given in table II.18 for the cost structures 1, 2 and 3. This same comparison was also made for the different alternatives considered in cost structure 4 as is shown in table II.19. Table II.20 then gives a comparison between the different heuristics when the best alternative is chosen for each subproblem in every heuristic. We will now discuss these results cost structure by cost structure.

Cost structure 1 is the cost structure in which the depot has a greater natural order period than the two identical retailers. We calculated the policy parameters of each heuristic in an independent way in the Ehrhardt and in the shortage costs vs. safety stock holding costs heuristics as we assumed that the retailers would be able in most cases to follow their locally optimal policy. The results in table II.18 clearly indicate that the modified Clark and Scarf heuristic is the best heuristic for this cost structure; it always is the best heuristic and the average cost deviation to the optimal solution only is 2.20 % whereas the cost deviation of the other heuristics to the optimal solution is around 5 %. The other heursitics have higher shortage costs because the retailers have a greater difference between the order point and the order up to level which makes that the number of orders at the retailers for every depot order is smaller which implies that the risk of imbalance between the different retailers, and thus of shortages, increases. We are however not sure whether this superior performance of the modified Clark and Scarf heuristic is a general rule when the natural order period of the depot is greater than the natural order period of all retailers or just is a by-product of these particular cost structures.

Cost structure 2 is the cost structure in which the depot's natural order period lies between the natural order period of the two retailers. We proposed to use adapted costs to calculate the policy parameters of the collapsed part consisting of the depot and the retailer with the greater natural order period in the Ehrhardt and in the shortage costs vs. safety stock holding costs heuristic; the retailer with the smaller natural order period was allowed to follow its locally optimal solution in both heuristics. We also gave an adapted version of the modified Clark and Scarf heuristic to cope with this cost structure. The results in table II.18 show that the different heuristics do not differ much with respect to the resulting costs though the Ehrhardt heuristic performs somewhat better than the other two heuristics. The cost difference between the optimal solution and the heuristic solution is mainly caused by higher shortage costs, partially offset by lower holding costs, which are incurred because the heuristic policies have a far more straightforward ordering policy; the optimal order points and order up to levels are a function not only of echelon inventory but also of the situation at the other facilities.

Cost structure 3 is the cost structure in which the depot's natural order period is smaller than the natural order period of the two identical retailers. All heuristics collapse this problem into a single facility problem which leads to a solution in which all facilities follow the same ordering policy. The allocation to the retailers then is a pure myopic allocation, i.e. one which tries to balance the inventories the first time they can be influenced. The results in table II.18 again show little difference between the heuristics considered though the Ehrhardt heuristic again performs somewhat better. The cost difference between the optimal solution and the heursitic solutions is mainly caused by higher shortage costs which are incurred because the depot's order point and the depot's order up to level are in the heuristic solutions not dependent on the situation at the retailers but are totally based on the echelon inventory position at the depot.

Cost structure 4 is the cost structure in which the depot's natural order period is smaller than the natural order periods of the two different retailers. We tested

Sub-Problem	Mod. Cl. & Sc.				Ehrhardt				SS vs. SHC			
	Dep	Ret2	Ret1	Costs	Dep	Ret2	Ret1	Costs	Dep	Ret2	Ret1	Costs
1	(9,14)	(3,4)	(3,4)	18.29	(8,13)	(3,6)	(3,6)	18.70	(7,13)	(3,5)	(3,5)	19.32
2	(8,16)	(3,4)	(3,4)	19.94	(7,15)	(3,6)	(3,6)	21.59	(7,15)	(3,5)	(3,5)	20.63
3	(8,18)	(3,4)	(3,4)	21.80	(7,17)	(3,6)	(3,6)	22.44	(7,17)	(3,5)	(3,5)	22.41
4	(8,20)	(3,4)	(3,4)	23.42	(7,18)	(3,6)	(3,6)	24.14	(7,18)	(3,5)	(3,5)	23.71
5	(8,21)	(3,4)	(3,4)	25.71	(7,21)	(3,6)	(3,6)	26.28	(6,20)	(3,5)	(3,5)	26.39
6	(8,23)	(3,4)	(3,4)	27.80	(7,23)	(3,6)	(3,6)	28.10	(6,22)	(3,5)	(3,5)	27.92

Table II.12 : Heuristic Solutions for the Problems with Cost Structure 1

Sub-Problem	Mod. Cl. & Sc.				Ehrhardt				SS vs. SHC			
	Dep	Ret2	Ret1	Costs	Dep	Ret2	Ret1	Costs	Dep	Ret2	Ret1	Costs
1	(6,15)	(3,4)	(2,8)	24.21	(7,15)	(3,6)	(3,9)	23.96	(7,15)	(3,5)	(2,8)	23.26
2	(6,15)	(3,4)	(2,8)	24.83	(7,16)	(3,6)	(3,9)	24.65	(6,15)	(3,5)	(2,8)	25.37
3	(6,16)	(3,4)	(2,8)	25.37	(7,16)	(3,6)	(3,9)	25.48	(6,16)	(3,5)	(2,8)	25.48
4	(6,16)	(3,4)	(2,8)	26.14	(7,17)	(3,6)	(3,9)	25.91	(6,16)	(3,5)	(2,8)	26.24
5	(6,17)	(3,4)	(2,8)	27.09	(7,17)	(3,6)	(3,9)	26.85	(6,17)	(3,5)	(2,8)	27.20

Table II.13 : Heuristic Solutions for the Problems with Cost Structure 2

Sub-Problem	Mod. Cl. & Sc.				Ehrhardt				SS vs. SHC			
	Dep	Ret2	Ret1	Costs	Dep	Ret2	Ret1	Costs	Dep	Ret2	Ret1	Costs
1	(7,13)	(2,6)	(2,6)	20.88	(7,13)	(3,7)	(3,7)	21.22	(7,13)	(2,6)	(2,6)	20.88
2	(7,13)	(2,6)	(2,6)	21.76	(7,13)	(3,7)	(3,7)	22.10	(7,13)	(2,6)	(2,6)	21.76
3	(6,13)	(2,6)	(2,6)	23.66	(7,14)	(3,7)	(3,7)	22.52	(6,13)	(2,6)	(2,6)	23.66
4	(6,14)	(2,6)	(2,6)	23.65	(7,14)	(3,7)	(3,7)	23.30	(6,13)	(2,6)	(2,6)	24.45
5	(6,14)	(2,6)	(2,6)	25.29	(7,15)	(3,7)	(3,7)	24.38	(6,14)	(2,6)	(2,6)	25.29

Table II.14 : Heuristic Solutions for the Problems with Cost Structure 3

Sub-Problem	Mod. Cl. & Sc.				Ehrhardt				SS vs. SHC			
	Dep	Ret2	Ret1	Costs	Dep	Ret2	Ret1	Costs	Dep	Ret2	Ret1	Costs
1	(6,18)	(2,7)	(2,12)	29.69	(7,18)	(3,8)	(2,12)	29.37	(6,17)	(2,6)	(2,11)	30.26
2	(6,18)	(2,7)	(2,12)	29.86	(7,18)	(3,8)	(2,12)	29.54	(6,17)	(2,6)	(2,11)	30.44
3	(6,19)	(2,7)	(2,12)	30.75	(6,18)	(3,8)	(2,12)	30.14	(6,18)	(2,6)	(2,11)	30.80
4	(6,19)	(2,7)	(2,12)	31.52	(6,19)	(3,8)	(2,12)	31.00	(6,18)	(2,6)	(2,11)	31.62
5	(6,20)	(2,7)	(2,12)	31.19	(6,19)	(3,8)	(2,12)	30.45	(6,19)	(2,6)	(2,11)	32.05

Table II.15 : Heuristic Solutions for the Problems with Cost Structure 4
(retailer 1 and the depot on the same cycle)

Sub-Problem	Mod. Cl. & Sc.				Ehrhardt				SS vs. SHC			
	Dep	Ret2	Ret1	Costs	Dep	Ret2	Ret1	Costs	Dep	Ret2	Ret1	Costs
1	(3,17)	(3,7)	(3,10)	26.85	(2,16)	(2,6)	(3,10)	27.45	(3,16)	(3,6)	(3,10)	27.36
2	(3,17)	(3,7)	(3,10)	27.19	(2,16)	(2,6)	(3,10)	27.67	(3,16)	(3,6)	(3,10)	27.76
3	(3,17)	(3,7)	(3,10)	28.22	(3,18)	(3,7)	(3,11)	28.82	(3,17)	(3,7)	(3,10)	28.22
4	(3,19)	(3,7)	(3,10)	29.82	(3,18)	(3,7)	(3,11)	30.46	(3,17)	(3,7)	(3,10)	29.94
5	(3,19)	(3,7)	(3,10)	31.27	(3,19)	(3,7)	(3,11)	32.05	(3,19)	(3,8)	(3,10)	31.27

Table II.16 : Heuristic Solutions for the Problems with Cost Structure 4
(independently treated retailers)

Sub-Problem	Mod. Cl. & Sc.				Ehrhardt				SS vs. SHC			
	Dep	Ret2	Ret1	Costs	Dep	Ret2	Ret1	Costs	Dep	Ret2	Ret1	Costs
1	(6,17)	(6,17)	(6,17)	29.99	(6,17)	(6,17)	(6,17)	29.99	(6,17)	(6,17)	(6,17)	29.99
2	(6,17)	(6,17)	(6,17)	30.16	(6,17)	(6,17)	(6,17)	30.16	(6,17)	(6,17)	(6,17)	30.16
3	(6,18)	(6,18)	(6,18)	30.82	(6,17)	(6,17)	(6,17)	30.69	(6,17)	(6,17)	(6,17)	30.69
4	(6,18)	(6,18)	(6,18)	31.64	(6,18)	(6,18)	(6,18)	31.64	(6,17)	(6,17)	(6,17)	31.58
5	(6,18)	(6,18)	(6,18)	32.45	(6,18)	(6,18)	(6,18)	32.45	(6,18)	(6,18)	(6,18)	32.45

Table II.17 : Heuristic Solutions for the Problems with Cost Structure 4
(real collapsed policy)

Heuristic	Modified Clark and Scarf	Ehrhardt	Shortage Costs vs. Safety Stock Costs
Cost Structure 1			
NTB	6	0	0
AOPT	2.20%	5.57%	4.97%
ABH	0.00%	3.30%	2.70%
MOPT	2.98%	9.37%	8.78%
MBH	0.00%	8.27%	5.63%
Cost Structure 2			
NTB	1	3	1
AOPT	5.36%	4.71%	5.23%
ABH	1.32%	0.69%	1.19%
MOPT	7.70%	6.58%	8.79%
MBH	4.08%	3.01%	2.92%
Cost Structure 3			
NTB	2	3	2
AOPT	7.24%	5.76%	7.89%
ABH	2.06%	0.64%	2.75%
MOPT	11.29%	8.65%	11.29%
MBH	5.06%	1.63%	5.06%

Table II.18 : Summary of the Results for Cost Structures 1, 2 and 3

Heuristic	Modified Clark and Scarf	Ehrhardt	Shortage Costs vs. Safety Stock Costs
Partial Collapsing			
NTB	0	5	0
AOPT	8.93%	7.14%	10.44%
ABH	1.66%	0.00%	3.10%
MOPT	11.66%	10.46%	13.80%
MBH	2.43%	0.00%	5.25%
Indep. retailers			
NTB	5	0	2
AOPT	1.85%	4.04%	2.74%
ABH	0.00%	2.15%	0.88%
MOPT	3.27%	5.85%	3.27%
MBH	0.00%	2.49%	2.10%
Total Collapsing			
NTB	3	4	5
AOPT	10.31%	10.22%	10.18%
ABH	0.12%	0.04%	0.00%
MOPT	12.79%	12.79%	12.79%
MBH	0.42%	0.42%	0.00%

Table II.19 : Summary of the Results for Cost Structure 4

Heuristic	Modified Clark and Scarf	Ehrhardt	Shortage Costs vs. Safety Stock Costs
NTB	4	1	1
AOPT	1.79%	2.99%	2.74%
ABH	0.49%	1.65%	1.42%
MOPT	3.01%	4.53%	3.27%
MBH	2.43%	2.23%	2.69%

Legend : NTB : Number of Times Best heuristic
         AOPT : Average cost deviation to OPTimal solution
         ABH : Average cost deviation to Best Heuristc
         MOPT : Maximum cost deviation to OPTimal solution
         MBH : Maximum cost deviation to Best Heuristic

Table II.20 : Summary of the Results for Cost Structure 4
              (best of seperate retailing and partial collapsing).

several alternative solutions for every heuristic in this situation : in the first
one we order at the depot and at the retailer with the greater natural order period
in the same cycle while the retailer with the smaller natural order period follows
its locally optimal policy (the partial collapsing principle of cost structure 2,
the cost structure in which the depot's natural order period lies between the natural
order period of the different retailers), in the second one we do as if the retailers
were independent, i.e. as if the depot were used only for one retailer, i.e. seperate retailing as it was defined by Schwarz, and in the third one we order the depot and both retailers in the same cycle (the collapsing principle of cost structure 3, the cost structure in which the depot's natural order period is smaller
than the natural order period of the two identical retailers). The results of these
different policies are shown in table II.19. We then chose the best alternative for
every heuristic in every subproblem; the performance of the resulting policy is
shown in table II.20 and looks promising; a maximum cost deviation, over all subproblems over all heuristics, compared to the optimal solution of only 4.53 %. Note
that the best alternative proved to be the seperate retailing solution when the
depot's setup cost was low and switched to the partial collapsing solution for higher
setup costs of the dept (this did not yet occur for the Ehrhardt heuristic). Note
that we made the same observation for cost structures 2 and 3 where the seperate
retailing solution also outperforms the (partial) collapsing solution when the depot's setup cost is very low. We did not investigate this further because we believe these very low setup cost at the depot as compared to the retailers' setup to
be a rather irrealistic assumption; furthermore this seperate retailing solution
rapidly becomes worse, compared to a collapsing solution when the number of retailers

increases as was already shown by Schwarz and the cost difference between the seperate retailing solution and the collapsing solution for the problems with cost structure 2 or 3 never is very high.

VII. CONCLUSION

In this paper we formulated the stochastic multi-echelon production/inventory distribution problem as a Markovian Decision Process. The only source of uncertainty considered is final demand uncertainty. We investigate the properties of an optimal solution to very simple distribution systems and find that the optimal policy at a given production facility cannot easily be expressed as a function of one decision variable as is the case in assembly problems.

We investigate the cost consequences of heuristics whose ordering decisions are solely based on the echelon inventory position at that particular facility; these cost consequences are much more severe as when the same heuristics are used in an assembly problem, mainly because they lead to more shortages as a result of imbalances which occur during implementation of the proposed heuristics. Seperate retailing seems to be a viable alternative when the depot's setup cost is very low and the natural order period of the depot is smaller than the natural order period of (some of) the retailers; we however donot advocate the use of seperate retailing but recommend collapsing strategies where the depot is set on the same cycle as (some of) the retailers because seperate retailing rapidly becomes worse as the number of retailers increases or the depot's setup cost becomes greater and because seperate retailing is more difficult to administer.

BIBLIOGRAPHY

[1] ARROW, K., KARLIN, S. and SCARF, H. : 'Studies in the mathematical theory of inventory and production', Stanford University Press, 1958.

[2] BERRY, W. and WHYBARK, D. : 'Research perspectives for MRP systems', Production and Inventory Management, 1975 (2), pp. 19-25.

[3] BIGGS, J., GOODMAN, S. and HARDY, S. : 'Lot-sizing rules in a hierarchical multi-stage inventory system", Production and Inventory Management, 1977 (1), pp. 104-115.

[4] BILLINGTON, P., Mc CLAIN, J. and THOMAS, L. : 'Mathematical approaches to capacity constrained MRP systems : Review, formulation and problem reduction', Cornell University, Graduate School of Business and Public Administration, Working Paper 81-17, July 1981, p. 31.

[5] BLACKBURN, J. and MILLEN, R. : 'Improved heuristics for multi-stage requirements planning systems', Management Science, 1982 (1), pp. 44-56.

[6] BLACKBURN, J. and MILLEN, R. : 'Heuristic lot-sizing performance in a rolling-schedule environment', Decision Sciences, 1980, pp. 691-701.

[7] BROWN, R. : 'Advanced Service Parts Inventory Control', Materials Management Systems, Norwich, Vermont, 1982, p. 436.

[8] CHAKRAVARTY, A. : 'Multi-stage production/inventory deterministic lot size computations', International Journal of Production Research, 1984 (3), pp. 405-420.

[9] CLARK, A. and SCARF, H. : 'Optimal policies for a multi-echelon inventory system', Management Science, 1960 (4), pp. 475-490.

[10] CLARK, A. and SCARF, H. : 'Approximate solutions to a simple multi-echelon inventory system', Studies in applied probability and management science, Stanford University Press, pp. 88-100.

[11] COLLIER, D. : 'The interaction of single-stage lot size models in a materials requirements planning system', Production and Inventory Management, 1980 (4), pp. 11-20.

[12] COLLIER, D. : 'Aggregate safety stock levels and component part commonality', Management Science, November 1982, pp. 1296-1303.

[13] EHRHARDT, R. : 'Easily computed approximations for (s,S) inventory system operating characteristics', Naval Research Logistics Quarterly, 1985, p.347-359.

[14] EHRHARDT, R. : 'The power approximation for computing (s,S) inventory policies', Management Science, August 1979, pp. 777-786.

[15] EHRHARDT, R. and MOSIER, C. : 'A revision of the power approximation for computing (s,S) policies', Management Science, May 1984, pp. 618-622.

[16] EPPEN, G. and SCHRAGE, L. : 'Centralized ordering policies in a multi-warehouse system with lead times and random demand', Chapter 2 in "Multi-level Production/ Inventory Control Systems: Theory and Practice", edited by L. Schwarz, North-Holland, 1981.

[17] FEDERGRUEN, A. and ZIPKIN, P. : 'Allocation policies and cost approximations for multilocation inventory systems', Naval Research Logistics Quarterly, 1984, pp. 97-129.

[18] FEDERGRUEN, A. and ZIPKIN, P. : 'Approximations of dynamic, multilocation production and inventory systems', Management Science, January 1984, pp. 69-84.

[19] FEDERGRUEN, A. and ZIPKIN, P. : 'Computational issues in an infinite-horizon, multi-echelon inventory model', Operations Research, July-August 1984, pp. 818-836.

[20] FREELAND, J. and PORTEUS, E. : 'Easily computed inventory policies for periodic review systems : Shortage costs and service level models', Stanford University, Graduate School of Business, July 1979, p. 20.

[21] GRAVES, S. and SCHWARZ, L. : 'Single cycle continuous review policies for arborescent production/inventory systems', Management Science, January 1977, pp. 529-540.

[22] GROSS, D., SOLAND, R. and PINKUS, C. : 'Designing a multi-product, multi-echelon inventory system', Chapter 1 in "Multi-level Production/Inventory Control Systems : Theory and Practice", edited by L. Schwarz, North-Holland, 1981.

[23] HOWARD, R. : 'Dynamic programming and Markov processes', M.I.T. Press, Cambridge, Massachussets, 1960.

[24] JACKSON, P. : 'What to do until your ship comes in : Ship up to S allocation policies in a two-echelon distribution system', Cornell University, School of Operations Research and Industrial Engineering, Technical Report No. 570, January 1983, p. 27.

[25] JACKSON, P. and MUCKSTADT, J. : 'A two-period, two-echelon inventory stocking and allocation problem', Cornell University, School of Operations Research and Industrial Engineering, Technical Report No. 616, 1984, p. 29.

[26] JACKSON, P. and MUCKSTADT, J. : 'Risk pooling in a two-period, two-echelon inventory stocking and allocation problem', Cornell University, School of Operations Research and Industrial Engineering, Technical Report No. 634, 1984, p. 47.

[27] LAMBRECHT, M., LUYTEN, R. and MUCKSTADT, J. : 'Safety stock policies for multi-echelon production systems', K.U.L.-T.E.W., Onderzoeksrapport No. 8208, 1982, p. 31.

[28] LAMBRECHT, M., LUYTEN, R. and MUCKSTADT, J. : 'Protective stocks in multi-stage production systems', Intnl. Journal of Production Research, 1984 (6), pp.1001-1025.

[29] LUYTEN, R. : 'System-Based Heuristics for Multi-Echelon Assembly Production Systems', Chapter 1 in "Protective Stocks in Multi-Stage Production/Inventory and MRP-Systems", Doctoral Dissertation (in progress), K.U. Leuven - T.E.W.

[30] MAGEE, J. : 'Production planning and control', Mc. Graw-Hill, New York, 1958.

[31] MAXWELL, W. and MUCKSTADT, J. : 'Establishing reorder intervals in multi-stage production-distribution systems', Cornell University, School of Operations Research and Industrial Engineering, Technical Report No. 561, 1982.

[32] SCHWARZ, L. and SCHRAGE, L. : 'A simple continuous review deterministic one-warehouse n-retailer inventory problem', Management Science, January 1973, pp. 555-566.

[33] SCHWARZ, L. and SCHRAGE, L. : 'Optimal and system myopic policies for multi-echelon production/inventory assembly systems', Management Science, July 1975, pp. 1285-1294.

[34] TIMMER, J., MONHEMIUS, W. and BERTRAND, J. : 'Production and inventory control with the base stock system', Report EUT/BDK/12, Eindhoven University of Technology, 1984, p. 30.

[35] WIJNGAARD, J. and WORTMANN, J. : 'M.R.P. an inventories', European Journal of Operational Research, 1985, pp. 281-293.

[36] WILLIAMS, J. : 'Heuristic techniques for simultaneous scheduling of production and distribution in multi-echelon structures : Theory and empirical comparisons', Management Science, 1981 (3), pp. 336-352.

[37] ZIPKIN, P. : 'On the imbalance of inventories in multi-echelon systems', Mathematics of Operations Research, August 1984, pp. 402-423.

A BRANCH AND BOUND ALGORITHM FOR THE MULTI ITEM SINGLE LEVEL CAPACITATED DYNAMIC LOTSIZING PROBLEM

Ludo F. GELDERS

Johan MAES

Luk N. VAN WASSENHOVE

Abstract

In this paper we present a branch and bound algorithm for the multi item capacitated lotsizing problem. The bounding procedure is based on a Lagrangean relaxation of the problem. The multipliers are updated using subgradient optimization.
Although this algorithm can solve the problem to optimality, it is mainly used as a heuristic. Extensive computational results are reported for a large number of problems.

Keywords: production, inventory, lagrange multipliers, heuristics

Katholieke Universiteit Leuven, Division of Industrial Management, Celestijnenlaan 300A, B-3030 Leuven, Belgium.

1. Introduction

The multi item single level capacitated dynamic lotsizing problem consists of scheduling N items over a horizon of T periods. Demands are given and should be satisfied without backlogging. The objective is to minimize the sum of setup costs and inventory holding costs over the horizon, subject to a single constraint on total capacity in each period. In its simplest form problem (P) can be stated as :

$$(P) : \min \sum_{i=1}^{N} \sum_{t=1}^{T} (s_i y_{it} + h_i I_{it}) \tag{1}$$

$$\text{s.t.} \quad I_{it-1} + x_{it} - I_{it} = d_{it} \qquad \forall\ i,t \tag{2}$$

$$\sum_{i=1}^{N} a_i x_{it} \leqslant C_t \qquad \forall\ t \tag{3}$$

$$x_{it} \leqslant (\sum_{t=1}^{T} d_{it})\ y_{it} \qquad \forall\ i,t \tag{4}$$

$$x_{it}, I_{it} \geqslant 0 \qquad \forall\ i,t \tag{5}$$

$$y_{it} \in \{0,1\} \qquad \forall\ i,t \tag{6}$$

$$I_{i0} = 0 \qquad \forall\ i \tag{7}$$

where x_{it}, respectively I_{it} represent production and end of period inventory for item i in period t and Y_{it} indicates whether a setup must be incurred for item i in period t or not (i.e. $x_{it} > 0$ implies $Y_{it} = 1$).

The parameters d_{it}, s_i, h_i, a_i, C_t are the demand, setup cost, unit holding cost, capacity absorption and available capacity respectively. Observe that a variable production cost $p_i x_{it}$ could be added to the objective function without substantially changing the problem formulation.

Problem (P), even in its simplest form, is known to be NP hard, since the single item capacitated dynamic lotsizing problem is NP-hard (see e.g. Florian et al. [7], Bitran et al. [2]). However, the problem is frequently encountered in practice. Consequently a lot of research effort has already been invested in the topic. Most of this research has concentrated on heuristic algorithms (e.g. Lambrecht and Vanderveken [9], Dixon and Silver [3],Dogramaci et al. [4], Karni and Roll [8],...). The performance of these heuristics is discussed in detail in Maes and Van Wassenhove [11,12]. As far as optimal solution algorithms are concerned, two approaches have been reported so far. The first was initiated by Manne [13] and was subsequently improved by different other researchers (e.g. Dzielinsky et al. [5], Lasdon and Terjung [10],...). Essentially the Manne approach is based on set partitioning in which the best solution is chosen from a given candidate set, taking into account the capacity constraints. Although the method is originally formulated as an optimal solution technique, it is most frequently used as a heuristic by rounding off the continuous (LP) solution of the set partitioning problem. This approach works reasonably well when the number of items is much larger than the number of periods since the latter determines the maximum number of fractional variables in the LP solution.

The second approach is based on a strong formulation of the problem (e.g. Barany et al. [1]). In this approach the solution space of the problem is restricted by adding new (and stronger) constraints to the problem (cuts). This new problem is then solved using a standard mixed integer programming package. There is only limited computational experience with this method although Barany et al. report to have solved some larger problems (20 items and 13 periods) to optimality.

The aim of the current paper is twofold. First to present a new branch and bound algorithm which can also be used as a heuristic and second, to use the method as a benchmark against which the solutions of previously tested heuristics can be evaluated [11,12]. In the following section we present the method and some computational refinements. Then computational results are given for a set of randomly generated problems. The results are compared with the solutions obtained by some commonly known heuristics.

2. The Branch and Bound Algorithm

The algorithm develops a binary search tree by fixing the setup variables Y_{it} to 0 or 1. Each node is therefore characterized by a set of Y_{it} which are fixed and a second set of free setup variables which can be determined by the lower bounding algorithm.

Search strategy

The branching variable is selected in a simple sequential fashion starting with item 1 and period 1 (i.e. Y_{11}) and fixing all setups for period 1 before moving to period 2, and so on. A node is created only if the partial setup pattern corresponding to it guarantees that at least one feasible solution exists. The search strategy is as follows. First a depth-first search is performed by following the path of setup variable values of an initial feasible solution as given by the application of a heuristic to the problem. We used Dixon and Silver's heuristic [3]. After the first backtracking step the search procedure always selects the newly created node with the smallest lower bound.

If at any iteration of the lower bounding algorithm at a given node the lower bound exceeds the incumbent upper bound, the node is fathomed. The algorithm then uses simple backtracking to select the next node to be explored. If no pending nodes remain, the algorithm terminates and the incumbent upper bound is optimal. If the attempts to fathom the node are unsuccessful after a given number of iterations, a branching step is invoked.

Lower bounding algorithm

The bounding method is based on a Lagrangean relaxation suggested by Thizy and Van Wassenhove [14]. In short the method works as follows :

Problem (P) decomposes into N uncapacitated single product lot sizing problems when using a Lagrangean relaxation of the capacity constraints (3) :

$$(P_u) : \min \sum_{i=1}^{N} \sum_{t=1}^{T} (s_i Y_{it} + h_i I_{it}) + \sum_{t=1}^{T} u_t (\sum_{i=1}^{N} a_i x_{it} - C_t) \qquad (8)$$

s.t. (2), (4), (5), (6), (7) and

$$u_t \geqslant 0 \qquad\qquad\qquad \forall\ t \qquad\qquad (9)$$

Each of these problems can be solved using the Wagner and Whitin algorithm [15]. It is a commonly known property that the optimal solution value of the relaxed problem P_u can serve as a lower bound to the original problem P for any set of $u_t \geqslant 0$ [6].

The problem then remains to choose the best Lagrangean multipliers, i.e. the ones providing the largest possible lower bound (the dual optimum). As suggested by Thizy and Van Wassenhove the initial multipliers are the optimal dual variables of a transportation problem constructed using the setup pattern from Dixon and Silver's solution. Subsequently the multipliers are updated in an iterative way using the subgradient optimization method :

$$u_t^{k+1} = \max \{0, u_t^k + s^k (\sum_{i=1}^{N} a_i\ x_{it}^k - C_t)\} \qquad (10)$$

$$\text{where}\quad s^k =\ k\ (z^0 - z_u^k)/ \sum_{t=1}^{T} (\sum_{i=1}^{N} a_i\ x_{it}^k - C_t)^2 \qquad (11)$$

x^k is an optimal solution of P_u^k

z^0 is a good approximation of the solution of the problem (an upper bound)

k is a scalar step size. $(0 < \lambda \leqslant 2)$

z_u^k is the optimal solution value to (P_u^k) i.e. the lower

bound at iteration k.

As we move down the search tree the multipliers of the last iteration on a given level are passed on as initial multipliers for the next lower level. However after backtracking these values are no longer known. The approach taken then is to restart from zero multipliers, and to perform a larger number of iterations.

The number of iterations to be used in the subgradient optimization algorithm is an important issue. Indeed, the larger the number of iterations, the sharper the bound and the more nodes will be fathomed. However longer computation times will be needed to calculate the bound at each node. It is therefore necessary to make a tradeoff between the time spent in calculating the bound at each node and the time spent in developing the enumeration tree.

Three different iteration limits were used. At the root node 30 iterations are performed in order to provide good initial Lagrangean multipliers. As we move down the tree, only three iterations are made at each node, such that the lower bounds are obtained very fast. This can be done since the (optimal) multipliers probably will not change very much as we move down the tree. After a backtracking step all multipliers are reset to zero, and 10 iterations are performed in order to obtain a new set of (hopefully) good multipliers. It is clear that setting these iteration limits is a largely heuristic process which requires some fine tuning in each practical setting.

Upper bounds

After each iteration k of the subgradient method an attempt is made to find a better primal feasible solution (to replace the incumbent upper bound) by solving a transportation problem. The transportation problem uses the fixed setups corresponding to the current node and, for the free setup variables, the values as determined by the solution to the Lagrangean problem P_u^k (the optimal Wagner and Whitin schedules for each item). Denoting these setup variables by Y_{it}^k, the transportation problem can be stated as [14]:

$$(P_t) = z_{ij} = \min \sum_{i=1}^{N} \sum_{t=1}^{T} \sum_{r=t}^{T} k_{itr} z_{itr} \tag{12}$$

$$\text{s.t.} \quad \sum_{t=1}^{r} z_{itr} \geqslant a_i \, d_{ir} \qquad \forall \, ir \tag{13}$$

$$\sum_{i=1}^{N} \sum_{r=t}^{T} z_{itr} \leqslant C_t \qquad \forall \, t \tag{14}$$

$$k_{itr} = h_i \, (r-t) \text{ for } t \leqslant r \text{ and } Y_{it}^{k} = 1$$

$$\infty \text{ otherwise} \tag{15}$$

The solution value of this transportation model yields an upper bound to the original problem. If this new solution is better than the incumbent one, it becomes the new incumbent solution.

Although the framework for the algorithm as described above works well, it contains a lot of inefficiencies. A large number of transportation problems will have to be solved, which in many cases are infeasible. Moreover one must realize that for a problem with N items and T periods a transportation problem with T sources and N*T destinations has to be solved. Reducing the number of transportation problems to be solved will therefore considerably reduce computation time.

Proposition 1. The setup pattern Y_{it}^{k} (of a Lagrangean solution) can lead to a feasible production schedule if and only if :

$$\sum_{i=1}^{N} \sum_{t=1}^{(t_i^*-1)} d_{it} \leqslant \sum_{t=1}^{q} C_t \qquad q = 1,\ldots,T \tag{16}$$

where t_i^* is the period in which the next setup for item i is planned (if no such period exists, then $t_i^* = T + 1$).

<u>Proof</u> : Trivial

It follows that if the above condition is not satisfied, the transportation problem (P$_t$) will have an unbounded solution value. In that case the construction and solution of problem (P$_t$) is skipped.

At each iteration three different tests are performed before a transportation problem is solved. The first test checks, based on proposition 1, whether the transportation problem is infeasible. If it is not, we check whether the setup pattern is identical to the one of the most recently solved transportation problem. If this is not the case and if we are still in the branch in which the incumbent solution was found, we check whether the new proposed setup pattern is identical to the setup pattern of the incumbent solution. If the answer is negative the transportation problem is solved. If any of the above tests yields a positive answer the transportation problem is skipped and the procedure simply performs the next subgradient iteration.
Proposition 1 is also used to check the feasibility of the partial setup pattern after a branching step. If the pattern is infeasible the new node is not created.

3.<u>Computational results</u>

In this section some computational results with the branch and bound algorithm are reported. The first problem set consists of 14 small problems from literature, while the second set considers 36 randomly generated 12 item, 12 period problems.

<u>E-optimality and the use of the algorithm as a heuristic</u>

Although the proposed algorithm will solve the problem to optimality if the tree is completely explored, this will in many cases consume inordinate amounts of CPU time. In order to speed up the pruning of the search tree, one could fathom a node if the deviation between its lower bound and the best upper bound, obtained so far, is less than a given percentage E :

i.e.   fathom if $(100 + E) * LB / 100 \geqslant UB$ (17)

The obtained solution will in this case be within E percent of optimality.

Another more drastic limitation of the computation time is to simply stop the procedure when a preset number of nodes has been explored. In this case the obtained solution will be within B percent of optimality where

$$B = 100 * (UB - LB_{min})/UB \tag{18}$$

with LB_{min} the smallest lower bound among the pending nodes.

Small problems from literature

Table 1 shows the results for 14 problems (for E = 0). The first 10 originate from Lambrecht and Vanderveken [9], the last 4 are slightly larger problems from Thizy and Van Wassenhove [14].
Besides some data on the characteristics of the problem, table 1 shows the total CPU time on IBM 4341 under CMS operating system, the number of nodes explored, number of transportation problems which were solved and the number which were not solved (i.e. which were eliminated by the tests of section 2). For the last 4 problems the CPU times needed by Barany et al's algorithm (on a Data General MV 8000 using the SCICONIC mixed integer programming software) are also given [1].

As one can see from the table, total CPU times required to find the optimal solution are quite high and highly unpredictable even for these small problems. The table also shows that the tests to decide whether or not a transportation problem should be solved are very useful indeed.

Results for the last four problems with the E-optimality feature are reported in table 2 for different values of E. It is obvious that the performance of the algorithm can be highly improved from a computational point of view at the cost of a little accuracy.

problem	size	CPU (s)	#nodes gene-rated	#tp solved	tp not solved	Barany et al[1] CPU (S)
1	3*4	1.22	56	26	102	
2		1.07	65	16	125	
3		0.79	55	6	103	
4		1.71	61	44	122	
5	4*4	2.94	134	48	246	
6		1.34	73	9	163	
7		1.32	69	17	134	
8		1.66	91	14	196	
9		1.56	98	12	180	
10	4*6	14.71	233	245	301	
11	8*8	4920	156071	1745	318771	2391
12		836	6870	2400	22363	493
13		195	1775	741	5094	163
14		69	680	439	1866	77

Table 1 : 14 problems from literature

Problem	E = 0			E = 1			E = 2			E = 3		
	CPU (S)	Nodes	Solution value	CPU (S)	Nodes	Solution value	CPU (S)	Nodes	Solution value	CPU (S)	Nodes	Solution value
11	4920	156071	8430	1201	25186	8430	479	8666	8430	155	2614	8480
12	836	6870	7910	63	678	7910	15	168	7910	0.38	2	7920
13	195	1775	7610	6.64	60	7620	4.20	22	7620	0.55	2	7870
14	69	680	7520	0.66	2	7520	0.66	2	7520	0.66	2	7520

Table 2 : Heuristic performance of E-bounding

Random 12 by 12 problems

To test the algorithm for more realistic problem sizes, 36 randomly generated problems were solved. In this experiment the search was always abandoned after 1000 nodes had been explored (for obvious budgetary reasons). The problems were generated as follows :
  - demand was generated from a normal distribution with mean 100 and standard deviation (SIGM) drawn uniformly from [5,10](L), [5,25](M) or [5,50](H) for each item (DEM = C)
  - for the lumpy demand pattern (DEM = L) the same rules were used except for the fact that demand was set equal to zero in 20% of the periods
  - the problem density (total demand/total capacity) was either 50% (CAP=L), 80% (M) or 90% (H)
  - holding cost for each item was set equal to 1, while the setup cost was calculated to obtain time between order values for each item between [1,2] for TBO = L and between [1,6] for TBO = H.

Table 3 summarizes the results from a computational point of view using E values of 5, 1 and 0%. For each case are reported : the number of feasible nodes explored (max 1000), the percentage of the transportation problems which were solved, the gap remaining after 1000 nodes have been explored and the computation time.

As can be seen from Table 3 the loosely capacitated problems are much easier to solve than those where the problem density is high. This is obviously due to the fact that the algorithm is based on Wagner and Whitin type of solutions, which will often be infeasible when capacity is tight.

TBO	CAP	SIGM	DEM	E = 5%				E = 1%				E = 0%			
				(1)	(2)	(3)	(4)	(1)	(2)	(3)	(4)	(1)	(2)	(3)	(4)
H	H	L	C	1000	0.03	10.0	146	1000	0.99	8.5	146	1000	15.04	8.0	278
H	H	M	C	1000	0.16	10.0	128	1000	0.39	10.0	145	1000	22.81	10.0	305
H	H	H	C	1000	0.03	8.0	141	1000	0.30	6.3	144	1000	15.38	6.3	210
H	H	L	L	1000	12.75	20.0	403	1000	15.27	10.0	490	1000	29.85	20.0	506
H	H	M	L	1000	1.00	6.5	161	1000	20.83	7.5	361	1000	26.39	8.6	406
H	H	H	L	1000	0.68	8.7	162	1000	7.66	10.0	230	1000	28.86	12.0	411
H	L	L	C	2	20.00		1	26	5.80		5	1000	1.80	0.2	200
H	L	M	C	28	2.82		5	28	2.82		5	1000	27.26	0.5	262
H	L	H	C	2	33.33		1	28	2.82		4	1000	8.83	0.1	157
H	L	L	L	2	7.14		1	2	9.52		2	1000	4.49	0.0	183
H	L	M	L	2	12.50		1	2	13.33		2	1000	5.81	0.3	172
H	L	H	L	2	20.00		1	2	11.11		2	1000	6.13	0.0	339
H	M	L	C	1000	4.18	7.5	211	1000	32.61	7.0	339	1000	28.78	7.0	366
H	M	M	C	1000	0.07	7.1	149	1000	6.58	5.8	207	1000	28.81	6.0	331
H	M	H	C	204	12.15		72	1000	6.32	2.9	236	1000	31.99	4.3	398
H	M	L	L	1000	0.11	6.8	153	1000	6.97	5.2	177	1000	20.19	6.4	225
H	M	M	L	1000	3.52	5.0	223	1000	30.96	5.6	436	1000	33.44	6.3	559
H	M	H	L	1000	19.97	7.0	440	1000	32.91	8.7	676	1000	35.46	8.4	483
L	H	L	C	2	6.67		1	162	47.09		39	1000	42.89	4.0	386
L	H	M	C	2	33.33		1	236	4.81		33	1000	41.90	0.8	324
L	H	H	C	94	0.54		9	419	8.95		88	1000	39.17	8.5	331
L	H	L	L	2	3.85		2	980	5.07		160	1000	28.86	2.6	389
L	H	M	L	2	14.29		1	2	7.69		2	1000	40.93	0.3	338
L	H	H	L	2	10.00		1	1000	10.44	2.0	283	1000	42.05	1.8	573
L	L	L	C	2	66.67		1	2	66.67		1	2	66.67		1
L	L	M	C	2	66.67		1	2	66.67		1	2	66.67		1
L	L	H	C	2	66.67		1	2	66.67		1	2	66.67		1
L	L	L	L	2	33.33		1	2	33.33		1	2	33.33		1
L	L	M	L	2	66.67		1	2	66.67		1	2	66.67		1
L	L	H	L	2	66.67		1	2	66.67		1	2	66.67		1
L	M	L	C	2	33.33		1	2	33.33		1	1000	51.99		360
L	M	M	C	2	33.33		1	2	33.33		1	1000	45.18		269
L	M	H	C	2	33.33		1	2	33.33		1	640	38.52	0.0	167
L	M	L	L	2	25.00		1	2	20.00		1	1000	41.17	0.5	360
L	M	M	L	2	33.33		1	2	25.00		1	1000	49.34	0.6	440
L	M	H	L	2	33.33		1	64	1.47		7	1000	38.61	1.1	328

Table 3 : 36 randomly generated problems - algorithmic performance

(1) : number of nodes (max. 1000)
(2) : number of transportation problems solved / total number of subgradient iterations
(3) : remaining gap when 1000 nodes are explored (eq. 18) blank entries indicate 0%
(4) : CPU time in seconds (rounded)

More interesting conclusions can be drawn from table 4, which compares the branch and bound algorithm to some commonly known heuristics, i.e. Lambrecht-Vanderveken [9], Dixon-Silver [3] and Dogramaci et al [4]. Notice that for our algorithm we used the Dixon and Silver heuristic as a starting solution. Table 4 reports the average improvements over the heuristics (with E values of 5, 1 and 0%) and in each case limiting the maximum number of nodes to 1000. For each of the problem classes, the percentage improvement of the branch and bound algorithm over the heuristics is given. Each entry is an average over 6 values.

In many cases remarkable improvements over the heuristics can be seen, especially for problems with a high TBO value. Note also that the method is highly dependent on the initial solution, since the branch and bound search sometimes does not find the solution obtained with Dogramaci et al.'s heuristic even after 1000 nodes. This also illustrates the limitations of this branch and bound algorithm.

Problem density		HIGH			MEDIUM			LOW		
TBO		0%	E 1%	5%	0%	E 1%	5%	0%	E 1%	5%
H	LV	2.69	3.3	3.01	2.24	2.82	2.22	3.97	3.95	1.51
	DS	2.99	3.58	3.29	3.54	4.12	3.54	3.68	3.66	1.23
	DPA	2.77	3.37	3.07	-0.27	0.28	-0.29	2.07	2.04	-0.36
L	LV	0.87	1.11	0.67	0.36	0.03	0.03	0.35	0.35	0.35
	DS	0.81	1.05	0.61	0.33	0	0	0.35	0.35	0.35
	DPA	1.04	1.29	0.84	0.69	0.37	0.37	1.03	1.03	1.03

Table 4 : Average improvement (%) of the branch and bound algorithms
(E = 0, 1 and 5%) over the heuristic of Lambrecht-Vanderveken (LV),
Dixon-Silver (DS) and Dogramaci et al. (DPA)

	E = 0			E = 1			E = 5		
	% improvement	times better	max. improvement	% improvement	times better	max. improvement	% improvement	times better	max. improvement
LV	1.75	32	8.26	1.93	31	8.26	1.3	26	9.7
DS	1.95	34	7.35	2.13	31	7.35	1.5	24	7.35
DPA	1.22	28	10.83	1.40	29	12.13	0.75	26	13.41

Table 5 : Performance of the branch and bound algorithms (E = 0,1 and 5%) as compared to the heuristics of Lambrecht-Vanderveken (LV), Dixon-Silver (DS) and Dogramaci et al. (DPA).

4. Conclusions

This paper has presented a branch and bound algorithm for the multi item single level capacitated dynamic lotsizing problem. The algorithm is based upon a Lagrangean relaxation of the capacity constraints and on subgradient optimization to find a lower bound at each node. This bounding procedure is described in detail in Thizy and Van Wassenhove [14]. At each iteration of the subgradient method a primal transportation problem may yield a feasible solution, i.e. an upper bound, provided the transportation problem has a bounded solution value. Since solving these transportation problems is expensive it is first checked whether the problem has been solved before and whether it has a bounded solution value. Our computational experience shows that these checks are very efficient. Like any other branch and bound algorithm, our algorithm is sensitive to the availability of a good starting upper bound. For practical reasons we selected the Dixon-Silver heuristic. Obviously, the procedure is also sensitive to the branching strategy. Again for convenience we selected a simple and straightforward strategy. It follows from the above that the algorithm could probably be substantially improved by designing more sophisticated search schemes and by further fine-tuning. This was not our purpose for various reasons.

It should be clear from our computational tests that (even when trying all the tricks in the book) the method, when run to optimality (i.e. E = 0) is not practical for solving larger problems. Computation times and search trees can be very large even for the moderate 12 item - 12 period problems we attempted to solve. This once again shows that the multi item single level capacitated lotsizing problem is a tough mathematical problem. However, our main purpose was to use the method as a heuristic and to compare it to other well-known heuristics. Indeed, in a branch and bound enumeration usually only a small part of the effort is spent in finding the optimal solution whereas inordinate amounts of work are often needed to prove optimality.

Therefore, when using our method as a heuristic, i.e. stopping when either 1000 nodes are investigated or E-optimality has been shown, one should have a fair chance of obtaining the optimal solution. As such our method could be used as a benchmark to get an idea on how far well-known heuristics are from optimality. These results are summarized in Table 5. The table shows that the average improvement of our method over well-known heuristics is of the order of 1 to 2 percent. Note that the maximum improvement is of the order of 10 percent in our experiments which shows that sometimes these well-known heuristics perform very badly. Table 5 also shows that our truncated branch and bound search finds better solutions for a large majority of the 36 test problems (even for E = 5%). This indicates that the heuristics of Lambrecht-Vanderveken, Dixon-Silver and Dogramaci et al. rarely find the optimal solution although their average performance may be satisfactory for some practical settings.

Bibliography

[1] Barani, I., Van Roy, T.J., and Wolsey, L.A., "Strong Formulations for Multi-item Capacitated Lot Sizing", Management Science, vol.30, n°10, October 1984, pp.1255-1261.

[2] Bitran, G., and Yannasse, H., "Computational Complexity of the Capacitated Lot Size Problem", Management Science, vol.28, n°10, October 1982, pp.1174-1186.

[3] Dixon, P.S., and Silver, E.A., "A Heuristic Solution Procedure for the Multi-item, Single Level, Limited Capacity, Lot Sizing Problem", Journal of Operations Management, vol.2, n°1, October 1981, pp.23-39.

[4] Dogramaci, A., Panayiotopoulos, J.E., and Adam, N.R., "The Dynamic Lot Sizing Problem for Multiple Items under Limited Capacity", AIIE Transactions vol.13, n°4, December 1981, pp.294-303.

[5] Dzielinsky, B.P., and Gomory, R.E., "Optimal Programming of Lot Sizes, Inventory and Labor Allocations", Management Science, vol.11, n°9, July 1965, pp.874-890.

[6] Fisher, M.L., "The Lagrangean Relaxation Method for Solving integer Programming Problems", Management Science, vol.27, n°1, Jan.1981, pp.1-18.

[7] Florian, M., Lenstra, J.K., and Rinnooy Kan A.H.G., "Deterministic Production Planning : Algorithms and Complexity", Management Science, vol.26, n°7, July 1980, pp.122-20.

[8] Karni, R., and Roll, Y., "A Heuristic Algorithm for the Multi-item Lot Sizing Problem with Capacity Constraints", IIE Transactions, vol.14, n°4, December 1982, pp.249-356.

[9] Lambrecht, M.R., and Vanderveken, H., "Heuristic Procedure for the Single Operation Multi-item Loading Problem", AIIE Transactions, vol.11, n°4, December 1979, pp.319-326.

[10] Lasdon, L.S., and Terjung, R.C., "An Efficient Algorithm for

Multi-item Scheduling", Operations Research, vol.19, n°2, July-August 1971, pp.946-969.

[11] Maes, J., and Van Wassenhove, L.N., "Multi-item Single Level Capacitated Dynamic Lot Sizing Heuristics : A Computational Comparison, part I", WP 84-27 K.U.Leuven, Department of Industrial Management.

[12] Maes, J., and Van Wassenhove, L.N., "Multi-item Single Level Capacitated Dynamic Lot Sizing Heuristics : A Computational Comparison, part II", WP 85-08 K.U.Leuven, Department of Industrial Management.

[13] Manne, A.S., "Programming of Economic Lot Sizes", Management Science, vol.4, n°2, January 1958, pp.115-135.

[14] Thizy, J.M., and Van Wassenhove, L.N., "A Subgradient Algorithm for the Multi-item Capacitated Lot Sizing Problem", Research Report EES, 83-14, Princeton University, December 1983, to appear in IIE-Transactions.

[15] Wagner, H.M., and Whitin, T.M., "Dynamic Version of the Economic Lot Size Model", Management Science, October 1958, pp.89-96.

Aggregating Items in Multi-Level
Lot Sizing

Sven Axsäter
Division of Transportation and
Material Flow Systems
Luleå University of Technology
Luleå, Sweden

and

Henry L.W. Nuttle
Dept of Industrial Engineering
North Carolina State University
Raleigh, North Carolina, USA

<u>Abstract</u>

One way of reducing a multi-level lot sizing problem is to identify
conditions on the cost parameters that will guarantee that a group of
items can under all circumstances be produced at the same time. This
means that this group of items can be treated as a single item. In
this paper we present such conditions and discuss their applicability.

Classification codes: Lot Sizing
                       Multi-Stage Systems

1   <u>Introduction</u>

In multi-stage production and distribution systems it is, in general,
very difficult to determine optimal lot sizes. The reason is that lot
sizes for different items can not be determined separately, since the
lot sizing for a parent item will affect the demand for its components.
In practice this is usually ignored and lot sizes are determined by
applying single-stage methods sequentially.

During the last two decades substantial research efforts have been devoted to multi-stage lot sizing problems. As a result of this research we have relatively efficient optimizing algorithms for special product structures. The simplest case is the serial structure i.e. when one item has at most one immediate predecessor and one immediate successor. A reasonably efficient algorithm for the serial problem has been given by Love [8]. The serial structure is a special case of an assembly structure. Such systems have a single end item used to satisfy customer demand, which is assembled from a number of component items which, in turn, may be assembled from other component items, etc. This means that component items may have several immediate predecessors but only one immediate successor. Efficient algorithms for assembly structures have been given by Afentakis et al [1], and recently by Rosling [11]. It is still an open question whether exact algorithms of this type can be justified in practice. Practitioners may regard them as too complex. Furthermore, we are of course, not talking about an exact solution of the real problem which usually involves also capacity constraints and stochastic demand (see Axsäter [2]). Therefore simple approximate procedures are an interesting alternative, especially when we are faced with more general product structures.

When demand is constant it is possible to derive solutions that are very close to optimum by restricting the order intervals to be powers of 2 times a certain base period (Maxwell and Muckstadt [9] and Roundy [10]). The simplest way to take the multi-stage structure into account is to apply single stage lot sizing procedures sequentially with modified cost parameters. See Blackburn and Millen [4] and Heinrich and Schneeweiss [6]. Other heuristics have been suggested by Graves [5] and Lambrecht et al [7].

Independent of whether an exact or approximate lot sizing algorithm is used, it is natural to simplify the problem as much as possible before applying the algorithm. One way is to identify conditions on the cost parameters that will guarantee that a group of items may be determined, a priori, to follow identical schedules in some optimal plan. If a group of items can be combined, this group may be treated as a single item in a material requirements planning system. Axsäter and Nuttle [3] have given a number of such conditions that will allow combination of items. The purpose of this paper is to discuss applications and extensions of these conditions.

2   Assembly systems

Let us consider an assembly system (see Figure 1).

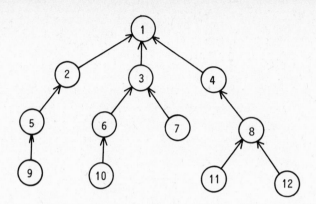

Figure 1. Assembly system.

Our objective is to generate a production/purchase plan to minimize total setup plus inventory carrying cost over a T-period horizon. End item demand in each period is known but may vary from period to period, cost parameters are constant over time, initial inventories are zero for all items and lead times are constant so that they may be ignored. Since we are dealing with assembly systems, we may also assume without loss of generality, that one unit of any item requires one unit of each of its immediate predecessor items. Let S_i be the setup cost and $e_i \geq 0$ the echelon carrying cost of item i.

The general assembly structure in Figure 1 can be viewed as a collection of two-level structures such as that shown in Figure 2.

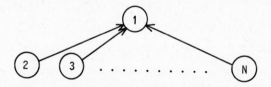

Figure 2. General two-level structure.

Let us now state the following proposition.

Proposition 1: The general two-level structure in Figure 2 will collapse if and only if

$$(\sum_{j\neq i} S_j)/(\sum_{j\neq i} e_j) \geq S_i/e_i \qquad i = 2, \ldots, N \qquad (1)$$

This means that if (1) is satisfied we can replace the whole structure by a single item with setup cost $\sum_j S_j$ and echelon holding cost $\sum_j e_j$. On the other hand if (1) is not satisfied there exists a demand sequence such that no optimal solution with common setups exists. We refer to [3] for a proof.

As a special case of (1) we can see that the serial structure in Figure 3

Figure 3. Two-item serial structure.

will collapse if and only if

$$S_1/e_1 \geq S_2/e_2 \qquad (2)$$

Going back to Figure 1 it is obvious that we can apply these results starting with the lowest level. For example, items 8, 11 and 12 may be combined if and only if

$$\frac{S_8 + S_{12}}{e_8 + e_{12}} \geq \frac{S_{11}}{e_{11}}$$

and

$$\frac{S_8 + S_{11}}{e_8 + e_{11}} \geq \frac{S_{12}}{e_{12}}$$

If this is the case these three items can be replaced by an item 8' with cost parameters $S_{8'} = S_8 + S_{11} + S_{12}$ and $e_{8'} = e_8 + e_{11} + e_{12}$. Next, we can check whether item 8' may be combined with item 4 i.e. if

$$\frac{S_4}{e_4} \geq \frac{S_{8'}}{e_{8'}}$$

etc.

It can also be shown that condition (2) can be applied to any serial substructure of a larger network, (as illustrated in Figure 4), i.e. not only to two items at the lowest level.

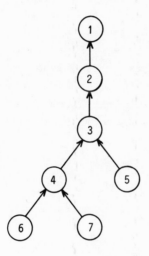

Figure 4. Items 1, 2 and 3 constitute a serial substructure.

It is easy to see that condition (1) implies that $S_1/e_1 \geq S_i/e_i$ (i = 2,...,N). This means that total collapse is only possible in some cases where the parent item has a higher ratio between setup cost and echelon carrying cost than all its component items. We will consequently very often face situations where our condition for total collapse is not satisfied. A natural question is then whether it is possible to combine some subset of the items. To be more specific let us consider conditions for combining item i and item 1 in the two-level structure of Figure 2. It turns out that the problem of partial collapse is more complicated than that of total collapse. It is possible though to state the following proposition which is proved in [3]:

Proposition 2: If in Figure 2

$$S_i/e_i \leq S_j/e_j \qquad\qquad j = 2, \ldots, N \qquad\qquad (3)$$

and

$$S_1 e_i - S_i e_1 \geq \sum_{j=2}^{N} (S_j e_i - S_i e_j) \qquad\qquad (4)$$

items 1 and i can be combined.

It is important to note that conditions (3) and (4) are sufficient but not necessary. There may therefore exist cases when the conditions are not satisfied while it is still possible to combine items 1 and i. For example, if $e_j = 0$ for all $j \neq 1,i$, in an optimal plan there will be just one setup for items $j \neq 1,i$ and items 1 and i may be combined provided that the serial condition $S_1/e_1 \geq S_i/e_i$ is satisfied. Furthermore, if $S_i = 0$ then items 1 and i can obviously be combined.

Let us now go back to Figure 1. Assume that items 8, 11 and 12 can not be combined. Using Proposition 2 we can combine items 8 and 11 if

$$S_{11}/e_{11} \leq S_{12}/e_{12}$$

and

$$S_8 e_{11} - S_{11} e_8 \geq S_{12} e_{11} - S_{11} e_{12}$$

Assuming that this is the case we have a new item 8" with $S_{8"} = S_8 + S_{11}$ and $e_{8"} = e_8 + e_{11}$, and we can apply the serial condition (2) to items 4 and 8".

3   Extensions

So far we have given some basic results for assembly systems and shown how these results can be applied in a straight-forward manner. The results and general methodology have, however, a wider applicability and we shall discuss some extensions.

Let us first consider the two-level arborescence structure in Figure 5

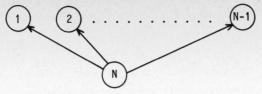

Figure 5.   Two-level arborescence structure.

We assume that the lead times are zero (or equal) and that items 1, 2, ..., N-1 have identical demand. This may, for example, be the case if the items are components of some other item. We can now prove:

<u>Proposition 3</u>:   The two-level arborescence structure in Figure 5 will collapse if and only if

$$(\sum_{j \neq i} S_j)/(\sum_{j \neq i} e_j) \leq S_i/e_i \qquad i = 1, 2, \ldots, N-1 \qquad (5)$$

<u>Proof</u>   Necessity is immediate. According to Proposition 1, if condition (5) is not satisfied there exists a demand sequence such that it is advantageous to have different schedules for item i on one hand and the other items on the other hand.

Too see that condition (5) is also sufficient, assume that it is satisfied and consider a relaxation of the structure in Figure 5 to one involving N-1 independent serial systems as shown in Figure 6, where the setup and carrying costs for item N in system i are taken to be $\alpha_i S_N$ and $\alpha_i e_i$, respectively, and

$$\alpha_i = \frac{S_i \sum_{j=1}^{N} e_j - e_i \sum_{j=1}^{N} S_j}{e_N \sum_{j=1}^{N} S_j - S_N \sum_{j=1}^{N} e_j} = \frac{S_i \sum_{j \neq i} e_j - e_i \sum_{j \neq i} S_j}{e_N \sum_{j \neq N} S_j - S_N \sum_{j \neq N} e_j}$$

Figure 6.   Relaxed structure.

It is an immediate consequence of (5) that

$$S_N/e_N \leq S_i/e_i \qquad\qquad i = 1, \ldots, N-1$$

The trivial case when all ratios are equal will evidently collapse and is disregarded. It is then clear that $\alpha_i > 0$. Furthermore it is easy to see that

$$\sum_{i=1}^{N-1} \alpha_i = 1$$

Applying Proposition 1 each two-level structure will collapse. The resulting ratio of setup and carrying cost for structure i is then

$$\frac{S_i + \alpha_i S_N}{e_i + \alpha_i e_N} = \frac{(S_i e_N - e_i S_N)\sum_{j=1}^{N} S_j}{(S_i e_N - e_i S_N)\sum_{j=1}^{N} e_j} = \frac{\sum_{j=1}^{N} S_j}{\sum_{j=1}^{N} e_j}$$

i.e. it is the same for each i. Thus there is an identical optimal schedule for each collapsed structure i and we can conclude that the whole structure will collapse.

The main idea in our proof of Proposition 3 was to <u>relax constraints</u> before applying our condition for total collapse. This idea can also be used in a more general way. To see this let us again go back to Figure 1. If the total structure will collapse the resulting ratio of setup and carrying cost will be $\Sigma S_j / \Sigma e_j$. Assume now that we can relax the constraints, for example according to Figure 7, such that $S_{1'} + S_{1''} = S_1$ and $e_{1'} + e_{1''} = e_1$ and

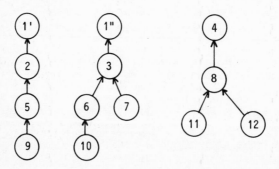

Figure 7.   Relaxation of the assembly system in Figure 1.

such that each substructure has a ratio of total setup and carrying cost equal to that of the original structure. If when applying Proposition 1 to each substructure, we find that each structure will collapse, we know that this is also the case for the original structure.

Finally, it is also of interest to note that the two-level assembly structure in Figure 2 with $e_1 = 0$ may be interpreted as a lot-sizing model for N-1 end items with identical external demand and a <u>joint setup cost</u> S_1 as well as individual setup and holding costs. Applying Propositions 1 and 2 we can check whether an item should be included in all the joint setups.

References

1. Afentakis, P., B. Gavish, and U. Karmarkar, "Computationally Efficient Optimal Solutions to the Lot-Sizing Problem in Multi-Stage Assembly Systems", <u>Management Science</u>, Vol. 30 (February 1984), pp 222-239.

2. Axsäter, S., "Evaluation of Lot-Sizing Techniques", <u>International Journal of Production Research</u> (to appear).

3. Axsäter, S., and H.L.W. Nuttle, "Combining Items in Multi-Level Assembly Systems", Luleå University of Technology, Research Report 1984:32, and NC State University, OR Report No. 205 (1984).

4. Blackburn, J.D., and R.A. Millen, "Improved Heuristics for Multi-Echelon Requirements Planning Systems", <u>Management Science</u>, Vol. 28 (January 1982), pp 44-56.

5. Graves, S.C., "Multi-Stage Lot-Sizing: An Iterative Procedure", Chapter 4 in <u>Multi-Level Production/Inventory Control Systems: Theory and Practice</u> (L.B. Schwarz, editor), North Holland, Amsterdam (1981).

6. Heinrich, C., and Ch. Schneeweiss, "Multi-Stage Lot-Sizing for General Production Systems", University of Mannheim (1985).

7. Lambrecht, M.R., J. Vander Eecken, and H. Vanderveken, "A Heuristic Method for the Facilities in Series Dynamic Lot Size Problem", Onderzoeksrapport 7817, Katholieke Universiteit Leuven (1978).

8. Love, S.F., "A Facilities in Series Inventory Model with Nested Schedules", <u>Management Science</u>, Vol. 18 (January 1972, Part 1), pp 327-338.

9. Maxwell, W.L., and J.A. Muckstadt, "Establishing Consistent and Realistic Reorder Intervals in Production-Distribution Systems", Technical Report No. 561, School of Industrial Engineering and Operations Research, Cornell University (1983).

10. Roundy, R.A., "A 98%-Effective Lot-Sizing Rule for a Multi-Stage Production/Inventory System", Technical Report No. 642, School of Industrial Engineering and Operations Research, Cornell University (1984).

11. Rosling, K., "Optimal Lot-Sizing for Dynamic Assembly Systems", Linköping Institute of Technology (1985).

OPTIMAL LOT-SIZING
FOR
DYNAMIC ASSEMBLY SYSTEMS

Kaj Rosling
Linköping Institute of Technology

Abstract

The simple case of a dynamic assembly system with no initial stocks is
investigated as a test case for some new ideas on lot-sizing for Materials Requirements Planning. The model relies on the facility location
formulation of Wagner's and Whitin's inventory problem. An iterative
procedure is proposed that derives close upper and lower bounds through
cost modifications based on Benders Decomposition and level-by-level
optimization. The bounding procedure is integrated into a branch and
bound scheme that outperforms by at least an order of magnitude its
probably best competitor, the algorithm due to Afentakis et al (1984).
The bounding procedure behaves excellently well as a heuristic and
relates interestingly to the well-known lot-sizing methods of Graves
(1981) and Blackburn and Millen (1982).

Classification codes: Lot Sizing
                      Assembly Systems

1   Introduction

Materials Requirements Planning (MRP) is a widely used technique to
determine production schedules in multi-stage manufacturing systems.
The idea is to use information on lead-times and precedence relations
among products ("bill of material") to translate schedules of finished
items into timed requirements of components (see e.g. Orlicky (1975)).

Most research on lot-sizing in MRP-systems has been carried out on
assembly inventory systems. These are multi-stage systems where the
manufacture of an item requires a certain number of components and in
turn, the item itself is a component of a single parent item. A single
final item satisfies the external demand. To simplify further for research purposes, initial stocks of all components are generally assumed
to be zero. The popularity of the assembly system is due to the fact
it is the only problem with some taste of realism for which at least
medium sized problems can be solved by present optimization techniques.

Research on the present kind of lot-sizing problems was initiated by
Wagner and Whitin (1958) who investigated the single-item problem and
found a very efficient dynamic programming algorithm to solve it. Their
dynamic programming framework was extended and applied to general systems by e.g. Zangwill (1967) and Veinott (1969). A dynamic programming
algorithm for assembly systems was devised by Crowston et al (1973).
Unfortunately, the algorithms resulting from the dynamic programming
framework have not proved very successful. As a matter of fact they
are notably inefficient except for the very special case of an assembly system with all items in series (Love (1972)).

As an alternative to the dynamic programming framework has emerged integer programming formulations for the general lot-sizing problem, e.g.
Steinberg and Napier (1980) and Billington et al (1983). Though their
formulations exhibit an amount of "structure" - i.e. generalized fixed-
charge networks - present techniques seem unable to solve general problems larger than 10-15 items, say. However, the assembly system was
successfully approached along similar lines by Afentakis et al (1984).
They were able to optimize systems with up to 50 items in reasonable
computing times, but as a matter of fact their time requirement is at
least hundred times in excess of the requirement for the same number
of independent single-item problems.

The purpose of the present paper is to develop an exact algorithm for the assembly system (with no initial stocks) based on the facility location formulation of the single-item problem investigated by Krarup and Bilde (1976), Barany et al (1984) and Rosling (1984). The potential of this formulation is felt to be properly tested on the assembly system - to be of any potential value for the general lot-sizing problem, the proposed concepts should work excellently well on this very simple system.

2   The Facility Location Formulation

The single-item lot-sizing problem of Wagner and Whitin (1958) may be modelled as a simple facility location problem, SFLP.

$$\text{SFLP:} \qquad \min \sum_{j=t}^{T} \sum_{t=j}^{T} c_{jt} \cdot X_{jt} + \sum_{j=t}^{T} S \cdot Y_j$$

$$\sum_{j=1}^{t} X_{jt} = 1 \qquad t = 1,2,\ldots,T \qquad (1)$$

$$X_{jt} \leq Y_j \qquad j = 1,2,\ldots,T, \ t = j,j+1,\ldots,T$$

$$X_{jt}, \ Y_j \in \{0,1\} \qquad j = 1,2,\ldots,T, \ t = j,j+1,\ldots,T$$

S is the set-up cost. It is incurred in period j if production of a lot then takes place. Then also $Y_j = 1$. X_{jt} is the proportion of period t's demand satisfied from the lot produced in period $j (j \leq t)$. Furthermore,

$$c_{jt} = h \cdot d_t \cdot (t-j) \qquad (2)$$

where h is the holding cost per unit and period and d_t is the demand of period t.

While problem SFLP generally is a very difficult problem, the special cost relationship (2) makes it very simple. Krarup and Bilde (1977) and later Barany (1984) and Rosling (1984) found that then the version of the problem where the integer requirements are relaxed ($Y_j \geq 0$) still has an optimal integer solution. They also devised algorithms that solve the relaxed version of SFLP and its dual in $O(T^2)$ time. The algorithms are very close to Wagner's and Whitin's original algorithm for the lot-sizing problem.

In the sequal a slightly reformulated version of SFLP denoted FLP is used.

$$\text{FLP: min} \sum_{j=1}^{T} \sum_{t=j}^{T} c_{jt} \cdot X_{jt} + \sum_{j=1}^{T} S \cdot Y_j$$

$$X_{1t} - s_{1t} = 0 \qquad\qquad t=1,2,\ldots,T$$

$$X_{jt} - s_{jt} + s_{j-1,t} = 0 \qquad\qquad t=2,\ldots,T, j=2,\ldots,t-1 \qquad (3)$$

$$X_{tt} + s_{t-1,t} = 1 \qquad\qquad t=1,2,\ldots,T$$

$$X_{jt} \leq Y_j \qquad\qquad j=1,2,\ldots,T,\ t=j,\ldots,T$$

$$s_{jt} \geq 0,\ X_{jt},\ Y_j \in \{0,1\} \qquad j=1,2,\ldots,T,\ t=j,\ldots,T$$

In problem FLP the variables s_{jt} should be understood as slack variables. The equivalence between FLP and SFLP is simply seen by adding the constraints (4) for each fixed t. The relaxed version of FLP has of course a natural integer solution just as SFLP and its dual can be solved in $0(T^2)$ time by a simple algorithm suggested by Rosling (1985). The reason for reformulating SFLP is the ease by which FLP can be integrated in an assembly framework. Suppose problem FLP intends to model the production planning situation for a component that is used for the production of a single successor item, s. Suppose d_t is the demand for s in period t and that for simplicity exactly one item of the component is required for each item assembled of the successor. The demand for the component is then also d_t. FLP is now a correct model for the component only if its successor is produced in each period. If this is not the case FLP should be further constrained by the fact that production of the successor assumes that the component is available. Thus, letting X^s_{jt}, $j \leq t$, denote the proportion of d_t produced in period t if the successor, if $X^s_{jt}=1$ then it is required that $X_{kt}=0$ for k=j+1, j+2,...,t or, equivalently, that $\sum_{k=1}^{j} X_{kt} = 1$. This kind of constraints is easily taken into account by a simple amendment to FLP. This generalized problem is denoted GFLP.

GFLP: $\min \sum\limits_{j=1}^{T} \sum\limits_{t=j}^{T} c_{jt} \cdot X_{jt} + \sum\limits_{j=1}^{T} S \cdot Y_j$

$$X_{1t} - s_{1t} = X_{1t}^S$$

$$\left. \begin{array}{l} X_{jt} - s_{jt} + s_{j-1,t} = X_{jt}^S \quad \text{for } j=2,\ldots,t-1 \\[2mm] X_{tt} + s_{t-1,t} = X_{tt}^S \end{array} \right\} \quad \text{for } t=1,2\ldots,T \quad (4)$$

$$X_{jt} \leq Y_j$$

$$s_{jt} \geq 0, \; X_{jt}, \; Y_j \in \{0,1\} \quad \text{for } j=1,2,\ldots,T \quad t=j,\ldots,T$$

The only modification made of FLP is that the right-hand side of (3) has been replaced by X_{jt}^S in (4). Since $\sum\limits_{j=1}^{t} X_{jt}^S = 1$ for the successor, the reader can easily verify, beginning with the last equation of (4), that $X_{jt}^S = 1$ actually implies that $X_{kt} = 0$ for $k=j+1,\ldots,t$.

Rosling (1985) demonstrates that also the relaxed version of GFLP has an optimal integer solution provided that $X_{jt}^S \in \{0,1\}$ and that the production plan of the successor is such that production takes place in a period only if the stock then is zero of the final product. An algorithm is also given that solves the dual of GFLP in $O(T^2)$ time. The dual is denoted DGFLP

DGFLP: $\max \sum\limits_{j=1}^{T} \sum\limits_{t=j}^{T} a_{jt} \cdot \lambda_{jt}$

$$\sum\limits_{t=j}^{T} \max(0, \lambda_{jt} - c_{jt}) \leq S \quad \text{for } j=1,2,\ldots,T \quad (5)$$

$$\lambda_{jt} \geq \lambda_{j+1,t} \quad \text{for } t=2,3,\ldots,T \text{ and } j=1,\ldots,t-1$$

The variables λ_{jt} of DGFLP could be interpreted as the cost of satisfying the demand of period t from production in period j (or an earlier period).

3   The assembly system

In an assembly system each component is assembled into exactly one successor product. Finally one single product results and all customer demands are only for this final item. Provided that the initial stocks of all products are zero, the assembly system can be modelled as a simple collection of problems GFLP. It is denoted NEW.

$$\text{NEW: min} \sum_{i=1}^{N} \left\{ \sum_{j=1}^{T} \sum_{t=j}^{T} c_{jt}^{i} \cdot x_{jt}^{i} + \sum_{j=1}^{T} s^{i} \cdot Y_{j}^{i} \right\}$$

$$\left. \begin{array}{l} x_{1t}^{i} - s_{1t}^{i} = x_{1t}^{s(i)} \\[2ex] x_{jt}^{i} - s_{jt}^{i} + s_{j-1,t}^{i} = x_{jt}^{s(i)} \quad j=2,3,\ldots,t-1 \\[2ex] x_{tt}^{i} + s_{t-1,t}^{i} = x_{tt}^{s(i)} \end{array} \right\} \text{ for all } i,t \qquad (6)$$

$$x_{jt}^{i} \leq Y_{jt}^{i} \qquad \text{for all } i,j,t$$

$$s_{jt}^{i} \geq 0, \ x_{jt}^{i}, \ Y_{jt}^{i} \in \{0,1\} \qquad \text{for all } i,j,t$$

In NEW a "successor" $s(1)$ appears to the final item. We define

$$s(1) = 0 \text{ and}$$

$$x_{jt}^{o} = \begin{cases} 1 & \text{for } j=t \\ 0 & \text{for } j \neq t \end{cases}$$

In NEW $s(i)$ denotes the immediate successor of item i in the assembly network and the cost coefficients c_{jt}^{i} are defined by (2) with h replaced by h^{i}. This coefficient should be interpreted as the echelon holding cost for component i, i.e. the holding cost that is in excess of the holding costs of all the components of which i is assembled. The echelon stock concept is originally due to Clark and Scarf (1960) and was recently exploited in the formulation of the present lot-sizing problem by Afentakis et al (1984). Compared to their formulation, NEW is an improvement in the sense that the bound on the minimal cost given by its relaxed version is at least as good as the one proposed by them (Rosling (1985)).

Problem NEW is a mixed integer programming problem of considerable size. Our solution approach is through branch and bound and our bounding device is the relaxed version of NEW ($X_{jt}^i \geq 0$, $Y_{jt}^i \geq 0$). This problem is an ordinary linear program but its size makes it rather complicated and it would persumably be very tedious to apply the Simplex algorithm. Instead an approximate solution procedure is proposed. It also has the merit of providing feasible, often optimal, solutions to the original problem NEW. The procedure handles the components level by level. Level one consists of only the final item and a component of level k has all its predecessors at various levels l, l>k. See fig. 1.

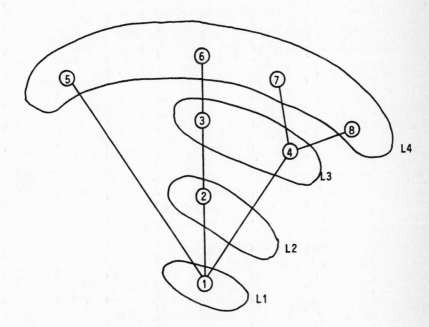

Fig 1   An assembly network with 8 items and 4 levels.

The procedure starts with a given feasible solution to NEW (we have generally selected the solution $X_{tt}^i = 1$ for all i,t). One single-item problem of the type GFLP is solved for each item i at the last level. The production plan for its successor, $X_{jt}^{s(i)}$, is then the given schedule. Actually the dual DGFLP is solved and the values λ_{jt}^i of the solution to item i are added to the cost coefficients $c_{jt}^{s(i)}$ of the successor of i. This procedure is then repeated level by level so that a single-item problem, GFLP, is solved for each item in the assembly network. In Rosling (1985) it is demonstrated that the procedure can be interpreted as multi-stage Benders decomposition. The minimal 'cost' of the final item is shown to be a valid lower bound for the optimal solution to NEW. This ends the first _dual phase_ of the approximate procedure. In the _primal phase_ the procedure is reversed and all the single-item problems of the dual phase are resolved level by level beginning with the final item. In this way a new feasible solution as well as an upper bound to NEW is obtained. If the upper and lower bounds coincide then an optimal solution to NEW has been found. If this is not the case then the latest feasible solution is the point of departure for a new dual and primal phase and so on. Convergence is not assured and consequently, the procedure can generally be used only as a bounding device. The true optimal solution is obtained by branch and bound.

The spirit of the bounding procedure is close to that of Van Roy's "Cross Decomposition" (1983). He circles around between subproblems and master problems exactly as we do (though only in two stages). However, Van Roy closes the optimization by solving some full Benders (or possibly Dantzig-Wolfe) master problems with all cuts generated during the circling-around phase retained. In contrast we close our optimization by branch and bound.

The spirit of the bounding procedure is also similar to that of Graves (1981). The difference between Graves' method and ours is that his correspondence to our "costs", λ_{jt}^i, are derived for a fixed set-up schedule for all predecessors (not only the immediate ones) of item i. Thus, the shadow costs contain only direct holding (and possibly production) costs but no distributed set-up costs and the methods coincide when set-up costs are absent. The great virtue of Graves' method is its generality, however. It is not confined to assembly systems but it is on the other hand a true heuristic, virtually useless in deriving close lower bounds.

A third reference that the bounding procedure should be compared to is the cost-modification heuristic of Blackburn and Millen (1982). Our approach may be understood as a holding cost modification procedure in the following way. Note that the total original echelon holding cost in period j for the demand of period t of item i is $(c_{jt}^i - c_{j+1,t}^i)$. In the subproblems GFLP of the bounding procedure this difference has been modified to $(c_{jt}^i - c_{j+1,t}^i) + \sum_{\ell \in B(i)} (\lambda_{jt}^\ell - \lambda_{j+1,t}^\ell)$, where $B(i)$ denotes the set of immediate predecessors of item i.

The original feature of our approach is that the modified cost of holding stock in period j is not the same for all items then in stock. To the contrary the modified holding cost (even if it is recomputed as a cost per unit) differs among items depending on the period, the demand of which the item is destined at. Blackburn and Millen take the more conventional view of making no difference among items stored in the same period. This is the lack of freedom of the conventional inventory model and exactly what makes the facility location formulation so attractive. However, it should be emphasized that Blackburn and Millen not only modify holding costs but also set-up costs. This feature is lacking in the present approach and so, it might be an idea by which the bounding procedure may be improved.

3   Computational results and conclusions

Details of the algorithm is found in Rosling (1985). It was realized in a FORTRAN 77 computer program that was run on the DEC 2065 of the Data Centre at Linköping Institute of Technology. The test problems were those of Afentakis et al (1984). There are basically three different assembly networks from which 90 lot-sizing problems with 5-50 items were constructed. The result on this problem set is summerized in table 1.

TABLE 1

Computational results of the branch & bound algorithm on the 90 twelve-periods problems of Afentakis et al (1984).

	First iteration	End of bounding	Branch and Bound
No. of proven optimal solutions	44	85	90
No. of optimal solutions	69	88	90
total CPU-time (sec. DEC2065)	9	41	48
Deviation from optimum % LB average	0.12	0.011	-
" % LB max	1.11	0.34	-
" % UB average	0.15	0.005	-
" % UB max	2.48	0.45	-

Afentakis et al required totally 896 CPU-seconds on the IBM 3032 of University of Rochester to optimize the same problems. The published experiences on similar problems by Afentakis and Gavish (1985) seem to indicate that IBM 3032 and DEC 2065 use roughly equivalent in speed on this kind of problem.

The bounding procedure seems to work well also as a heuristic device. The errors shown at the end of the bounding procedure at the initial node (after a maximum of 15 and an average of 2.7 main iterations) are at least as good as those of Afentakis (1982) and the errors are neg-ligable. None of the 88 optimal solutions were found within more than 5 iterations. Even the first iteration of the bounding procedure seems to be a fully acceptable heuristic. This is most interesting since the first iteration of the bounding procedure requires the solution of only two single-item inventory problems per item which should make it competitive even to the simplest level-by-level heuristics. However, it requires the use of an exact dual single-item algorithm and can not possibly use a heuristic like that of Silver and Meal (1973) which persumably is about five times faster on twelve-periods problems.

There was little indication of any relation between algorithmic performance and problem structure. All the five-items problems were however solved by the first main iteration. The bounding procedure failed on two 20-items problems, two 40-items problems and one 50-items problem. The only one of the three basic assembly structures on which the bounding procedure succeeded on all problems was the most serial one (= network B of Afentakis et al (1984)).

At the outset of this study the assembly system was considered a test case on which some new ideas on lot-sizing may advantageously be assessed. The first idea is to model the basic single-item inventory model as a facility location problem. Extended to the assembly lot-sizing problem this idea created an integer linear program that compared favourably to previous models in so far as the relaxed version with no integer requirements gave improved bounds. A computational study on a problem set of 90 cases due to Afentakis et al (1984) revealed that the bounds of the new approach coincided with the optimal values for at least 88 cases, a result achieved for only 46 cases by their more conventional approach.

The second idea is a truely computational one. Through solution of series of single-item problems lower as well as upper bounds and feasible solutions were found to the assembly lot-sizing problem. The approach is approximate, but for 85 out of 90 test problems it still found a proven optimal solution after at most five main iterations. The bounding procedure was integrated into a branch and bound algorithm that solved the problems of the test set in a computer running time that is at least an order of magnitude times less than that of its probably best competitor, the algorithm due to Afentakis et al (1984). The bounding procedure works well as a heuristic. After its first main iteration 69 out of 90 optimal solutions were found. The average deviation from the minimal cost was less than 0,15%.

Thus, the test case apparently turned out very fabourable to the suggested concepts. Consequently, they seem indeed worthy of further investigation.

References

Afentakis, P., "A Class of Heuristic Algorithms for Lot-Sizing in Multistage Assembly Systems", Working Paper, The Graduate School of Management, University of Rochester, Rochester, N.Y., 1982.

Afentakis, P. and B. Gavish, "Optimal Lot-Sizing Algorithms for Complex Product Structures", Working Paper Series No. QM 8318, The Graduate School of Management, University of Rochester, 1985.

Afentakis, P., B. Gavish and U. Karmarkar, "Exact Solutions to the Lot-Sizing Problem in Multistage Assembly Systems", Management Sci., 30 (1984), 222-239.

Barany, I., J. Edmonds and L.A. Wolsey, "Packing and Covering a Tree by Subtrees", Core Discussion Paper No 8434 (1984) Center of Operations Research and Econometrics, Université Catholique de Louvain, Belgium.

Billington, P.J., J.O. Mc Clain and L.J. Thomas, "Capacity-Constrained MRP Systems", Management Sci., (1983), 1126-1141.

Blackburn, J.D. and R.A. Millen, "Improved Heuristics for Multi-Stage Requirements Planning Systems", Management Sci., 28 (1982), pp. 44-56.

Clark, A. and H. Scarf, "Optimal Policies for Multi-Echelon Inventory Problems", Management Sci., 6 (1960), pp 475-490.

Crowston, W.B., M.H. Wagner and J.F. Williams, "Economic Lot Size Determination in Multi-Stage Assembly Systems", Management Sci., (1973), pp. 517-527.

Graves, S.C., "Multi-Stage Lot Sizing: An Iterative Procedure", Ch. 4 in Schwarz, L.B. (Ed). Multi-Level Production/Inventory Control Systems: Theory and Practice, North Holland, Amsterdam 1981.

Krarup, J. and O. Bilde, "Plant Location, Set Covering and Economic Lot Sizing: An 0(mn) Algorithm for Structured Problems", in Collatz, L. et al (eds) Optimierung bei Graphentheoretischen und Ganzzahligen Probleme, Birkhauser, Basel, 1977, 155-180.

Love, S.F., "A Facility in Series Inventory Model with Nested Schedules", Management Sci., 18 (1972), 327-338.

Orlicky, J., Materials Requirements Planning, McGraw-Hill, New York, 1975.

Rosling, K., "The Dynamic Inventory Model and the Uncapacitated Facility Location Problem", to appear in Chikán, A., Proceedings of the Third International Symposium on Inventories held in Budapest 1984, Also available unabridged as Research Report 102, Dep of Production Economics, Linköping Institute of Technology, Sweden.

Rosling, K., "Optimal Lot-Sizing in Assembly Systems", Linköping Institute of Technology, 1985.

Silver, E.A. and H. Meal, "A Heuristic for selecting Lot-Size Quantities for the Case of a Deterministic Time-Varying Demand Rate and Discrete Opportunities for Replenishment, Production and Inventory Management, 14 (1973), 64-74.

Steinberg, E. and H.A. Napier, "Optimal Multi-Level Lot Sizing for Requirements Planning Systems", <u>Management Sci.</u>, 26 (1980) 1258-1271.

Van Roy, R.J., "Cross Decomposition for Mixed Integer Programming", <u>Mathematical Programming</u>", 23 (1983), pp. 46-63.

Veinott, A.F., "Minimum Concave-Cost Solutions of Leontief Substitution Models of Multi-Facility Inventory Systems", <u>Oper. Res.</u>, 17 (1969), 262-291.

Wagner, M.H. and T.M. Whitin, "Dynamic Version of the Economic Lot-Sizing Model", <u>Management Sci.</u>, 5 (1958), 89-96.

Zangwill, W.I., "A Deterministic Multiproduct, Multi-Facility Production and Inventory Model", <u>Oper. Res.</u>, 14 (1967), 486-507.

John A. Muckstadt
School of Operations Research
and Industrial Engineering
Cornell University
Ithaca, New York 14853

ABSTRACT

Lot sizes for externally purchased components used in assemblies are often
determined so that total inventory carrying costs and fixed ordering costs are
approximately minimized. By focusing primarily on this criterion, a number of
constraints relating to receiving dock capacity and storage area capacities are
usually ignored. The goals of this paper are to develop a model and an algorithm
that can be used to establish the time between external procurements and between
movement of stock from stage to stage for each component in a multi-stage assembly
system recognizing the presence of these capacity constraints.

I.   INTRODUCTION

Lot sizes for externally purchased components used in final assemblies are often
computed using simple rules. For example, when production rates for final
assemblies remain relatively constant over time, some variation of the Wilson lot
size formula is frequently used to determine component procurement lot sizes. If
the demand rates for final products change over time, then some other technique
might be used, such as the part period balancing method, the least unit cost
approach, or the Silver-Meal heuristic [8]. All of these methods establish
component lot sizes so that inventory carrying costs are compared to fixed ordering
costs in such a way that total component procurement costs are approximately
minimized. By focusing primarily on this criterion, a number of issues of practical
significance are often ignored. The purposes of this paper are to present a model
and to describe an algorithm for planning component lot sizes for assembly plants
recognizing some of these factors such as limitations on available labor, equipment
and space.

Frequently the amount ordered from a vendor for a component may not be delivered
at one time, but is scheduled to be delivered in several lots. This concept is
central to the so-called "Just-in-Time" inventory control philosophy. For example,
an order may be for 52,000 units with weekly deliveries of 1000 units. The

component order quantities are normally based on demand projections for final assemblies as stated in a master production schedule; however, as in the example, the delivery quantities may be smaller than the order quantities. If the production rate for the final product is approximately constant, then the order quantity is often an integer multiple of the delivery quantity. Delivery quantities, and the time between the receipt of such quantities, called the delivery intervals, are set based on other considerations such as receiving dock capacity, warehouse space, storage space on the shop floor, storage and delivery container capacities, material handling capacities between a receiving dock and a warehouse and between a warehouse and the shop floor, and any fixed ordering costs and inventory carrying costs. The capacities we have mentioned can be related to both equipment and labor. In addition, the selection of an optimal delivery interval should take into account the lot splitting possibilities that can take place after a delivery is made (e.g. the quantity of a component sent from a warehouse to the shop floor can be less than that component's delivery quantity). We call the optimal delivery quantity the economic delivery quantity and the optimal delivery interval the economic delivery interval.

Our specific goal in this paper is to develop a model and an algorithm that can be used to establish consistent and realistic economic delivery intervals for each component while recognizing the presence of some of the capacity constraints mentioned earlier.

There are a number of reasons for formulating the model in terms of delivery intervals rather than lot sizes. First, in many real environments that we have observed, planners think in terms of the frequency of receipt of components and the frequency of material movements within a plant rather than in terms of lot sizes. Second, when the production plan for each final product varies, it is easy to determine the delivery quantities knowing the value of the delivery intervals. There are also some mathematical simplifications present when formulating the problem in this way. Additional discussion concerning the reasons for choosing delivery intervals to be the decision variables rather than the delivery quantities can be found in Maxwell and Muckstadt [6].

We also stated that the economic delivery intervals must be chosen so that a consistent flow of material will result. By this we mean that the delivery interval between the receipt of a shipment from an external supplier and between successive stages in the assembly plant should be planned so that schedules can be effectively implemented. For example, a solution is not practical if a delivery interval for a component from an external supplier is $\sqrt{5}$ times as long as the delivery interval of that component from the main warehouse to the shop floor. Therefore, we have limited attention to a particular class of policies.

To insure that the economic delivery quantities are both consistent and realistic, the class of policies we consider are nested and stationary. By stationary we mean that the time between deliveries from one stage to the next is always the same. By nested we mean that a delivery will not arrive at a stage unless a delivery is also made from that stage to a successor stage. Nested policies are used in practice to prevent the build up of in-process inventories. While stationary and nested policies need not be optimal in more general situations [7,11], they are appropriate for the situation we model since we assume a constant and continuous consumption rate for each component and assume a serial flow for a component through the assembly plant [5]. These and other assumptions will be subsequently discussed more completely. For certain extensions of the present model, the nestedness assumption may be inappropriate. Non-nested policies can be introduced using ideas presented by Maxwell and Muckstadt [6] and Roundy [9].

We also restrict attention to solutions for which the delivery interval for a component to a given stage must be $1,2,4,8,\ldots,2^k$ times as long as the delivery interval for that component to a successor stage, where k is a non-negative integer. Restricting attention to such policies greatly simplifies the detailed scheduling problem for component deliveries to and throughout a plant [6]. Furthermore, limiting the solutions to this class of policies has little affect on the objective function value. For unconstrained distribution type system structures including serial systems Roundy [9] and Maxwell and Muckstadt [6] have proven that by restricting solutions to this class, the objective function can never be more than 6% higher than the value obtained by following any other policy. We show that a similar result holds for the constrained problem considered here.

Finally, we assume a base planning period exists for each component. This period can be an hour, shift, day, week, etc. Each component delivery interval must be a power of two multiple of this base planning period. The notion of a base planning period is frequently used in practice. For example, a certain minimal amount of inventory is often moved to a line station on a delivery. This amount could correspond to a specific number of hours of work for a laborer. The length of a base planning period may also reflect the capabilities of an information system. We note that the base planning period can be set arbitrarily small if no constraints exist on the minimum length of the delivery intervals. Thus a variety of applications can be represented based on this concept.

The remainder of this paper is organized in the following way. In the next section we present the assumptions and nomenclature used in the paper. The model is stated in Section III and an algorithm is developed and analyzed in Section IV.

II. MODELING THE ECONOMIC DELIVERY INTERVAL PROBLEM

In this section we develop a model of the economic delivery interval problem described in Section I. The model is a planning model, which is used only to find delivery intervals for each type of component. Detailed scheduling of the exact arrival and shipping times from stage-to-stage cannot be accomplished using the model. Consequently only aggregate activity is considered in each stage of the system.

The model is based on the following assumptions.

1. The assembly rate for all final products is constant and continuous and equals λ_p units per year.

2. The material flow for component p can be represented by a graph G_p that corresponds to a serial system. The nodes in the graph represent storage areas and the arcs indicate the movement of component p from one storage area to the next. $N(G_p)$ and $A(G_p)$ represent the node and arc sets corresponding to G_p, respectively. The first and final nodes have special attributes. The first node in G_p is a receiving area through which all components must flow. The receiving area is designated node 1. Hence $1 \in N(G_p)$ for all p. The final node in G_p (the one without a successor node) is called a line station.

3. Each component is ultimately consumed (placed into an assembly) at only one line station. This assumption is made only to reduce notational complexity. Minor modifications to both the model and algorithm must be made if this and the preceding assumption are relaxed.

4. There is a fixed cost associated with the placement and receipt of a delivery from an external supplier for component p, call it K_p.

5. The cost of holding one unit of component p for one year is h_p.

6. Capacities exist for each storage area and the receiving area.

    a) The total number of deliveries to the receiving area per year cannot exceed e.

    b) The time available for operating each storage area per year is fixed. We assume the time to process a lot of component p entering and leaving storage area i has both a fixed and variable component. The total annual average material flow through storage area i is proportional to $\sum_{p\ i \in N(G_p)} \lambda_p$. Thus the total variable processing time is unaffected by the lot sizing/delivery interval decisions. Deducting this projected known time from the total available time results in an estimate of the total annual hours available for the fixed portion of the processing activity associated with placing units into and taking them out of storage area i. Let c_i be this amount and let a_{ip} and b_{ip} represent the fixed times required to process a lot of any size of component p into and out of storage area i, respectively, where a_{ip} and b_{ip} are also measured in hours.

    c) Storage capacity is limited at each storage area, including line stations. Let s_i represent the storage capacity at area i at any point in time.

d) There is no storage capacity in the receiving area. Hence each arriving lot for component p moves immediately to storage area i, where $(1,i) \in A(G_p)$.

7. We assume a storage area at line station ℓ is dedicated to only one component; furthermore, we assume that $a_{\ell p} = 0$ for $\ell \in N(G_p) \cap I_L$, where I_L is the set of line stations; that is, there is no fixed processing time at a line station.

8. Delivery intervals are restricted to be a powers of two multiple of some base planning period of length B.

9. Since we assume a serial nature for graph G_p, only nested policies are considered.

Additionally, let T_{ip} represent the delivery interval for component p (measured in years) into storage area i, $i \in N(G_p)$; $g_p = h_p \lambda_p / 2$, the average yearly holding cost for component p if $T_{1p} = 1$; and M_{ip} represent the powers of two multiple of the base planning period B per delivery interval for component p into storage area i, $i \in N(G_p)$. Note that since there is no storage capacity in the receiving area (assumption 6d), $T_{1p} = T_{ip}$ for $(1,i) \in A(G_p)$. Let i_p represent the storage area i for which $(1,i_p) \in A(G_p)$.

Also, let d_{ip} represent the amount of storage capacity of area i, $i \in N(G_p)$, consumed per unit of component p. The value of d_{ip} depends on the storage system being used (e.g. dedicated storage for a component, random storage, etc.) in combination with the sequencing rules used to process the flow of components. Thus we allow the space factors to differ by storage area. For example, the factor would be 1 for the line station at which component p is used; however, it would have another value for a large automatic storage/retrieval system (ASRS). We assume the storage capacity consumed at storage area i for component p is measured proportional to the maximum inventory, that is, $\lambda_p(T_{ip} - T_{jp})$, where $(i,j) \in A(G_p)$. Thus if the entering and departing lots of component p at storage area i are of equal size, then no storage capacity is consumed. The storage capacity used at storage area i corresponding to a delivery interval plan is measured by

$$\sum_{p \ni i \in N(G_p)} d_{ip} \lambda_p (T_{ip} - T_{jp}).$$

and $(i,j) \in A(G_p)$

For notational simplicity, let $f_{ip} = d_{ip} \lambda_p$.

We close this section by describing an example system. The example illustrates the notion of a storage area and the structure of the graphs G_p. Suppose there are four components each of which is stored in storage area 1. Upon leaving this area, components 1 and 2 are sent to storage area 2 and components 3 and 4 are sent to storage area 3. From the storage areas, each component is sent to a line station. Figure 1 illustrates this system's structure. There are 7 storage areas.

Each component graph G_p is displayed in Figure 1. Then, G_1 has $N(G_1) = \{1,2,4\}$ and $A(G_1) = \{(1,2),(2,4)\}$, G_2 has $N(G_2) = \{1,2,5\}$ and $A(G_2) = \{(1,2),(2,5)\}$, G_3 has $N(G_3) = \{1,3,6\}$ with $A(G_3) = \{(1,3),(3,6)\}$, and G_4 has $N(G_4) = \{1,3,7\}$ and $A(G_4) = \{(1,3),(3,7)\}$.

Storage Area 1 (i = 1)

Component 1   Component 2   Component 3   Component 4

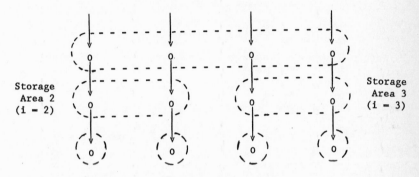

Storage
Area 2
(i = 2)

Storage
Area 3
(i = 3)

Line Station   Line Station   Line Station   Line Station
1   2   3   4
(i = 4)   (i = 5)   (i = 6)   (i = 7)

EXAMPLE SYSTEM STRUCTURE

Figure 1

III. THE MODEL OF THE ECONOMIC DELIVERY INTERVAL PROBLEM

In this section we state a model of the economic delivery interval problem (EDIP) that is based on the assumptions and notation discussed in Section II. We also present some observations concerning the model and its solution.

The EDIP can be stated as follows.

$$\min \quad \sum_p \{K_p/T_{1p} + g_p T_{1p}\} - \min \sum_p \{K_p/T_{i_p p} + g_p T_{i_p p}\} \tag{1}$$

$$\text{subject to} \quad \sum_p 1/T_{1p} \le e, \tag{2}$$

(Receiving Area Constraint, Assumption 6d)

$$\sum_{\substack{p \ni i \in N(G_p) \\ \text{and } (i,j) \in A(G_p)}} (a_{ip}/T_{ip} + b_{ip}/T_{jp}) \leq c_i, \ i \notin I_L, \tag{3}$$

(Fixed Time Constraint for Storage
Area i, Assumption 6b)

$$\sum_{\substack{p \ni i \in N(G_p) \\ \text{and } (i,j) \in A(G_p)}} f_{ip}(T_{ip} - T_{jp}) \leq s_i, \ i_i \notin I_L, \tag{4}$$

(Storage Capacity Constraint for
Area i, Assumption 6c).

$$f_{ip}T_{ip} \leq s_i, \ i \in N(G_p) \cap I_L, \tag{5}$$

(Line Station Storage Capacity,
Assumption 7)

$$T_{ip} = M_{ip} \cdot B \qquad i \in N(G_p) \qquad \text{(Assumption 8)} \tag{6}$$

$$M_{ip} \geq M_{jp} \qquad (i,j) \in A(G_p) \ \text{(Assumption 9)} \tag{7}$$

$$M_{ip} \in \{1,2,4,8....\}. \qquad \text{(Assumption 8)} \tag{8}$$

Since $T_{1p} = T_{i_p p}$, we can remove T_{1p} from the problems's formulation.

We note that the EDIP is a large-scale, non-linear integer programming problem. Consequently, it is not necessarily solved in an easy manner. Also observe that if $K_p = 0$ for all p, e is large and $a_{ip} = b_{ip} = 0$ for all i, then the EDIP is a linear integer program whose solution is $T_{ip} = B$. Thus if the fixed costs and times can be eliminated, or made relatively small, and the receiving area can accommodate $\sum_p 1/B$ shipments per year, the solution to the EDIP is immediate. In this case, virtually all storage area space could be eliminated. Furthermore, the solution in this situation indicates that the "Just-in-Time" principle is optimal. Thus Just-in-Time policies are optimal whenever fixed costs and times are inconsequential and the receiving area capacity is adequate. Note that if the fixed processing times and/or fixed procurement costs are not relatively small, then the optimal value for T_{ip} can be greater than B, that is, the Just-in-Time solution can be suboptimal.

IV. FINDING A SOLUTION TO THE EDIP

Rather than solving the EDIP directly, we first show how a solution to a relaxed version of this problem can be obtained. Then we discuss how the solution to this relaxed problem can be used to obtain values for the M_{ip} variables.

A. Relaxation of the EDIP

Suppose we relax the assumptions that M_{ip} must be a power of two and that a base planning period exists. The resulting relaxed problem, which we designate

REDIP, can be stated as

$$\min_{p} \ \Sigma \ \{K_p/T_{i_p p} + g_p T_{i_p p}\}$$

subject to constraints (1) - (5) of the EDIP and $T_{ip} \geq T_{jp} \geq 0$, $(i,j) \in A(G_p)$.

This problem is also not easy to solve. We propose obtaining its solution using an infinitely convergent procedure, each iteration of which consists of two steps. The first step requires solving a Lagrangian relaxation of the REDIP; the second step obtains new estimates for the multiplier values.

The Lagrangian relaxation used in the first step is obtained by dualizing with respect to certain capacity constraints. Let γ be the multiplier corresponding to the receiving area constraint, α_i be the multiplier for the storage area i ($i \notin I_L$) fixed time constraint, and β_i be the multiplier corresponding to the area i storage space capacity constraint ($i \notin I_L$). Then the relaxation, which we call the LREDIP, is

$$\min_{p} \ \Sigma \ \left\{ (K_p + \gamma)/T_{i_p p} + g_p T_{i_p p} \right\}$$

$$+ \ \Sigma_{p} \left[\ \Sigma_{\substack{i \geq 2 \\ i \in N(G_p), \ i \notin I_L \\ (k,i) \in A(G_p)}} [(\alpha_k b_{kp} + \alpha_i a_{ip})/T_{ip} + (\beta_i f_{ip} - \beta_k f_{kp}) \cdot T_{ip}] \right\}$$

subject to
$$T_{ip} \geq T_{jp} \geq 0, \ (i,j) \in A(G_p),$$
$$T_{ip} \leq s_i/f_{ip}, \ i \in N(G_p) \cap I_L,$$

where, by definition, $\alpha_1 - b_{1p} - \beta_1 - 0$. This LREDIP is chosen, as we will subsequently show, because it is easily solved given the values of γ, α_i and β_i.

To simplify notation, let

$$\bar{K}_{ip} - K_p + \gamma + \alpha_i a_{ip}; \ \bar{g}_{ip} - g_p + \beta_i f_{ip}, \qquad i - i_p, \ i \geq 2,$$

$$\bar{K}_{ip} - (\alpha_k b_{kp} + \alpha_i a_{ip}); \ \bar{g}_{ip} - \beta_i f_{ip} + \beta_k f_{kp}, \ i \neq i_p, \ i \geq 2, \ (k,i) \in A(G_p),$$

$$\bar{s}_i - s_i/f_{ip}, \ i \in N(G_p) \cap I_L,$$

where $\alpha_i - \beta_i - 0$, $i \in I_L$. Then, for fixed values of γ, α_i, and β_i, the LREDIP can be stated as

$$\min_{i \geq 2, p} \Sigma \ (\bar{K}_{ip}/T_{ip} + \bar{g}_{ip}T_{ip})$$

$$T_{ip} \geq T_{jp} \geq 0, \ (i,j) \in A(G_p),$$

$$T_{ip} \leq \bar{s}_i, \qquad i \in N(G_p) \cap I_L.$$

Observe that this problem is separable by component since the constraints reflect the precedence and line station capacity conditions by component. Furthermore, by assumption, the precedence relationships for component p can be represented by a graph of a serial system. We next show how this mathematical structure can be exploited to find an optimal solution to the LREDIP. To reduce notation, we temporarily drop the subscript p in the discussion in the next subsection.

B. Finding a Solution to the LREDIP

In this section we show how a solution to the LREDIP can be obtained. Since the LREDIP is separable by component, its solution can be found by solving p independent problems. We show in two steps how an optimal solution can be determined for each component.

In the first step, we consider the problem

$$\min_{i=2}^{n} \Sigma \ (\bar{K}_i/T_i + \bar{g}_iT_i)$$

$$T_i \geq T_j \geq 0, \ (i,j) \in A(G), \qquad \qquad \text{Problem 1}$$

where G is the graph of the serial system corresponding to component p. We begin by showing the relationship between a solution to Problem 1, and the ordered partitions of the graph G. The notion of an ordered partition is developed in Jackson, Maxwell and Muckstadt [2] and is discussed in the following subsection.

In the second step, we establish the relationship between the solution to Problem 1 and an optimal solution to the following problem, which we call Problem 2.

$$\min_{i} \Sigma \ (\bar{K}_i/T_i + \bar{g}_iT_i)$$

$$T_i \geq T_j, \ (i,j) \in A(G), \qquad \qquad \text{Problem 2}$$

$$T_\ell \leq \bar{s}_\ell.$$

We show how the solution to Problem 1 can be used to find a solution to Problem 2 and then present an algorithm for finding the solution to this problem and hence to the LREDIP.

B.1 Properties of an Optimal Solution to Problem 1

Define a subgraph G' of the graph G to consist of a subset N(G') of the node set N(G) together with the associated arc set A(G'), where $(i,j) \in A(G')$ if and only if $i \in N(G')$, $j \in N(G')$, and $(i,j) \in A(G)$. An ordered collection of subgraphs $(G_1, G_2, \ldots, G_N)$ of G is said to be ordered by precedence if for any $1 \leq \ell < k \leq N$ there does not exist a node $j \in N(G_\ell)$ and a node $i \in N(G_k)$ such that $(j,i) \in A(G)$. That is, no node in $N(G_\ell)$ precedes any node in $N(G_k)$ if $k > \ell$. We say that a collection of subgraphs $(G_1, G_2, \ldots, G_N)$ forms an ordered partition of the graph G if

(a) the node subsets $N(G_1), N(G_2), \ldots, N(G_N)$ form a partition
of the node set N(G), and

(b) the subgraphs are ordered by precedence.

A directed cut of a subgraph G' is simply an ordered (binary) partition (G'^+, G'^-) of the subgraph G'.

Suppose we have an arbitrary feasible solution to Problem 1 in which there are N distinct delivery intervals in the solution. Each delivery interval corresponds to a subset of the storage areas. Each storage area in that subset shares a common delivery interval. These subsets partition N(G). Define $G_1, \ldots, G_N$ to be the subgraphs of G corresponding to the subsets. Note that $G_1, \ldots, G_N$ must form an ordered partition of the graph G. Furthermore, the solution to Problem 1 can be optimal only if the delivery interval for G_k, call it $T(G_k)$, satisfies

$T(G_k) = (K(G_k)/g(G_k))^{1/2}$, $k = 1, \ldots, N$, where $K(G_k) = \Sigma_{i \in N(G_k)} \bar{K}_i$ and

$g(G_k) = \Sigma_{i \in N(G_k)} \bar{g}_i$.

Suppose $(G_1, \ldots, G_N)$ is an ordered partition of G with $T(G_k) = (K(G_k)/g(G_k))^{1/2}$ and $T_i = T(G_k)$ for all $i \in N(G_k)$, $k = 1, \ldots, N$. Then the solution $\{T_i\}$ is a feasible solution to Problem 1 if $T(G_1) \leq T(G_2) \leq \ldots \leq T(G_N)$; that is, if

$$\frac{K(G_1)}{g(G_1)} \leq \frac{K(G_2)}{g(G_2)} \leq \ldots \leq \frac{K(G_N)}{g(G_N)} .$$

The relationship between an optimal solution to Problem 1 and ordered partitions of the graph G is specified by the following theorem that is proved in Jackson, Maxwell and Muckstadt [2].

Theorem 1: Consider an arbitrary collection of N delivery intervals, $T(G_1), \ldots, T(G_N)$. The following three conditions are necessary and sufficient for these delivery intervals to correspond to an optimal solution to Problem 1:

(1) There exists an ordered partition $(G_1, \ldots, G_N)$ of the graph G such that
$T(G_k) = (K(G_k)/g(G_k))^{1/2}$ for each $k = 1, \ldots, N$;

(2) The sequence of ratios $\{K(G_k)/g(G_k); k = 1, \ldots, N\}$ is nondecreasing; and

(3) For each $k = 1, \ldots, N$, there does not exist a directed cut (G_k^-, G_k^+) of G_k such that

$$\frac{K(G_k^-)}{g(G_k^-)} < \frac{K(G_k^+)}{g(G_k^+)} \; .$$

Properties (2) and (3) are called the <u>convexity property</u> and <u>concavity property</u> of an optimal solution, respectively.

B.2 Finding an Optimal Solution to Problem 1

The optimal solution to Problem 1 is particularly easy to find due to the serial structure of the graph G. We will not present an algorithm here. Procedures are described in Maxwell and Muckstadt [6], Jackson and Roundy [3], or Schwarz and Schrage [10] that can be used to solve this problem. We note that due to the serial nature of G, the solution time is proportional to the number of nodes in G.

B.3 The Relationships Between Problem 1 and Problem 2

Suppose we have an optimal solution to Problem 1. This implies that we have found an ordered partition $G_1, \ldots, G_N$. Furthermore, since line station ℓ is the final node in the serial graph G, assume $\ell \in N(G_1)$ and $T_\ell = T(G_1) = \bar{K}(G_1)/\bar{g}(G_1)$. If $T_\ell \leq \bar{s}_\ell$, then this solution to Problem 1 is also an optimal solution to Problem 2. However, if $T_\ell > \bar{s}_\ell$, then this solution is not feasible to Problem 2. As we establish in the following theorem, even in this case the solution to Problem 1 is the basis for a solution to Problem 2.

<u>Theorem 2</u>: Suppose $G_1, \ldots, G_N$ is an optimal partition to Problem 1 and $T_\ell > \bar{s}_\ell$. Then there exists an ordered partition of G_1, say $G_1^1, \ldots, G_1^Q$ having the following properties:

(a) $T(G_1^1) > \bar{s}_\ell$.

(b) For any directed cut of G_1^1, say (G_1^{1+}, G_1^{1-}), such
that $\ell \in N(G_1^{1-})$,

$T(G_1^{1+}) \leq \bar{s}_\ell$.

(c) $\bar{s}_\ell < T(G_1^2) < T(G_1^3) < T(G_2) < \ldots < T(G_1^Q) < \ldots < T(G_N)$

and

(d) For each $k = 2, \ldots, Q$, for any directed cut (G_1^{k+}, G_1^{k-}),

$T(G_1^{k+}) < T(G_1^{k-})$.

Furthermore, an optimal solution to Problem 2 is given by

$$T_i - \bar{s}_\ell, \qquad i \in N(G_1^1),$$

$$T_i - T(G_1^k), \quad i \in N(G_1^k), \ k - 2,\ldots,Q,$$

and

$$T_i - T(G_j), \quad i \in N(G_j), \ j - 2,\ldots,N.$$

The proof of this theorem is lengthy and for that reason is omitted.

Observe that the above theorem does not rely on the serial nature of G. However, the following specialized algorithm for finding G_1^1 does take advantage of the serial structure of G_1.

Suppose there are n elements in $N(G_1)$. For ease of notation assume the nodes in this serial system are numbered 1 through n, where n corresponds to the appropriate line station. The algorithm builds a subgraph G_1^1 having the properties stated in Theorem 2. Note that a subgraph in a serial system can be described by two nodes; i.e. G' is a subgraph iff $N(G') - \{j,j+1,\ldots,k\}$ for $j \le k$. The algorithm searches for a j^* such that $N(G_1^1) - \{j^*,\ldots,\ell\}$.

PARTITIONING ALGORITHM FOR

FINDING G_1^1 (Algorithm 1)

Step 1. Set $N(G_1^1) - \{\ell\}$

Step 2. Set $j \leftarrow \ell-1$

$k \leftarrow \ell-1$

Step 3. While $(j \ge 1)$

$\{$If $\Sigma_{i-j}^k (\bar{K}_i/\bar{g}_i) \le s_\ell$, then $\{N(G_1^1) \leftarrow N(G_1^1) \cup \{j,j+1,\ldots,k\}$

$k \leftarrow j-1$

$j \leftarrow j-1$

$\}$

else $j \leftarrow j-1$

$\}$

End

B.4 An Algorithm for Finding an Optimal Solution to Problem 2

By combining the results developed in the preceding portions of this section, it is clear that the following algorithm finds an optimal solution to Problem 2 and hence can be used to find an optimal solution to the LREDIP.

ALGORITHM FOR FINDING THE
OPTIMAL SOLUTION FOR PROBLEM 2
(Algorithm 2)

Step 1. Find an optimal solution to Problem 1, which establishes an optimal
partition $G_1, \ldots, G_N$.

Step 2. Using Algorithm 1, find the graph G_1^1.

Step 3. Find the optimal partition of $G_1 - G_1^1$ using the same algorithm as used in
Step 1.

Step 4. Determine the optimal reorder intervals as follows:

$$T_i = \bar{s}_\ell, \; i \in N(G_1^1),$$

$$T_i = (\sum_{j \in N(G_1^k)} \bar{K}_j)/(\sum_{i \in N(G_1^k)} \bar{g}_j), \; i \in N(G_1^k), \; k = 2, \ldots, Q,$$

$$T_i = (\sum_{j \in N(G_k)} \bar{K}_j)/(\sum_{j \in N(G_k)} \bar{g}_j), \; i \in N(G_k).$$

V. A SOLUTION METHOD FOR THE EDIP

In this section we present a two step method for obtaining a solution to the
EDIP. First, we describe a procedure that finds a solution to the REDIP. This
method depends heavily on the results developed in the preceding section. Second,
we apply an optimal powers of two rounding rule for unconstrained problems to
generate a solution to the EDIP. We then briefly discuss the quality of the rounded
solution.

A. Finding a Solution to the REDIP

The procedure we propose for solving the REDIP has two steps. The first step
assumes the existence of values for the Lagrangian multipliers γ, α_i, and β_i.
Given these values, delivery intervals are established for each component using
Algorithm 2. If the solution satisfies the constraints of the EDIP (i.e., if the
left and right hand side values for each active constraint do not differ by more
than $\epsilon > 0$), then the procedure terminates. If not, step 2 is employed in which
new estimates of the multiplier values are calculated. Their values are found using
a large scale programming technique called column generation. References 1 and 4
contain a complete discussion of this method. We briefly summarize the idea behind
the procedure.

Each time the second step is entered, the column generation technique requires
solving a linear program. The rows of the linear program correspond to the
constraints on space and fixed time availability for the receiving area and all
storage areas except the line stations. Each column represents the space and time

requirements corresponding to a solution for Problem 2 for all components generated in Step 1. The variables in the linear program are weights that correspond to each column, or proposed solution generated in Step 1. One additional constraint exists in the formulation of the linear program that forces the sum of the weights to equal 1. The solution found to this linear program at each iteration yields a feasible solution to the REDIP (we assume the procedure is started with a known feasible solution) and a solution to its dual, that is, it yields an estimate of γ, α_i, and β_i.

The line station space constraints are not included in the Step 2 linear program. Recall that the linear program assigns optimal weights to each proposed solution so that feasibility to the REDIP is assured. Since all solutions obtained from Step 1 satisfy the line station space constraints, any convex combination of them also satisfies these constraints. Hence these constraints are not needed in the formulation of the linear program.

We now state the algorithm for obtaining a solution to the REDIP. The algorithm finds an $\in$ optimal solution. This procedure guarantees convergence of the multipliers to their optimal values. However, convergence is infinite. A complete discussion of the convergence properties of this type of algorithm can be found in References 1 and 4.

ALGORITHM FOR FINDING AN $\in$-OPTIMAL SOLUTION TO THE REDIP
(Algorithm 3)

Step 0. Generate initial values for γ, α_i, β_i, and a feasible solution for the REDIP.

Step 1. (a) Given the values of γ, α_i and β_i, find delivery intervals for each storage area for each component using Algorithm 2.

(b) For each constraint, compute the capacity utilization ratio corresponding to the solution generated in the first portion of this step. The utilization ratio measures capacity used corresponding to the proposed solution divided by the available capacity. Let U_i measure the fixed time constraint utilization ratios for area i, $i \notin I_L$ and V_i measure the utilization ratio for the area i storage capacity constraint, $i \notin I_L$. For $\in > 0$, if $U_i - 1 < \in$ for all i for which $\alpha_i = 0$ (and $\gamma = 0$) and $V_i - 1 < \in$ for all i for which $\beta_i = 0$ and $|U_i - 1| < \in$ for all i for which $\alpha_i > 0$ ($\gamma > 0$) and $|V_i - 1| < \in$ for i for which $\beta_i > 0$, then stop, the solution is $\in$-optimal; otherwise go to step 2.

Step 2. Find new values for γ, α_i and β_i. Generate a new column and weighting variable for the linear program. The components of this column reflect the respective total capacities required corresponding to the solution generated for all components in step 1. The final component is a 1, which appears in the weighting constraint. The new column has the following form.

$$
\begin{bmatrix}
\text{(total receiving area capacity consumed)} \\
\text{(storage area 1 fixed time capacity used)} \\
\text{(storage area 1 storage space used)} \\
\cdot \\
\cdot \\
\cdot \\
1
\end{bmatrix}
$$

Solve the linear program with the addition of this new column. Obtain new estimates for γ, α_i and β_i and return to Step 1.

The above algorithm works well for practical problems in which a component passes through only a few storage areas. The time required to solve the step 1 problem is proportional to $P \cdot J$, where J is the maximum number of storage areas a component actually enters and P is the number of components. Consequently, Step 1 can be accomplished very quickly. The total number of storage area constraints present in the Step 2 linear program should rarely exceed 25. Thus the basis and its inverse can be computed easily. Furthermore, the solution to the Step 2 linear program can often be obtained in one or a few pivots so that Step 2 is also accomplished rapidly. The number of iterations will, of course, vary depending on the problem and the selection of initial values for the multipliers and the quality of an available initial feasible solution to the REDIP.

We have assumed that an initial feasible solution can be obtained relatively easily. In real situations we have examined this has been possible. However, if one cannot be found quickly, the proposed algorithm can still be used by adding artificial variables to the formulation of the linear program used in Step 2. More iterations will most likely be required when an initial feasible solution is not available.

B. Finding an Approximate Solution to the EDIP

The solution obtained to the REDIP need not satisfy the powers of two restrictions stipulated in the formulation of the EDIP. The solution to the REDIP yields optimal values for the multipliers γ^*, α_i^* and β_i^* and values for the delivery intervals, T_{ip}. Assume $\overline{K}_{ip}$ and $\overline{g}_{ip}$ are computed using γ^*, α_i^* and β_i^*. Then $\{T_{ip}\}$ solves

$$\min_{i,p} \ \Sigma \ \{\overline{K}_{ip}/T_{ip} + \overline{g}_{ip}T_{ip}\}$$

$$T_{ip} \geq T_{jp} \geq 0, \ (i,j) \in A(G_p),$$ 　　　　　　　　(Problem 3)

$$T_{\ell p} \leq \overline{s}_\ell, \ \ell \in N(G_p) \cap I_L.$$

Assume, without loss of generality, that $\overline{s}_\ell$ is set so that it is a power of two multiple of B.

The power of two solutions T^*_{ip} and $T^*(G_{kp})$ can be obtained as follows. For component p, if $T_{\ell p} = \overline{s}_\ell$, then set $T^*_{ip} = \overline{s}_\ell$ for all i for which $T_{ip} = T_{\ell p}$, $i \in N(G_p)$, in the solution of Problem 3. Corresponding to the solution to Problem 3 there is an ordered partition of the graph for component p, G_p, which we designate $G_{1p}, \ldots, G_{N_p p}$. Let $i \in N(G_{kp})$ for which the corresponding delivery interval $T(G_{kp})$ is greater than $\overline{s}_\ell$. Then, as shown by Maxwell and Muckstadt [6], the optimal delivery interval for component p and storage area i is the smallest power of 2, M_{ip}, for which

$$M_{ip} \geq \frac{1}{B} \sqrt{\frac{1}{2} \left(\sum_{i \in N(G_{kp})} \overline{K}_{ip} \right) / \left(\sum_{i \in N(G_{kp})} \overline{g}_{ip} \right).}$$

Then $T^*_{ip} = T^*(G_{kp}) = M_{ip} \cdot B$ for $i \in N(G_{kp})$. Assume $M_{ip} = 2^{n_{ip}}, \ n_{ip} \in \{0,1,\ldots\}$. It is easy to show that in the worst case the cost of the powers of two solution cannot exceed the value found from the solution to the REDIP by more than roughly 6%.

Let us now turn our attention to the feasibility of the powers of two solution. It is easy to prove that $\sqrt{2} \cdot T(G_{kp}) \geq T^*(G_{kp}) \geq T(G_{kp})/\sqrt{2}$. A worst case analysis shows that a powers of two solution cannot exceed capacity by more than 41%, that is, the solution could use up to $\sqrt{2}$ times the available capacity. The worst case occurs for the fixed time constraints when all $T^*(G_{kp}) = \sqrt{2} \ T(G_{kp})$ and for the storage area constraints only if each $T^*(G_{kp})$ assumes its lowest possible value, a highly unlikely event. If the total number of component partitions is large, we would expect that the powers of two solution should consume about the same amount of capacity as the solution to the relaxed problem, the REDIP.

Assume $T^*(G_{kp})$ is uniformly distributed over the interval $[T(G_{kp})/\sqrt{2}, T(G_{kp}) \cdot \sqrt{2}]$. Then for the fixed time constraints that were active in the solution to the REDIP,

$$
E\left[\sum_{\substack{p\ni i\in N(G_p)\\ \text{and} \quad (i,j)\in A(G_p)}} \{a_{ip}/T^*_{ip} + b_{ip}/T^*_{jp}\}\right] - \sum_{\substack{p\ni i\in N(G_p)\\ \text{and} \quad (i,j)\in A(G_p)}} \left\{a_{ip}E[1/T^*_{kp}]\right.
$$

$$
\left. + b_{ip}E[1/T^*_{jp}]\right\}
$$

$$
= c_i\sqrt{2}\ \log\ 2.
$$

If the $T^*(G_{kp})$ are independent, then the strong law of large numbers implies that the limit of the left hand side of the active fixed time constraints approaches $.98c_i$ as the number of components and partitions grows large. Hence for a large number of components we would expect the solution to be feasible.

The storage area capacity use that results from the powers of two rounding can be analyzed similarly. Take the expectation of the left hand side capacity use for an active storage area i constraint, $i \notin I_L$.

$$
E\left[\sum_{\substack{p\ni i\in N(G_p)\\ \text{and} \quad (i,j)\in A(G_p)}} f_{ip}(T^*_{ip} - T^*_{jp})\right] - \sum_{\substack{p\ni i\in N(G_p)\\ \text{and} \quad (i,j)\in A(G_p)}} \left\{f_{ip}E[T^*_{ip}] - E[T^*_{jp}]\right\}
$$

$$
= 3/4\cdot\sqrt{2}\cdot s_i \approx 1.06s_i.
$$

Again we can apply the strong law of large numbers. The analysis shows that for a large number of components we would expect to use about 106% of the available capacity and therefore would expect the power of two solution to exceed the storage area constraints. However, by appropriately adjusting the value of s_i, that is, by setting s_i equal to 94% of the actual capacity, a feasible solution would be expected.

In summary we have seen that the power of two solution cannot increase the objective function by more than 6% above the value obtained when solving the REDIP. Furthermore, for a large number of components we expect the power of two solution to yield a feasible solution to the problem assuming the s_i values are properly adjusted.

ACKNOWLEDGEMENTS

I would like to thank Professors Peter Jackson and William Maxwell for their assistance during the development of this paper.

REFERENCES

[1] Dantzig, G.B., _Linear Programming and Extensions_, Princeton University Press, Princeton, NJ, 1963.

[2] Jackson, P.L., W.L. Maxwell and J.A. Muckstadt, "Determining Optimal Reorder Intervals in Capacitated Production-Distribution Systems," Technical Report 624, School of Operations Research and Industrial Engineering, Cornell University, Ithaca, NY, February 1984.

[3] Jackson, P.L. and R.O. Roundy, "Constructive Algorithms for Planning Production in Multi-Stage Systems," Technical Report 632, School of Operations Research and Industrial Engineering, Cornell University, Ithaca, NY, August 1984.

[4] Lasdon, L.S., _Optimization Theory for Large Systems_, MacMillan, New York, NY, 1970.

[5] Love, S.F., "A Facilities in Series Inventory Model with Nested Schedules," _Management Science_, Vol. 18, No. 5, January 1972.

[6] Maxwell, W.L. and J.A. Muckstadt, "Establishing Consistent and Realistic Reorder Intervals in Production-Distribution Systems," Technical Report 561, School of Operations Research and Industrial Engineering, Cornell University, Ithaca, NY, January 1983.

[7] Muckstadt, J.A. and H.M. Singer, "Comments on Single Cycle Continuous Review Policies for Arborescent Production/Inventory Systems," _Management Science_, Vol. 24, No. 16, December 1978.

[8] Peterson, R. and E.A. Silver, _Decision Systems for Inventory Management and Production Planning_, John Wiley & Sons, New York, NY, 1979.

[9] Roundy, R.O., "98%-effective Integer-ratio Lot sizing for One-warehouse Multi-retailer Systems," Technical Report No. 35, Department of Operations Research, Stanford University, Stanford, CA, September 1983.

[10] Schwarz, L.B. and Schrage, L., "Optimal and System Myopic Policies for Multi-Echelon Production/Inventory Assembly Systems," _Management Science_, Vol. 21, No. 11, July 1975.

[11] Williams, J.F., "On the Optimality of Integer Lot Size Ratios in Economic Lot Size Determination in Multi-Stage Assembly Systems," _Management Science_, Vol. 28, No. 11, November 1982.

MULTI-STAGE LOT-SIZING
FOR GENERAL PRODUCTION SYSTEMS

Claus E. Heinrich
and
Christoph Schneeweiss*

University of Mannheim
D-6800 Mannheim, Schloss

Summary

In this paper the multi-stage lot-sizing problem for general production structures is considered. General production structures are characterized by the fact that each stage may have several predecessor or successor stages. The objective is to minimize total costs which consist of a fixed charge per lot at each stage and linear holding costs. Time varying demand for final products is assumed to be known and has to be satisfied. A simple heuristic procedure is presented consisting of two phases. In the first phase a "basic policy" is determined which derives reorder times under the assumption of demand being constant. These reorder intervals are then in a second phase used to solve the time varying problem. In doing so a first possibility is to realize a cyclic policy simply according to the "basic policy". A second possibility of taking into account non-stationarity is to take adjusted cost parameters and apply single-stage inventory models. A simulation study shows that considerable cost improvements can be realized using this heuristic.

1. Introduction

Lot-sizing decisions for final items within material requirements planning (MRP) determine set-up and holding costs and establish the requirements of the needed components. Therefore, a lot-size decision on a certain stage reduces considerably the freedom of possible lot-size decisions of preceding stages; (the terms item and stage will be used synonymously).

In practice, generally this fact is not well understood. Lot-sizing is often done by applying single-stage models (like EOQ-Formula, Part-

---

* The authors gratefully acknowledge very helpful comments by Professor John. A. Muckstadt, Cornell University and Mr. Bob Harris, University College of Swansea on a preliminary draft of this paper.

Period-Balancing etc.). Although a great number of methods have been proposed to solve the multi-stage lot-sizing problem (a detailed survey is given by DeBodt/Gelders/VanWassenhove [10]), the acceptance of these methods is relatively poor. In our opinion this has two major reasons. First, the computional requirements are too demanding for most real world problems especially for methods generating optimal solutions. Second, most models can only be applied for special product structures which limits considerably the number of possible implementations.

In Fig. 1 examples of the most important special structures as well as the corresponding major references (in brackets) are given. Each structure is represented by a graph whose nodes are stages and whose arcs represent material flows.

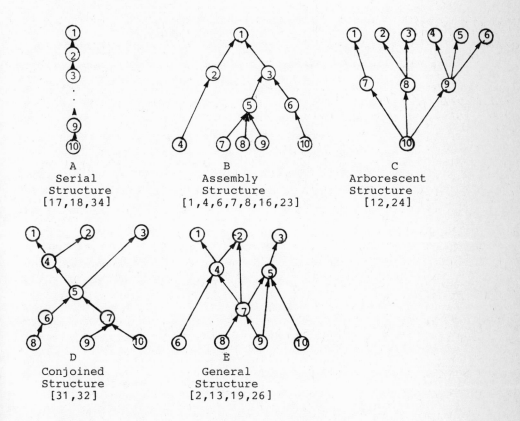

A
Serial
Structure
[17,18,34]

B
Assembly
Structure
[1,4,6,7,8,16,23]

C
Arborescent
Structure
[12,24]

D
Conjoined
Structure
[31,32]

E
General
Structure
[2,13,19,26]

Fig. 1: Examples of special product structures

The main point of this paper is to develop heuristic procedures for general structures and hence for all special structures as well. These procedures should easily fit into the existing software packages (like COPICS (IBM), HMS (Honeywell-Bull) etc.), i.e. the main parts of the existing lot-sizing models should not have to be changed.

The paper is organized as follows. In Sec. 2, the dynamic multi-stage lot-sizing problem (DMSLSP) is formulated and existing solution methods for special product structures are discussed. For general structures a simple heuristic is developed in Sec. 3. To test this heuristic an extensive simulation study was performed. The obtained results are presented and discussed in Sec. 4. Finally, a summary and general conclusions are given in Sec. 5.

2. The Dynamic Multi-Stage Lot-Sizing Problem
2.1 Problem Description

Usually the lot-sizing problem within MRP is characterized as follows. Production quantities (lot-sizes) $x_{i,t}$ are determined over a finite horizon H for each stage i (i=1,2,...,N) and each period t (t=1,2,...,H) in order to minimize total costs denoted by TC, consisting of setup and inventory holding costs for all stages and periods. Each setup at a certain stage i results in fixed setup costs S_i. The holding costs are calculated as a linear function according to the end of period inventory level , where h_i denotes the holdig costs per unit per unit time at stage i. The time varying demand $d_{i,t}$ for final products is known and has to be satisfied. Since lead times within MRP are assumed fixed, the timing of the lot-sizes can be ignored. Thus we assume production is instantaneous. No account is taken of capacity restrictions. The number of units from any stage required in the production of one unit of immediate successor stages is assumed to be one.

The problem for all product structure graphs can be mathematically formulated as follows

Model DMSLSP (Dynamic Multi-Stage Lot-Sizing Problem)

Minimize total costs

$$TC = \sum_{i=1}^{N} \sum_{t=1}^{H} (\delta_{i,t} S_i + h_i I_{i,t})$$

regarding the following restrictions

$$I_{i,t} = I_{i,t-1} + x_{i,t} - d_{i,t} \qquad \forall t; \ \forall i \ \text{with} \ s(i) \neq \emptyset$$

$$I_{i,t} = I_{i,t-1} + x_{i,t} - \sum_{j \in s(i)} x_{j,t} \qquad \forall t; \ \forall i \ \text{with} \ s(i) = \emptyset$$

$$I_{i,t} \geq 0 \qquad \forall i,t$$

$$x_{i,t} \geq 0 \qquad \forall i,t$$

$$\delta_{i,t} = \begin{cases} 1 & \text{if } x_{i,t} > 0 \\ \\ 0 & \text{otherwise} \end{cases}$$

where $I_{i,t}$: inventory level of stage i at the end of period t

$s(i)$: set of immediate successor stages of stage i
(for example in Fig. 1 structure E:
$s(1) = \emptyset$; $s(5) = (3)$))

$p(i)$: set of immediate predecessor stages of stage i
(for example in Fig. 1 structure E:
$p(1) = (4)$; $p(5) = (7 , 9 , 10)$))

2.2. Solution Methods

The formulation derived in the preceding section is a mixed integer programming problem that could be solved using standard mixed integer programming software such as MIPS (IBM). However, the required CPU-time for solving realistic problems is excessive. Therefore, faster procedures have been developed. Unfortunately most of the procedures are restricted to special product structures like the algorithms of Zangwill [34] and Love [18] for serial structures, the algorithms of Crowston/Wagner [8], Schwarz/ Schrage [23], and Afentakis/Gavish/- Karmarkar [1] for assembly structures. General structures can be optimally solved with the approaches of Steinberg/Napier [26] and Afentakis/Gavish [2] where the general structure is converted into simple but expanded assembly structures with additional constraints.

In spite of considerable improvements, however, optimal solution methods are not relevant for practice. Therefore, we concentrate on heuristic procedures. In principle, two main approaches exist in addition to the optimal solution methods where all stages and periods are regarded simultaneously. The first approach is a period-by-period concept in which the lot-sizes are simultaneously determined sequentially for all stages, for each period. Heuristics based on this approach have been suggested by Lambrecht/Vander Eecken/Vanderveken for serial [17] and assembly systems [16]. For general structures, however, no heuristic is known up to now.

The other approach determines the lots for each stage. This is called the level-by-level approach. A trivial level-by-level approach often is used in practice which simply applies single stage models. To take the multi-stage behaviour into account, properly however, additional information is necessary when isolated lot-sizes are calculated. As well as the direct costs of the stage (in question) also the affected costs of predecessor stages should be regarded.

This is done in a multi-pass heuristic which has been developed by Graves [13]. The affected costs of the predecessor stage are considered on a marginal basis as time variable production costs. The variable production cost $\mu_{i,t}$ reflect the holding costs of all predecessor stages which occur by producing one additional unit at stage i in period t. The calculation is based on the actual production schedules of the predecessor stages. Therefore $\mu_{i,t}$ can be interpreted as shadow prices for these schedules. The variable production costs are recalculated passing several times through the product structure. The determination of the lot-sizes for the stages is carried out by a modified Wagner-Whitin algorithm. The production plan is revised in an iterative fashion until no further improvements are possible.

Empirical investigations performed by Graves for assembly structures resulted in average cost deviations of about 0.4% from optimum. The computional effort required for this heuristic is extremely reduced in comparison to the optimal methods. Due to the multi-pass character, however, and the use of the highly sophisticated single-stage lot-size model the effort is still considerable.

Another way to consider the multi-stage behaviour is to adjust the given cost parameters. The advantage of this method is that no additional cost component must be taken into account and that the system may be calculated in one pass. McLaren [20] recommended the modification of the setup cost parameters and Blackburn/Millen [4] extended this approach to the holding cost parameters. The adjustments of the cost parameters are made regarding the cost relations between the stages. Empirical investigations carried out by Blackburn/ Millen [4], Lambrecht/Vander Eecken/Vanderveken [16] as well as Wemmerlöv [30] show considerable improvements using adjusted cost parameters.

3. A Heuristic Procedure
3.1 Principle Idea

The above mentioned approach shows that by considering the cost relations between the stages can result in remarkable cost improvements. Furthermore our experience shows that the variability of the demand does not have the assumed strong effect on the quality of solutions of multi-stage lot-sizing problems. Most approaches require considerable effort to take demand variability into account. Sometimes this is done by using the Wagner-Whitin algorithm disregarding the multi-stage character of lot-sizing. Hence the question arises, whether one should better ignore the demand variability and concentrate more intensely on the multi-stage behaviour. This approach seems to be very promising particularly for general structures as we will show.

These considerations lead us to construct a heuristic consisting of two phases. First, a basic policy is determined as guide to dynamic multi-stage lot-sizing . For this policy reorder intervals T_i of each stage are calculated assuming (external) demand to be constant. Second, these T_i (i=1,...,N) are then used to solve the time variant problem. Two different procedures are proposed for accomlishing this. First, the T_i can be used directly, i.e. the lot-sizes can be determined simply by the demand requirements within T_i. The other possibility would be to take adjusted cost parameters and apply one stage inventory models. By means of the relations of the reorder intervals between the stages the average effect of set-ups at the stage with respect to their predecessor stages is obtained. According to this effect the cost induced in the predecessor stages can be this assumption the Integrality-Theorem is often used in literature. This theorem specifies that the lot-size at each stage must be an integer multiple of the lot-size at its successor stage. The theorem has been established by Crowston and Wagner in [7] for assembly structures. Although in principal not applicable [27,28,33] it is further applied also to other structures by adapting it to time between orders T_i. The Integrality theorem may then be stated as follows:

$$T_j/T_i \geq 1 \quad \text{and integer} \quad ; \; \forall i, \; \forall j \in p(i).$$

By applying this theorem one receives so-called nested schedules. This means that the stages are linked such that a setup on a certain stage induces automatically setups of all successor stages. The nested schedule property is for general structures not necessarily optimal. However, it reduces complexity considerably leading still to comperatively good results.

Maxwell/Muckstadt [19] investigated general structures and found that a further restriction of the T_i can be made without considerable increases of costs. They propose not to consider all possible nested schedules but restricting the T_i to be a power of two times a base planning period B. Maxwell/Muckstadt provide a very efficient algorithm that finds optimal solutions for general structures in time that at worse is proportional to N^4, where N is the number of stages. Furthermore they proof that when restricting the solutions to the mentioned power-of-2-policy the average cost can never be more than 6% higher than can be achieved following any other nested schedules.

Hence for us it appears to be reasonable to restrict the reorder interval in a similiar manner. In contrast to Maxwell/Muckstadt we set our base planning period according to the original problem to be one. Furthermore we restrict the reorder intervals to a more general base M. Hence the reorder intervals are restricted as follows:

$$T_i = M^{k_i} \quad ; \quad M = 2,3,\ldots \quad k_i = 0,1,2,3,\ldots$$

I.e. T_i is a power of M which one has still to determine. Thus k_i will now be used as a decision variable. For M = 2 we have the well known power-of-2-policy. Using the echelon concept with echelon holding cost parameters e_i the problem can now be stated as follows calculated. The adjusted cost parameters are then determined by adding the affected costs of all predecessor stages to the cost parameters of stage i. The determination of the lots is then carried out by single stage lot-sizing models using these adjusted cost parameters. The stages are calculated sequentially (level-by-level approach) starting with the end-item stages.

3.2 Phase I: Determination of a Basic Policy

As a starting point of the first phase of the proposed heuristic constant demand is obtained by simply taking averages, i.e. demand per period D_i at stage i is given by (note that in the following i will always be used as the stage in question whereas j will be used as an index describing preceding or succeeding stages)

$$(1) \qquad D_i = 1/H \sum_{t=1}^{H} d_{i,t} \qquad ; \quad \forall i \text{ with } s(i) = \emptyset$$

$$D_i = \sum_{j \in s(i)} D_j \qquad ; \quad \forall i \text{ with } s(i) \neq \emptyset$$

Alternatively, in practice other averaging procedures could of course be used. The basic policy will have to be adapted only when major changes occur.

Assuming an infinite horizon we can now take as a criterion for the reduced problem (all problem parameters except the demand and the horizon are equal to the problem DMSLSP) the average cost C per period.

However, the assumption of constant demand and an infinite horizon do not reduce the problem significantly. Further restrictive assumptions concerning the time between orders T_i have to be introduced in order to reduce the problem complexity. The difficulty is therefore to restrict the T_i such that the problem is becoming tractable without being unrealistic.

The effort solving a multi-stage lot-sizing problem with constant demand depends heavily on calculating the relevant costs. Allowing time varying (cyclic) T_i this calculation is rather difficult [23]. Therefore we concentrate on constant T_i (single cycle policies). Under

Model NSP (<u>N</u>ested <u>S</u>tationary <u>P</u>roblem)

Minimize the average period costs

$$(2) \qquad C = \sum_{i=1}^{N} (S_i/T_i + (T_i-1)D_ie_i/2)$$

under the restrictions

$$(3) \qquad T_j \geq T_i \quad ; \quad \forall i, \forall j \in p(i)$$

$$(4) \qquad T_i = M^{k_i} \quad ; \quad k_i = 0,1,2,3,......$$

Let us now propose a procedure to determine the basic policy of phase I. This heuristic will consist of two parts. In the first part the time interval T_i is set stage-by-stage ensuring that the new generated solution is nested. If the modification of T_i results in a cost improvement the reorder interval of this stage will be further changed; otherwise the next stage $T_{i'}$ will be investigated. (Note that $T_{i'}$ might already be modified by T_i according to the nested schedule condition, cf. equs. (3), (4)).

Two passes through the product structure will be performed. In the first pass we consider increasing T_i and in the second pass we try decreasing them. A consideration of a possible decrease is reasonable, since by the nested schedule condition the T_i may blow up undesirably. The change of the time between orders is carried out by means of the variable k_i. (A similar procedure is suggested by Crowston/Wagner [6] for assembly systems. They use as decision variables the lot-size ratios between the stages. In contrary to serial and assembly structures these ratios cannot be applied for general structures since they do not insure nested schedules.)

The choice of the sequence in which the stages are regarded in the heuristic is an important fact referring to the computational burden. The stages are regarded according to their disposition level. The disposition level of a certain stage can be defined as maximum number of operations that are still necessary to obtain the end item. All stages with no successors therefore have disposition level 0, whereas the longest chain in the product structure determines the maximum number of disposition levels. (Fig. 2 illustrates this concept for structure E of Fig. 1.)

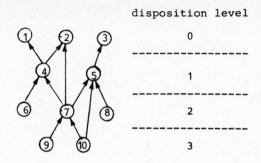

Fig. 2: Disposition levels of structure E

The sequence of the stages is determined by means of these disposition levels, that is first all stages with disposition level 0 are regarded, then all stages with disposition level 1 follow etc. The sequence of stages within the same disposition level is irrelevant. Thus the structure can be worked through in a rather effective way.

After these remarks part I of the procedure leading to the basic policy of phase I may be now stated as follows:

Part I
Step 1: Initial Solution

$$k_i = 0 \Rightarrow T_i = 1 \; ; \quad \forall i$$

$$\text{Costs:} \quad C = \sum_{i=1}^{N} S_i$$

Step 2: Increase of the reorder intervals

Consider sequentially all stages i according to their disposition levels.

a) Increase of T_i i.e. $\Delta k_i = 1$ and $\Delta k_j = 0$, $\forall j \neq i$

b) Ensure nested schedules (cf.eq.(3)). Check for all predecessor stages $j \in p(i)$

If $M^{k_i + \Delta k_{i+}} > M^{k_j}$

then determine Δk_j such that

$k_i + \Delta k_i = k_j + \Delta k_j$

c) Determine costs of the new solution

$$CN = \sum_{i=1}^{N} (S_i / M^{k_i + \Delta k_i} + (M^{k_i + \Delta k_i} - 1) D_i e_i / 2)$$

d) Check advantage

If $CN < C \Rightarrow C = CN$

$k_i \leftarrow k_i + \Delta k_i ; \quad \forall i$

Goto 2a)

Step 3: Decrease of the reorder interval

Consider sequentially all stages i according to their disposition levels.

a) Decrease T_i i.e. $\Delta k_i = -1$ for $k_i < 0$

$\Delta k_j = 0 , \quad \forall j \neq i$

b) Ensure nested schedules. Check for all successor stages $j \in s(i)$

If $M^{k_i + k_i} < M^{k_j}$

then determine Δk_j such that

$k_i + \Delta k_i = k_j + \Delta k_j$

c) Determine costs of the new solution

$$CN = \sum_{i=1}^{N} (S_i / M^{k_i + \Delta k_i} + (M^{k_i + \Delta k_i} - 1) D_i e_i / 2)$$

d) Check advantage

If $CN < C \Rightarrow C = CN$

$k_i \leftarrow k_i + \Delta k_i ; \quad \forall i$

Goto 3a)

(All steps of this algorithm are illustrated by an example given in Sec. 3.4.)

This first part of the procedure (performing only two passes) already yields a considerable cost reduction. Empirical investigations for the product structures of Fig. 1 show a mean cost deviation of only 0.7% from optimum and a maximum deviation of 7% for an ensemble of 30 simulation runs.

Part 2

In the second part of the procedure in obtaining a basic policy it is intended to improve the above solution. We noticed that especially for arborescence but also for general structures with a high degree of commonality (this measure indicates the average number of immediate successor stages in the product structure - for an exact definition see [5]) it is often better to ignore for certain stages the multi-stage character and to treat the stages independently. Especially for stages with relative small demand and a high set-up to holding cost ratio (S_i/h_i), longer reorder intervals than those of the preceding stages are favourable.

These remarks lead us to extend the possible solutions to non-nested schedules. However, the restriction of the reorder intervals (cf. equ.(4)) will still be valid. By allowing for such non-nested schedules we have the problem of determining holding costs. Maxwell/Muckstadt propose to solve this problem with the echelon cost principle by recalculating all echelon-stocks of the stages i and j for which $T_i \geq T_j$ which, however, may be a rather extensive procedure. Because of these difficulties no exact holding costs will be determined. Instead we approximate cost savings which result by changing the time between orders of the stages . As a performance measure for a change of T_i we use the following expression (A detailed explanation is given in Heinrich [15]):

$$C_i(\Delta k_i) = S_i / M^{k_i} - S_i / M^{k_i + \Delta k_i}$$

change of set-up costs

$$+ \sum_{j \in s(i)} \max (M^{k_i} - M^{k_j} ; 0) D_j h_i / 2$$

initial holding costs at stage i

$$- \sum_{j \in s(i)} \max (M^{k_i + \Delta k_i} - M^{k_j} ; 0) D_j h_i / 2$$

new holding costs at stage i

$$+ \sum_{j \in p(i)} \max (M^{k_j} - M^{k_i} ; 0) D_i h_j / 2$$

initial holding costs at the immediate
predecessor stages

$$- \sum_{j \in p(i)} \max (M^{k_j} - M^{k_i + \Delta k_i} ; 0) D_i h_j / 2$$

new holding costs at the immediate
predecessor stages

This value has to be calculated for all stages i for increase ($\Delta k_i = 1$) and decrease ($\Delta k_i = -1; k_i > 0$) of the reorder interval yielding 2N saving values. The maximum value determines stage i^* und the change Δk_i^* which has to be done, provided this maximum value is positive. The procedure continues as long as cost savings are realized. Summarizing we thus may state the following steps comprising the second part of the procedure to obtain the basic policy.

Step 4: Determination of cost savings
        Calculate $C_i(\Delta k_i)$; $\forall i$, $\Delta k_i = 1$, $\Delta k_i = -1$ for $k_i > 0$

Step 5: Check advantage
        If max $C_i(\Delta k_i) < 0$ Stop

Step 6: Revision
        Determine stage i^* und change Δk_i^* with maximal cost savings
        $k_i^* \leftarrow k_i^* + \Delta k_i^*$: Goto 4

(These steps are illustrated in the example given in Sec. 3.4). The improvements which can be realized in this second part of the heuristic heavily depend on the product structure. It is evident that the degree of possible improvements increases with the degree of commonality. No improvements are possible for serial and assembly structures. For conjoined and arborescence structures, however, the solution of part 1 can often be improved. In the average, improvements for our tests were about 3%.

3.3 Phase II. Adaption of the Basic Policy to Time Varying Demand

The reorder intervals T_i calculated under the assumption of constant demand, serve as basic information for the solution of the original dynamic problem DMSLSP. As already mentioned the T_i can either be used directly or they are used to adjust the cost parameters which on their part then determine lot sizes on a stage-by-stage basis.

3.3.1 Direct Use

The determination of lot-sizes will be performed sequentially starting with the stages of the end-items using the T_i values found in the constant demand case. The lot-size $x_{i,t}$ at stage i during T_i is

$$x_{i,t} = \sum_{k=t}^{t+T_i-1} d_{i,t} \qquad ; \forall i, \ t=1, T_i+1, \ldots, (\lceil H/T_i \rceil -1) \cdot T_i+1$$

$$x_{i,k} = 0 \qquad ; \forall i, \ \forall \ k \neq t$$

The demands $d_{j,t}$ of the predecessor stages j are then given by

$$d_{j,t} = \sum_{m \in s(j)} x_{m,t} \qquad ; \forall t$$

In the following the procedure will be referred to as FTBO (Fixed Time Between Orders).

3.3.2 Adjustment of Cost Parameters

The principle of calculating cost parameters has been mentioned in Sec. 2.2. The cost parameters are adjusted according to the multi-stage behaviour, i.e. set-up and holding costs that reflect the consequences of costs for all stages are determined. An adjusted set-up cost parameter $\hat{S}_i$ indicates the set-up cost of the whole system that arise as a consequence of a set-up at stage i. Besides the direct set-up costs of stage i all the affected set-up costs of preceding stages have to be considered. An adjusted holding cost parameter $\hat{h}_i$

gives the holding costs of stage i and reflect the costs of the subsystem consisting of all preceding stages.

To calculate these costs it is necessary to know the set-up costs of these stages. McLaren [20] and Blackburn/Millen [4] estimate lot-size ratios and adjust the parameters based on these ratios. For general structures, however, this adjustment is not possible, because for these structures the proposed estimation of the ratios does not lead to a feasible policy.

The knowledge of the reorder intervals T_i from phase I of our heuristic, however, will now allow us to adjust the cost parameters also for general structures. To adjust for general systems there are two main difficulties. First, the set-up costs of a stage cannot be unambiguously ascribed to a succeeding stage in case of common usage of this item by succeeding stages. Therefore the well known problem arises of allocating set-up costs to several succeeding stages. Second, it seems not always suitable to penalize the stages with the costs of all preceding stages. A ratio of reorder intervals T_j/T_i which is less than one for $j \in p(i)$ can be interpreted such that i is being decoupled from j. Therefore the cost of stage j should not be considered when adjusting the cost parameters of stage i.

Hence for general systems the cost parameters can be adjusted as follows:

$$\hat{h}_i = e_i + \sum_{\substack{j \in p(i) \\ T_i \leq T_j}} T_j/T_i \ \hat{h}_j + \sum_{\substack{j \in p(i) \\ T_i > T_j}} h_j$$

$$\hat{S}_i = S_i + \sum_{\substack{j \in p(i) \\ T_i \leq T_j}} T_i/T_j \ f_{j,i} \ \hat{S}_j$$

where $f_{j,i}$: fraction of set-up costs of stage j which is to allocate to stage i

The determination of $\hat{h}_i$ and $\hat{S}_i$ has to be carried out sequentially beginning with the stages which have no preceding stages. For these stages it is evident that $\hat{h}_i = e_i = h_i$ and $\hat{S}_i = S_i$.

Regarding the partition of set-up costs we propose two alternatives. The simplest way is the stage proportional partition, which assumes that each stage being an immediate successor of stage j is equally responsible for a set-up at stage j. Due to the already mentioned reasons this allocation has of course only to be performed for $T_i \leq T_j$. Hence one obtains

$$
f_{j,i} = \begin{cases} 1/A_j & \text{if} \quad T_i \leq T_j \\ \\ 0 & \text{otherwise} \end{cases}
$$

where A_j is the number of immediate successor stages m of stage j for which $T_m \leq T_j$.

Cost adjustments being based on these fractions will henceforth be denoted by SPCA (Stage Proportional Cost Adjustments).

As a second possibility to divide set-up costs we propose a demand proportionally partition. This proposal is being suggested by the fact that stages with higher demand usually cause more set-ups than stages with lower demand. Therefore the stages with higher demand should be charged with a higher fraction of the set-up costs of the preceding stages, yielding

$$
f_{j,i} = \begin{cases} D_i \Big/ \sum_{\substack{m \in s(j) \\ T_m < T_j}} D_m & \text{if} \quad T_i < T_m \\ \\ 0 & \text{otherwise} \end{cases}
$$

Cost adjustments being based on these fractions will henceforth be denoted by DPCA (Demand Proportional Cost Adjustment).

After the adjustment of the cost parameters the lot-sizes are determined sequentially by means of single stage lot-sizing models. This concludes phase II of the heuristic. Fig. 3 summarizes again the main steps of the complete algorithm.

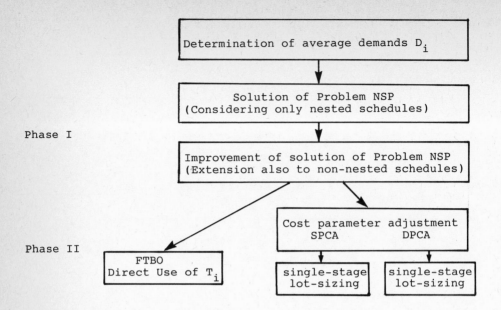

Fig. 3: Global Flow Chart of the Heuristic

Before presenting some simulation tests with the proposed general structure heuristic let us illustrate all steps by a simple example.

3.4 Simple Example

Consider the following dynamic multi-stage lot-sizing problem:

Product structure

Cost set (RC):

i	S_i	h_i	e
1	400	2.0	1.0
2	200	6.0	1.0
3	50	1.0	1.0
4	100	4.0	4.0

Demand rates:

t / i	1	2	3	4	5	6	7	8
1	5	12	8	9	7	19	11	9
2	38	45	34	40	42	48	35	38

Stages 3 and 4 have no independent demand. The initial inventories of all stages equal zero. Lead-times are not considered.

Phase I:

Calculation of the average requirements D_i

$$D_1 = \sum_{t=1}^{8} d_{1,t} = 10$$

$$D_2 = \sum_{t=1}^{8} d_{2,t} = 40$$

$$D_3 = D_1 + D_2 \qquad = 50$$

$$D_4 = D_2 \qquad\qquad = 40$$

Procedure to determine a Basic Policy (Base M = 2)

Part 1:

Steps	Iteration	best current values				changes in k_i				CN	C
		k_1	k_2	k_3	k_4	Δk_1	Δk_2	Δk_3	Δk_4		
1	0	0	0	0	0	0	0	0	0		750
2	1					1*	0	1+	0	555	555
2	2	1	0	1	0	1*	0	1+	0	502	502
2	3	2	0	2	0	1*	0	1+	0	566	502
2	4					0	1*	0	1+	452	452
2	5	2	1	2	1	0	1*	0	1+	577	452
2	6					0	0	1*	0	546	452
2	7					0	0	0	1*	587	452
3	8					-1*	0	0	0	542	452
3	9					0	-1*	0	0	532	452
3	10					-1+	0	-1*	0	505	452
3	11					0	-1+	0	-1*	502	452

* independent change

+ dependent change (caused by restriction to nested schedules)

Part 2:

Step 4:

Determination of the lower bounds for cost savings $C_i(\Delta k_i)$

i	$C_i(1)$	$C_i(-1)$
1	10.00	-90
2	-150.00	-80
3	- 93.75	27.5
4	-135.00	-50

Step 4:

$\max\ C_i(\Delta k_i) = C_3(-1) = 27,5 > 0$

Step 6:

Revision : $k_3 = 1$

Step 4:

Determination of the lower bounds for cost savings $C_i(\Delta k_i)$

i	$C_i(1)$	$C_i(-1)$
1	10	-80
2	-190	-80
3	- 27,5	-25
4	-135	-50

Step 5:

$\max\ C_i(\Delta k_i) = C_1(1) = 10 > 0$

Step 6:

Revision : $k_1 = 3$

Step 4:

Determination of the lower bounds for cost savings $C_i(\Delta k_i)$

i	$C_i(1)$	$C_i(-1)$
1	- 55	-10
2	-190	-80
3	- 27,5	-25
4	-135	-50

Step 5:

$$\max \ C_i(\Delta k_i) \ = \ C_1(1) \ = \ -10 \ < \ 0$$

Hence the basic policy is: $T_1 = 8$, $T_2 = 2$, $T_3 = 2$, $T_4 = 2$

Phase II:

Possibility 1: Direct taking-over (FTBO)

Production plan

t \ i	1	2	3	4	5	6	7	8	Costs
1	80	–	–	–	–	–	–	–	1014
2	83	–	74	–	90	–	73	–	1826
3	163	–	74	–	90	–	73	–	200
4	83	–	74	–	90	–	73	–	400

Total: 3440

Possibility 2: Adjustment of cost parameters

Stage 4:

$$\hat{S}_4 = S_4 = 100 \ : \ \hat{h}_4 = e_4 = h_4 = 4$$

Stage 3:

$$\hat{S}_3 = S_3 = 50 \ : \ \hat{h}_3 = e_3 = h_3 = 1$$

Stage 2:

$$\hat{S}_2 = S_2 + T_2/T_3 \ f_{3,2} \ \hat{S}_3 + T_2/T_4 \ f_{4,2} \ \hat{S}_4$$

The division of the set-up costs from stages 3 and 4 is carried out stage-proportional (SPCA-cost-modification). The fractions $f_{j,i}$ are as follows:

$$f_{3,2} = A_3 = 1$$
$$f_{3,1} = 0$$
$$f_{4,2} = A_4 = 1$$

Therefore $\hat{S}_2 = 200 + 2/2 \cdot 1 \cdot 50 + 2/2 \cdot 1 \cdot 100 = 325$

$$\hat{h}_2 = e_2 + T_3/T_2 \ \hat{h}_3 + T_4/T_2 \ \hat{h}_4$$
$$= 1 + 2/2 \cdot 1 + 2/2 \cdot 4 = 6$$

Stage 1:

$$\hat{s}_1 = s_1 + T_1/T_3 \, f_{3,1} \quad \hat{s}_3 = 400$$
$$\hat{h}_1 = e_1 + \hat{h}_3 = 1 + 1 = 2$$

Single-stage lot-sizing (as an example the Wagner/Whitin Algorithm is taken) with adjusted cost parameters SPCA

Production plan

i \ t	1	2	3	4	5	6	7	8	Costs
1	80	–	–	–	–	–	–	–	1014
2	38	79	–	82	–	83	–	38	1666
3	118	79	–	82	–	83	–	38	250
4	38	79	–	82	–	83	–	38	500

Total: 3430

Note that this schedule is identical to the schedule received by the multi-pass- heuristic MPH.

As a comparison: Wagner/Whitin with real cost parameters RC, i.e. the decoupled stage by stage procedure:

Production plan

i \ t	1	2	3	4	5	6	7	8	Costs
1	80	–	–	–	–	–	–	–	1014
2	38	45	34	40	42	48	35	38	1600
3	118	79	–	82	–	83	–	38	361
4	38	45	34	40	42	48	35	38	800

Total: 3775

4. Simulation Tests

The heuristics FTBO, SPCA and DPCA (s. flow chart Fig. 3) are examined by an extensive study. Since single-stage lot-sizing models with real cost parameters are widely used in practice the simulation study concentrates on this situation as a reference heuristic. I.e. in comparing different heuristics we adopt the point of view of the practitioner who is more interested in an improvement of his status quo than knowing the distance from a theoretical optimum. Along with the direct taking over of the reorder intervals (FTBO) and the two cost parameter adjustments, Graves multi-pass heuristic (MPH) was included because for general structures it is probably the best heuristic in case of time varying demand.

4.1 Experimental Design

For the calculation of the costs which result from the lot-sizing models a simulation program was implemented on a personal computer. The demands for the end-items were generated randomly. The requirements of the lower stages were determined by explosion of the bill of material and netting. For reasons of simplification all initial inventories were set equal to zero.

The experiment was limited to the five structures depicted in Fig. 1. The performance of the lot-sizing models was measured by the sum of the resulting set-up and inventory costs. The set-up costs S_i are assumed to take values (150, 300, 900, 1500, 3000) all having the same probability. The holding costs h_i were generated by the echelon costs which were also randomly generated taking values 0.1, 0.5, 1.0 and 2.0. For each product structure A to E we created in this way 6 cost sets.

External demand $d_{i,t}$ of end-items is limited to be normally distributed. Tests for similar problems show that other distributions including seasonal patterns do not essentially influence the cost performance. The average demands are depicted in the following table:

Structure \ Stage	1	2	3	4	5	6	7	8	9	10
A	150	–	–	–	–	–	–	–	–	–
B	150	–	–	–	–	–	–	–	–	–
C	80	80	100	–	–	–	–	–	–	–
C	50	100	20	20	80	50	30	–	–	–
E	40	30	80	–	–	–	–	–	–	–

Table 1: Average demands

We generated demands with these averages taking coefficients of variation to be 0.0, 0.25, 0.5 and 1. The length of the planning horizon was set to 24 periods being long enough to reduce the "last batch" effect.

The following lot-size methods were investigated:

a) Graves'multi-pass heuristic   (MPH)
b) Reorder model from section 3.1   (FTBO)
c) Single-stage lot-sizing models
   - Economic-Order-Quantity   (EOQ)
   - Period-Order-Quantity   (POQ)
   - Part-Period-Balancing   (PPB)
   - Silver/Meal-Heuristic   (SMH)
   - Groff-Heuristic   (GRO)
   - Axsäter-Heuristic   (AXS)
   - Wagner-Whitin Algorithm   (WW)

EOQ and POQ were adapted to time varying demand as described in Orlicky 21 . Concerning the methods PPB, SMH, GRO, AXS and WW we refer to the literature ([11],[25],[14],[3],[29]).

As cost parameters for the single-stage lot-sizing models we used three different cost sets

   - real cost set   (RC)
   - stage proportional adjusted cost set (SPCA)
   - demand proportional adjusted cost set (DPCA)

Hence it follows that 21 different lot-sizing policies had to be tested. A policy is characterized by the single-stage lot-sizing procedure and the used cost set. A policy GRO/SPCA for example implies that the lot-sizes are determined by means of the Groff heuristic using a stage proportional adjusted cost set. Of course the adjusted cost sets SPCA and DPCA were only used for determining the lot-sizes. The calculation of the costs was always carried out by means of the real cost set RC.

The size of the experiment can be described as follows. With 5 product structures, 6 different cost sets for each structure and 4 coefficients of demand variation there are 120 basic problems. Each basic problem was calculated by 23 different lot-sizing policies (21 single-stage procedures, MPH and FTBO) and for each problem the demands of the end-items (except for variability of zero) were repeatedly generated 10 times. Therefore 21.390 simulations runs were necessary. In each run 10 stages were considered and therefore in total 213.900 single-stage lot-sizing problems with 24 periods had to be solved.

4.2 Numerical Results

In the following the perfomance of the lot-sizing methods will be discussed in relation to the different product structures and demand variations. First we concentrate on the single-stage lot-sizing procedures mentioned in Sec. 4.1 c). For reasons of presentation we compare only the procedures that performed well with the reorder model FTBO and Graves'multi-pass heuristic MPH.

The improvements which can be realized by using the adjusted cost sets SPCA and DPCA in comparison to the use of real costs RC are shown in table 2. The values have to be considered as an average of all single-stage lot-sizing models.

Structure / Adjustment	A	B	C	D	E
SPCA	24.9	8.2	1.2	3.5	5.3
DPCA	24.9	8.2	1.7	4.0	5.8

Table 2: Cost decrease (in percent) associated with using adjusted cost sets SPCA and DPCA in relation to RC

It can be seen that improvements are achieved for each product structure. But the degree of improvements varies considerably. The ranking is as follows: A (serial) - B (assembly) - E (general) - D (conjoined) - C (arborescence). This ranking can be explained by the problem of set-up cost partition. No partition is necessary for serial and assembly structures (this is also the reason why SPCA and DPCA lead to the same results). The higher the degree of commonality the more severe the problem of allocating the set-up costs to the succeeding stages. Therefore the cost savings for structures C, D and E are not as high as for A and B. The improvements for structure A are substantial, this being caused by its considerable production depth. Taking the multi-stage behaviour into account the improvements for such structures are obviously greater than for structures with lower production depth.

The next step was to investigate the effects of choosing single-stage lot-sizing models. We found out, that for all tested cost sets the Wagner-Whitin algorithm was the best. The cost increases (in percent) of the other lot-sizing models are shown for the different cost sets in the following table.

Procedure Cost set	EOQ	POQ	PPB	SMH	GRO	AXS
RC	12.4	12.0	1.7	4.4	2.8	0.9
SPCA	18.3	17.1	2.8	4.5	2.8	0.3
DPCA	18.9	17.1	3.2	4.6	2.8	0.5

Table 3: Cost increases (in percent) in relation to Wagner/Whitin

The savings procedure of Axsäter (AXS) offers a real alternative to the Wagner/Whitin algorithm. It should be pointed out that the cost deviation is reduced by using the adjusted cost sets. Considering the smaller computational effort the procedure seems to be suitable when using adjusted cost parameters. A little bit surprising is the good performance of Part-Period-Balancing, because in some investigations this procedure is either not used [30] or rejected [4]. In our investigation PPB was in nearly all cases better than the Silver-Meal-Heuristic (SMH). Also Lambrecht/Vander Eecken/Vanderveken [16] and Choi/Malstrom/Classen [9] obtained similar results.

For the subsequent analysis only PPB, AXS and WW are considered. These models are compared with the fixed time between order model (FTBO) and the multi-pass heuristic (MPH). First the comparison is performed in relation to the different product structures.

Policy Structure	FTBO	PPB --- RC	PPB --- SPCA	PPB --- DPCA	AXS --- RC	AXS --- SPCA	AXS --- DPCA	WW --- RC	WW --- SPCA	WW --- DPCA
A	5.6	25.4	2.0	2.0	26.5	0.9	0.9	24.8	-0.2	-0.2
B	4.4	10.3	2.4	2.4	10.8	0.7	0.7	8.8	0.1	0.1
C	2.0	7.7	7.0	6.7	4.7	3.2	2.6	3.3	2.7	1.7
D	2.9	12.2	8.8	8.9	11.1	6.3	6.0	11.2	6.7	6.1
E	1.3	12.2	7.8	7.1	9.8	3.5	3.1	8.9	3.7	2.9

<u>Table 4:</u> Cost increases (in percent) in relation to MPH (considering all demand variations)

As expected the multi-pass heuristic turned out to be best in nearly all cases. This being due to the repeated recalculation of lot-sizes. The single-stage Wagner/Whitin algorithm using the adjusted cost sets is, however, very close to MPH. In 2 cases the results are even better than Graves'heuristic. Surprising is the performance of the reorder model FTBO. The results for FTBO are nearly always better than the results achieved by the dynamic single-stage lot-sizing models PPB, AXS and WW when these are used with real cost sets. However, one can suppose that the performance of FTBO heavily depends on the degree of demand variability.

This is shown in table 5 which gives the sensitivity of the different models with respect to the demand variability.

Policy Variation	FTBO	PPB --- RC	PPB --- SPCA	PPB --- DPCA	AXS --- RC	AXS --- SPCA	AXS -- DPCA	WW --- RC	WW --- SPCA	WW --- DPCA
0.0	-0,1	13.1	3.0	2.9	14.5	0.4	0.3	13.2	2.2	1.3
0.25	1.1	14.7	6.8	6.6	13.8	5.0	4.1	12.5	3.5	3.1
0.5	3.4	15.1	6.6	6.4	12.7	4.0	3.8	11.7	2.7	2.6
1.0	9.9	12.9	7.3	7.1	10.4	3.6	3.1	9.8	2.7	2.4

<u>Table 5:</u> Cost increases (in percent) in relation to MPH (considering all product structures)

Whereas in case of constant demand FTBO is even better than MPH the cost deviation increases by the growth of demand variability. Note that FTBO is still better than all dynamic single-stage lot-sizing models used with real cost sets at variation 0.5. Even at a value of 1.0 which can be interpreted as lumpy demand FTBO is better than PPB/RC and AXS/RC.

Considering the single-stage lot-sizing models which are used with adjusted cost sets it can be seen that these procedures are worse than FTBO for low demand variability (0.0 and 0.25). Increasing the coefficient of variability (0.5 and 1.0) this fact changes. In all cases a significant cost decrease compared to the use of real sets can be observed.

5. Concluding Remarks

Summarizing consider Fig. 4 at the next page (for a similar presentation in the pure inventory field s. [22], p. 124). The starting point for a lot-sizing heuristic in production is a situation being characterized by a general multi-stage production structure with capacity constraints and stochastic non-stationary disturbances. (problem (0)). Concentrating on the non-capacitated problem and restricting stochastics to external demand one may reduce problem (0) to a rolling horizon model. This model consists of a sequence of models each describing the decision window for the time being. These models, denoted by (1) in Fig. 4, are the starting point of our heuristic. They consist of a forecasting model F and a multi-stage general structure deterministic dynamic lot-sizing model DM as generally described in Sec. 2.

We may now look in a slightly different way at the above proposed multi-stage heuristic. One of the main premises in constructing the heuristic was its capability of being easily implementable into existing software packages. Hence, except for major adaptations only a one-stage (one pass) type of heuristic would be suitable. Having this in mind we separated the two properties of being time variant and multi-stage into a time constant multi-stage problem and a time variant one-stage problem. These two problems were treated by phases I and II of the described heuristic as depicted by the left and right hand sides of Fig. 4 respectively.

The relaxation of demand variability allowed us in phase I to calculate reorder intervals T_i thus taking into account the structural properties of the production system. In a second phase these T_i were then used to cope also with the more short termed effects of time variability.

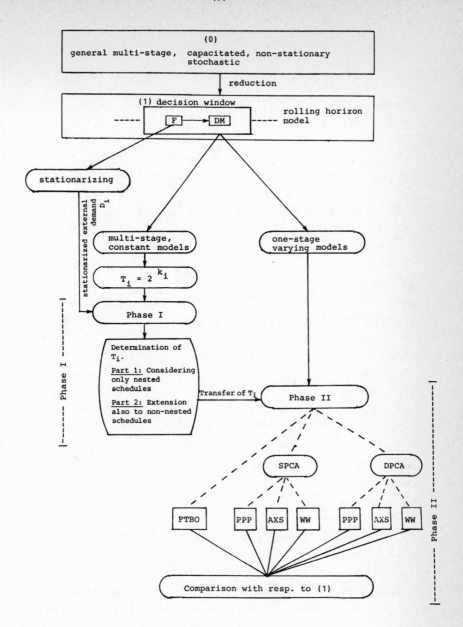

Fig. 4: Modellogram of the heuristic

The calculation of T_i was greatly simplified employing ideas related to the integrality theorem which led to special reorder intervals $T_i = 2^k i$. The k_i were then calculated with respect to the nested schedule restriction. Note, however, that for general structures also non-nested schedules have to be considered.

Phase II then determines the final lot-sizing policy. It turned out that for not too high a time variation of demand the T_i gave already very accceptable results. For higher fluctuations a cost adjustment for non-constant single-stage lot-sizing heuristics has to be performed. Note that for general structures in contrary to serial and assembly systems the problem of allocating set-up costs occurs which led us to propose the two procedures depicted in Fig. 4.

Finally considering special features of the product structure and demand variability the algorithm results in the following advice for its use in practice:

For the solution of smaller problems for general product structures having a high degree of commonality and high demand variability Graves'multi-pass heuristic should be applied. For complex product structures, however, this heuristic is too extensive. Therefore we propose the application of the reorder model FTBO or isolated single-stage lot-sizing using adjusted cost sets. The application of fixed time between orders FTBO has another advantage: Production planning is more stable and MRP system nervousness can be reduced. The practitioner should choose the FTBO for low demand variability whereas for increasing variability he should change to one-stage lot-sizing models with adjusted cost parameters. Summarizing the heuristic has the following appealing aspects:

- It may easily be implemented in existing software packages since only cost-parameters and reorder intervals T_i have to be changed.

- Additional computational effort is only necessary if the mean values of external demand change considerably.

As for all algorithms which only take into account special aspects of the broader production lot-sizing problem summarized in (0) one should of course always be aware that all considerations and comparisions were performed only with respect to model (1) which, however, often only reflects a limited part of the total lot-sizing problem (See also: "Some Modelling Theoretic Remarks on Multi-Stage Production Planning" in this proceedings).

References

[1] Afentakis, P., Gavish, B. and Karmarkar, U.:Computationally Efficient Optimal Solutions to the Lot-Sizing Problem in Multi-Stage Assembly Systems, Management Science, 30(2), 1984, pp 222-239

[2] Afentakis, P .and Gavish, B.: Optimal Lot-Sizing Algorithms for Complex Product Structures, Working Paper Series No. QM 8318, Industrial Engineering and Operations Research Department, Syracuse University, 1983

[3] Axsäter, S.: Economic Lot-Sizes and Vehicle Scheduling, European Journal of Operations Research, (4), 1980, pp 395-398

[4] Blackburn, J.D. and Millen, R.A.: Improved Heuristics for Multi-Echelon Requirements Planning Systems, Mangement Science, 28(1), 1982, pp 44-56

[5] Collier, D.A.: Aggregate Safety Stock Levels and Component Part Commonality, Management Science, 28(11), 1982, pp 1296-1303

[6] Crowston, W.B., Wagner, M.H. and Henshaw, A.: A Comparison of Exact and Heuristic Routines for Lot Size Determination in Multi-Stage Assembly Systems, AIIE Transactions, 4(4), 1970, pp 313-317

[7] Crowston, W.B., Wagner, M. and Williams, J.F.: Economic Lot Size Determination in Multi-Stage Assembly Systems, Management Science, 19(5), 1973, pp 517-527

[8] Crowston, W.B. and Wagner, M.H.: Dynamic Lot Size Models for Multi-Stage Assembly Systems, Management Science, 20(1), 1973, pp 14-21

[9] Choi, H., Malstrom, E. and Classen R.: Computer Simulation of Lot-Sizing Algorithms in Three Stage Multi-Echelon Inventory Systems, Journal of Operations Management, 4(3), 1984, pp 159-277

[10] De Bodt, M., Gelders, L. and Van Wassenhove, L.N.: Lot-Sizing Under Dynamic Demand Conditions: A Review, Engineering and Production Economics, 8, 1984, pp 165-187

[11] De Matteis, J.J. and Mendoza A.G.: An Economic Lot-Sizing Technique, IBM System Journal, 7, 1968, pp 30-46

[12] Graves, S.C. and Schwarz, L.B.: Single Cycle Continous Review Policies for Arborescent Production/Inventory Systems, Mangement Science, 23(5), 1977, pp 529-540

[13] Graves, S.C.: Multi-Stage Lot-Sizing: An Iterative Procedure, in Schwarz, L.B. (Ed), Multi-Level Production/Inventory Control Systems: Theory and Practice, North Holland, 1981, Chapter 4, pp 95-110

[14] Groff, G.K.: A Lot Sizing Rule for Time-Phased Component Demand, Production and Inventory Management, First Quarter 1979, pp 47-53

[15] Heinrich, C.: Mehrstufige Losgrößenplanung für allgemeine Produktionstrukturen, Ph.D. Dissertation,University of Mannheim, to appear

[16] Lambrecht, M., Vander Eecken, J. and Vanderveken, H.: A Comparative Study of Lot-Sizing Procedures for Multi-Stage Assembly Systems, OR-Spektrum, 5(1), 1983, pp 33-43

[17] Lambrecht, M., Vander Eecken, J. and Vanderveken, H.: Review of Optimal and Heuristic Methods for a Class of Facilities in Series Dynamic Lot-Size Problems, in: Schwarz, L.B. (Ed), Multi-Level Production/Inventory Control Systems: Theory and Practice, North Holland 1981

[18] Love, S.F.: A Facilities in Series Inventory Model with Nested Schedules, Mangement Science, 18(5), 1972, pp 327-338

[19] Maxwell, W. and Muckstadt, J.: Establishing Consistent and Realistic Reorder Intervals in Production - Distribution Systems, Technical Report No 561, School of Operations Research and Industrial Engineering, Cornell University, September 1984

[20] McLaren, B.J.: A Study of Multiple-Level Lot-Sizing Procedures for Material Requirements Planning System, Ph.D. Dissertation, Purdue University 1977

[21] Orlicky, J.: Material Requirements Planning, McGraw-Hill, New York 1975

[22] Schneeweiss, Ch.: Modellierung industrieller Lagerhaltungs-systeme, Einführung und Fallstudien, Berlin-Heidelberg 1981

[23] Schwarz, L.B. and Schrage, L.: Optimal and Systems Myopic Policies for Multi-Echelon Production/Inventory Assembly Systems, Management Science, 21(11), 1975, pp 1285-1294

[24] Schwarz, L.B.: A Simple Continous Review Deterministic one Warehouse N Retailer Inventory Problem, Mangement Science, 19(5), 1973, pp 555-566

[25] Silver, E.A. and Meal, H.C.: A Heuristic for Selecting Lot Size Quantities for the Case of a Deterministic Time-Varying Demand Rate and Discrete Opportunities for Replenishment, Production and Inventory Mangement, 2nd Quarter, 1973, pp 64-74

[26] Steinberg, E. and Napier, H.A.: Optimal Multi-Level Lot Sizing for Requirements Planning System, Management Science, 26(12), 1980, pp 1258-1271

[27] Szendrowits, A.Z.: Comments on the Optimalitiy in: Optimal and System Myopic Policies for Multi-Echelon Production/Inventory Assembly Systems, Management Science, 27(9), 1981, pp 1081-1087

[28] Szendrovits, A.Z.: Non Integer Optimal Lot-Size Ratios in two Stage Production Inventory Systems, Int. Journal of Production Research, 21(3), 1983, pp 323-336

[29] Wagner, H.M. and Within, T.: Dynamic version of the Economic Lot Size-Model, Management Science, 5, 1958, pp 89-96

[30] Wemmerlöv, U.: An Experimental Analysis of the Use of Echelon Costs and Single Stage Lot-Sizing Procedures in Multi-Stage Production/Inventory Systems, International Journal of Production Mangement, 2(3), 1982, pp 42-54

[31] Williams, J.F.: A Hybrid Algorithm for Simultaneous Scheduling of Production and Distribution in Multi-Echelon Structures, Management Science, 29(1), 1983, pp 77-92

[32] Williams, J.F.: Heuristic Techniques for Simultaneous Scheduling of Production and Distribution in Multi-Echelon Structures, Management Science, 27(3), 1981, pp 336-352

[33] Williams, J.F.: On the Optimality of Integer Lot Size Ratios in: Economic Lot Size Determination in Multi-Stage Assembly Systems, Management Science, 28(11), 1982, pp 1341-1349

[34] Zangwill, W.I.: A Backlogging Model and a Multi-Eechelon Model of a Dynamic Economic Lot Size Production System - A Network Approach, Management Science, 15(9), 1969, pp 506-527

PRACTICAL APPLICATION OF THE ECHELON
APPROACH IN A SYSTEM WITH DIVERGENT
PRODUCT STRUCTURES

K. van Donselaar

J. Wijngaard

Eindhoven University of Technology

Eindhoven, Netherlands

Abstract

This paper deals with problems met in modelling a particular multi-echelon production and inventory situation in practice. These problems include process uncertainties, the influence of scheduling, a capacity-level decision and divergence in the last part of the product structure. First, echelon stocknorms are computed for the linear part of the product structure. These stocknorms are compared with the currently used stocknorms. To solve the last problem, the divergence, a simple heuristic is proposed.

1. Introduction

At Philips' product division for electronic components and materials (Elcoma) the need arised to check whether it would be possible to lower inventories in production chains by introducing the echelon-concept. For this purpose they created a small working-group, which used the ceramic plate capacitor (CPC) as a test-case. This case is considered in this paper. The first Section is used to describe some general features concerning CPC-production and control.

1.1 The product
The CPC is a small electronic component (5x18 mm), used in various applications, e.g. televisions, video's and electric drills. Total production is about 1.6 billion pieces a year, distributed over some 4000 different designs. Annual sales is about 15 million ECU. The CPC's product structure is depicted in Figure 1.

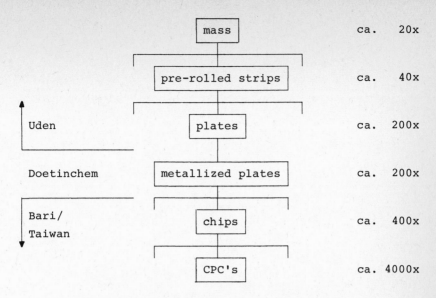

Figure 1. The CPC's product structure

1.2 The production process

Starting from raw materials, mass is being made in Uden (NL). This mass
is kneaded and rolled several times. Then ceramic plates are cut, which
are being stoked in kilns. After inspection these plates go to
Doetinchem (NL), where they are being metallized. In Bari (Italy) or
Taiwan the metallized plates are being cut into pieces (chips) and then
assembled in CPC's. One type of metallized plate goes either to Taiwan
or to Bari. The final products are collected in a central distribution
point in Veldhoven (NL).
This production process can be depicted as in Figure 2.
The scope of this case included the stockpoints in Doetinchem, Bari,
Taiwan and Veldhoven. From Figures 1 and 2 it appears, that the product
structure for this case is linear up to and including the stockpoints
in Bari and Taiwan, while the last part of the product structure is
divergent.

1.3 The planning process

The goodsflow is controlled integrally from the release point for
plates in Uden up to and including the stockpoints in Bari and Taiwan.
At the moment the last part of the goodsflow is controlled separately.
However, it is envisaged to adopt a goodsflow control system, where
both parts are integrated.

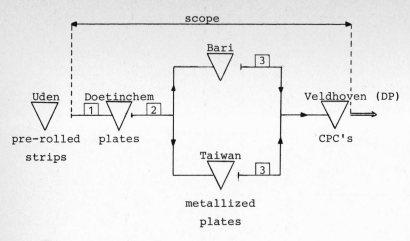

Figure 2. The CPC-production process

For the first part of the system an integral goodsflow control procedure is run every month. By means of the computerprogram SEMT this
procedure yields setupadvises for Uden and Doetinchem, based on
differences between a) the sum of cumulative demand and stocknorms and
b) the content of the "pipeline" (work in progress and actual stock).
Measuring the content of the pipeline is a first step towards an
echelon approach. The stocknorms in this method, however, are still
computed for each stockpoint individually. Based on these SEMT-setup-
advises the integral goodsflow controller makes the final proposals.
Bottlenecks are discussed in a MPS-meeting together with the production
plan for Bari and Taiwan for the next 5 months. This production plan is
specified per product-group and is derived from a production plan per
CPC, which is based on sales-forecasts.

For Bari-sourced products the average total leadtimes are approximately
2 months for Bari-Veldhoven, 4 months for Doetinchem-Bari-Veldhoven and
6 months for Uden-Bari-Veldhoven. The leadtimes for Taiwan-sourced
products are resp. 2.5, 5 and 7 months.
One should bear in mind here, that the leadtime, used for determination
of a stocknorm is equal to the sum of the throughputtime, the information and scheduling delay and the review period.

1.4 The current method to determine stocknorms

At this moment the norms for safety stock are based on classical theory:
One calculates the norms for safety stock for each stockpoint separately
by multiplying 1.) the standard deviation (σ) of the demand (D) during
the leadtime (ℓt) with 2.) a safety factor (k), depending on the
desired service level:

$$\text{safety stock} = k \cdot \sigma\left(\sum_{i=1}^{\ell t} D_i\right).$$

However, because one felt, that this norm was too low, the stocknorm
for the fastmovers in Bari and Taiwan was raised up to 1.5 month
average demand.

1.5 The new method to determine stocknorms

Instead of individual stocknorms, the new method will make use of
echelon stocknorms, whereas the objective to achieve a pre-specified
service level remains the same. Here echelon stock for an item on a
release point at a certain moment is defined as: The total number of
that item, which is in the pipeline from that release point up to and
including the last stockpoint in the system.

1.6 The approach

Since the production process in the first stage (where the product
structure is linear) has some special features, and because that part
of the goodsflow is already controlled integrally, the problem of
determining echelon stocknorms is split up in two: First of all, the
first part of the system is considered. Section 2 describes how stocknorms can be determined for this particular linear subsystem, where-
after Section 3 compares the echelon stocknorms with the currently used
stocknorms for this subsystem. Secondly, in Section 4 a heuristic is
developed to determine stocklevels in systems, which are partly linear,
partly divergent. If Veldhoven will be included in the integrally
controlled system, this heuristic can be applied to control the total
system.

2. Modelling the linear subsystem

The subsystem considered in this Section includes the stockpoints of
Doetinchem, Bari and Taiwan. Since the plates are used exclusively
either in Bari or Taiwan, the subsystem is a linear two-echelon system.
Section 2.1 describes how stocknorms for this kind of system can be

determined. Since in the CPC-case some special features occur, the general method has to be adapted. How this is accomplished, is described in Sections 2.2 - 2.5.

2.1 Determining stocknorms in linear two-echelon systems

For linear two-echelon systems echelon stocknorms can be calculated using the distribution function of demand during the echelon leadtime. To see how this is accomplished, the general linear two-echelon system in Figure 3 is considered. L and ℓ represent the leadtime from the supplier to stockpoint 2, resp. the leadtime from stockpoint 2 to stockpoint 1. The system is reviewed each period and follows a (S,S)-type ordering-policy with respect to both echelons.

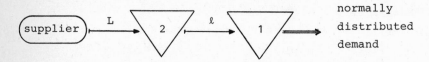

Figure 3. A linear two-echelon system

The first echelon can be seen as a single-level production unit, meeting normal demand. Its stocknorm S_1 is determined by the desired service level α_1: $S_1 = (\ell+1) \cdot \mu + k_1 \sigma \sqrt{(\ell+1)}$, with $\Phi(k_1) = \alpha_1$, where $\Phi(.)$ is the standard normal distribution function and μ is the average demand. That means that S_1 is determined so, that the distribution function of the demand during leadtime and review period equals the value of the service level.

The same reasoning can be applied to determine the stocknorm for the second echelon (S_2): Let S_2 be such, that $\Psi^{L+\ell+1}(S_2) = \Phi(k_2) = \alpha_2$, where $\Psi^{L+\ell+1}(.)$ is the distribution function of demand during the second-echelon leadtime and the review period. It can be shown, that the resulting stock-out probability for the total system is larger than $\max(1-\alpha_1, 1-\alpha_2)$, but smaller than $1-\alpha_1\alpha_2$.

The exact stock-out probability is given by (see Appendix) β, where:

$$\beta = 1 - \int_{-\infty}^{S_1} \Psi^L(S_2-y) \cdot \psi^{\ell+1}(y) \, dy$$

$$= 1 - \int_{-\infty}^{k_1} \Phi\left(\frac{k_2 \cdot \sqrt{(L+\ell+1)} - v \cdot \sqrt{(\ell+1)}}{\sqrt{L}}\right) \cdot \phi(v) \, dv \qquad (1)$$

In case of normal demand and S_1 and S_2 having the same safety factor k, with $\Phi(k)=\alpha$, this probability can well be approximated by:

$$\hat{\beta} = (1 + \alpha \cdot \sqrt{\{L/(L+\ell+1)\}}) \cdot (1-\alpha) \tag{2}$$

Empirical tests show, that the relative error of $\hat{\beta}$ is less than min.$[10\%,(1-\alpha)\cdot100\%]$.

The above has been derived for the case of fixed leadtimes, stationary demand and an infinite capacity. These conditions are not satisfied in the CPC-situation. In Sections 2.2 - 2.5 this is discussed and it is shown how the approach can be adapted.

2.2 Process uncertainties

In the first stage production is in batches. Due to several causes, this production process may fail, which may lead to failure of the entire batch. Because this causes a delay in leadtime, the natural solution is to include this failure-probability in the leadtime. The probability, that the process goes well is denoted by p. The extra leadtime caused by one process-failure is 1 month. Then, if the process fails i times before it performs well, the leadtime will be the original leadtime (when there are no process-failures) + i·1. This happens with probability $(1-p)^i \cdot p$.

So if for example the original leadtime equals 4 months and if the probability, that the process goes well equals 80%, the probability density function (p.d.f.) of the leadtime can be depicted as in Figure 4.

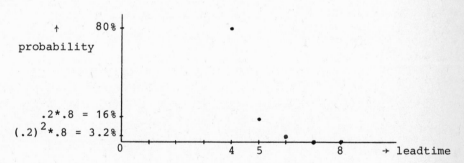

Figure 4. The impact of process-uncertainties on leadtime

2.3 Scheduling

With respect to the first stage (a stoke-process) scheduling is necessary to reduce capacity- and energy-losses. This scheduling, however, makes the leadtimes vary. The only information available beforehand is, that every product can be scheduled once every month.

Therefore it seems a reasonable solution to consider the leadtime as a
stochastic variable, which is uniformly distributed on the interval
[a-.5,a+.5) with a the average leadtime when there are no process-
failures.
This, combined with the influence of process-failures, leads to the
following p.d.f. for the leadtime:

$$h_a(x) = \begin{cases} p \cdot (1-p)^i & \text{if} \quad a-.5+i \le x < a+.5+i, \quad i=0,1,2,\ldots \\ \\ 0 & \text{if} \quad x < a-.5 \end{cases}$$

This p.d.f. of the leadtime is shown in Figure 5 for the case where the
probability that the process goes well equals 80% and where a equals 4
months.

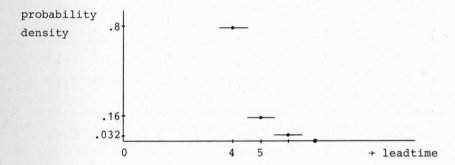

Figure 5. The combined impact of process-uncertainties
and scheduling on leadtime

With this p.d.f. and the normal p.d.f. of demand it is possible to
construct the distribution function ($F_a(.)$) of the demand during the
leadtime. It is assumed, that the demand during any fixed leadtime x is
normally distributed with mean $x \cdot \mu$ and standard deviation $\sigma \cdot \sqrt{x}$. Then:

$$F_a(z) = \int_0^\infty \Phi((z-x \cdot \mu)/\sigma\sqrt{x}) \cdot h_a(x) \, dx.$$

By using $F_a(.)$ instead of convolutions of $\Psi(.)$, it is possible to apply
the method of Section 2.1 in the CPC-situation, whereas (2) is a good
approximation of the system stock-out probability for p close to 1.

2.4 Non-stationary demand
As usual in practice, demand isn't stationary. In every period
forecasts are available. These should be used instead of the average

historical demand in the formulae for the stocknorms. The safety stock for echelon 1 and 2 should be chosen to be equal to $k \cdot \sigma 1$ and $k \cdot \sigma 2$, where $\sigma 1$ and $\sigma 2$ are the standard deviation of the forecast error of the total demand during the leadtime of echelon 1 resp. echelon 2.

A more severe cause of non-stationarity in the CPC-case is that the CPC is going to phase out within the next years. It is not known, however, when this will happen exactly. The influence of this on the capacity-level decision is discussed at the end of Section 2.5.

2.5 Infinite capacity

With three kilns operating, there is many capacity unoccupied. Since the demand is about enough to fully occupy 2.2 kilns, it is very expensive to have the third kiln on. Fortunately the condition to have infinite capacity available can be solved in another (cheaper) way also: by storing capacity in inventory and putting the third kiln off as long as there is sufficient stored capacity available. Here a separation is made between fastmovers and slowmovers. Only fastmovers are used for storage of capacity, since they are the most suitable products for that purpose. So, while the stocknorms for the slowmovers, determined by the method of Sections 2.1 to 2.4, are used in the normal way, the norms for the fastmovers will only be used to determine the moment, when the third kiln is put on. In fact, the following strategy with respect to the third kiln is followed: When stored capacity reaches a critical level m, which equals the sum of the fastmovers' stocknorms, the third kiln is put on to produce up to a quantity M. These kind of models are studied by De Kok [6], who uses the following approximation for M-m (analogous to Camp's formula):

$$
M - m = \left[\frac{2K(\pi_2 - \mu)(\mu - \pi_1)}{h(\pi_2 - \pi_1)} \right]^{1/2}
$$

where μ : average demand

π_1 : low production rate (2 kilns operating)

π_2 : high production rate (3 kilns operating)

K   : switch-over cost for a switch from π_1 to π_2

h   : holding cost of one unit

For the CPC-case, M-m appears to be sufficient to meet the shortage of production capacity for about 16 months, while producing with only two kilns.

As mentioned earlier, the demand for CPC's is not stationary: It is

decreasing at a 10%-rate a year. From the moment on where demand equals
the production capacity of two kilns, no extra capacity is required
anymore and any stored capacity still left then is useless. So the
approach may result in too much stored capacity. Therefore in this case
a rule of thumb is taken at hand. Let CUM be the excess demand, cumulated over the period where demand is larger than the production capacity of two kilns (see Figure 6). Now the production strategy with
respect to the third kiln will be to produce up to the minimum of CUM+m
and M.

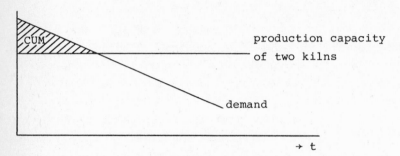

Figure 6. Demand versus production capacity of two kilns
as a function of time

3. Results

After thus modelling the CPC-situation, a comparison is made between
the current and the echelon safety stocknorms, using recent data.
In fact, two comparisons are made; the first one excludes the Uden
process-disturbances, whereas the second one includes them. In all
calculations the required service level of the system is fixed at 99%.

3.1 Comparison of safety stocks, excluding process-disturbances
In the first comparison process-disturbances are excluded. For the
current method the extra stock of 1.5 month average demand for the
fastmovers is neglected, whereas for the new approach p (= probability
of no process-failures) is chosen to be one.
The results for the current method (first column in Figure 7) are
derived from SEMT. The figures for the new approach (second column) are
approximations (based on the average coefficient of variation), because
the method is not yet incorporated in SEMT.

	Current Method	Echelon stocks	
Bari	172	202	
Taiwan	114	116	
Doetinchem	376	78	(= 396 - (202+116))
Whole system	<u>662</u>	<u>396</u>	(= 60%)

Figure 7. Safety stocknorms in thousands of plates,
excluding Uden process-disturbances

3.2 Comparison of safety stocks, including process-disturbances

The second comparison includes the process uncertainties in Uden. The
first column of Figure 8 represents the actual figures from the SEMT-
run in March '85 (including the rule of an extra safety stock of 1.5
month for the fastmovers). The second and third columns give the
results of the echelon approach with a probability of 97% resp. 90%,
that the process in Uden does not fail.

	Current Method	Echelon stocks p = 97%	Echelon stocks p = 90%
Bari	334	202	202
Taiwan	193	116	116
Doetinchem	376	189	381
Whole system	<u>903</u>	<u>507</u>	<u>699</u>

Figure 8. Safety stocknorms in thousands of plates,
including Uden process-disturbances

Figures 7 and 8 both indicate, that introduction of the echelon-
concept can be worthwile.

4. Divergent systems

As mentioned in Section 1, it is envisaged to extend the integral
goodsflow control procedure to include Veldhoven as well. To do so, a
heuristic is needed to determine the stocklevels in divergent systems.
After an evaluation of some of these heuristics in Section 4.1, a
simple heuristic is developed in Section 4.2. Section 4.3 describes how
this heuristic can be applied to the CPC-situation.

4.1 Evaluation of heuristics

The heuristics in [1], [3], [4] and [5] determine stocklevels, which are optimal up to the approximation of no imbalance between inventories of different final products. Two heuristics, which keep account of imbalance, are those of Zipkin [13] and Wijngaard [12].

Whereas the former heuristics all minimize expected costs, there is also some literature, concerning the influence of stocklevels on service level for multi-echelon systems: Simon [11] and Deuermeyer and Schwarz [2] and Rosenbaum [8] all consider a system, which is (partly) reviewed continuously. They derive approximations by means of which the system service level can be determined. The relation between stock-levels and service level is treated from a more practical point of view by Lawrence [7]. The formulae used for approximating the relation between stocklevels and service level, however, are not stated.

Since the CPC-case is dealing with a periodic review system, none of the available results is directly applicable. Eppen and Schrage [3] minimize expected costs for a system, which does not carry inventory at the central stockpoint. The idea of their heuristic can be used also in the service level case with a central stockpoint, which does carry inventory. This is worked out in the next Section.

4.2 A simple heuristic for divergent systems

Consider a two-echelon divergent system (see Figure 9).

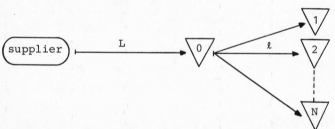

Figure 9. A divergent two-echelon system

The leadtimes are identical for all lower level products. Demand is stationary. The system is assumed to be controlled by an (S,S)-type ordering policy. The stocknorms for echelon 1 and 2 are chosen analogously to the stocknorms derived by Eppen and Schrage [3, page 61]. If S_{1j} is the stocknorm of the j-th lower level product, then

$$S_{1j} = (\ell+1)\mu_j + k_1\sigma_j\sqrt{(\ell+1)} \quad , \quad j=1,\ldots,N.$$

If σ_1 and σ_2 are defined as $\sigma_1^2 := (\ell+1)\cdot(\Sigma\ \sigma_j)^2$ and $\sigma_2^2 := L\cdot\Sigma\ \sigma_j^2 + (\ell+1)\cdot(\Sigma\ \sigma_j)^2$, then S_1 and S_2 can be written as:

$$S_1 = \sum_{j=1}^{N} S_{1j} = (\ell+1)\Sigma\mu_j + k_1\sigma_1 \quad \text{and} \quad S_2 = (L+\ell+1)\Sigma\mu_j + k_2\sigma_2.$$

Imbalance is assumed not to take place. That is, the echelon inventories of the lower level products all have the same stock-out probability at the start of any period. The service level of all lower level products is kept equal to each other. That implicates that this service level is equal to $P(x_{t+1} \geq z)$, where x_{t+1} is the content of the first echelon and z is normally distributed with mean $(\ell+1)\cdot\Sigma\mu_j$ and variance $(\ell+1)\cdot(\Sigma\sigma_j)^2$. The following formula for system stock-out probability β can be derived analogous to (1), where $\psi_b^a(.)$ is the normal distribution function with mean $a\cdot\Sigma\mu_j$ and variance $a\cdot b$.

$$\beta = 1 - \int_{-\infty}^{S_1} \psi_{\Sigma\sigma_j^2}^{L}(S_2-y)\cdot\psi_{(\Sigma\sigma_j)^2}^{\ell+1}(y)\,dy$$

$$= 1 - \int_{-\infty}^{k_1} \Phi\left(\frac{k_2\sigma_2-v\sigma_1}{\sqrt{(\sigma_2^2-\sigma_1^2)}}\right)\cdot\phi(v)\,dv. \tag{3}$$

Comparing formula (3) with (1) it appears, that (3) is identical to (1) if L and $\ell+1$ are chosen to be $\sigma_2^2-\sigma_1^2$ resp. σ_1^2. So, if the safety factor for both echelons is equal ($k_1 = k_2 = k$, with $\Phi(k)=\alpha$), the stock-out probability for the divergent system can be approximated by $\hat{\beta}$:

$$\hat{\beta} = (1+\alpha\cdot\sqrt{(1-\sigma_1^2/\sigma_2^2)})\cdot(1-\alpha)$$

$$= (1+\alpha\cdot\frac{\sqrt{L\cdot\Sigma\sigma_j^2}}{\sqrt{(L\cdot\Sigma\sigma_j^2 + (\ell+1)(\Sigma\sigma_j)^2)}})\cdot(1-\alpha) \tag{4}$$

Since (3) is identical to (1), the relative error of $\hat{\beta}$ is the same as in Section 2.1, that is: less than min.$[10\%,(1-\alpha)\cdot100\%]$.

The quality of (3) as an estimate of the service level depends on the probability, that the system is in balance. The probability, that the system will be in balance in the next period, given the fact, that it is in balance now, is indicated by Eppen and Schrage [3, table 1] for systems without a central stock-keeping unit at the second echelon. Their results show, that this probability is high for systems consisting of few lower level products with small coefficients of variation. The system studied here does have a central stock-keeping unit. This only improves the probability of being able to keep the stocks in balance. So this approximation of the service level will be a good one in case of a situation with few medium and high-volume items. In cases of many items at the lower echelon and/or large coefficients of variation the possibility of imbalance may be too large to neglect. On the other hand, if imbalance becomes sufficiently large, it can be eliminated as discussed in the next Section.

4.3 Application of the heuristic

In a stationary situation with batchsizes equal to one all products will order some stock (equal to the demand from the previous period) from the central stockpoint. Imbalance arises if the central stockpoint is unable to raise all lower level inventories up to an equal stock-out probability.

In a non-stationary situation with batchsizes larger than one, however, it can happen that some products do not need any extra stock. Due to the batchsize or a change in forecasts, the inventory position of a product may be so large in a certain period, that it needs no extra stock to meet demand for the next $\ell+1$ periods. All products with such excess stock should be excluded from the system when an order is placed at the central stockpoint. In that way it is avoided, that in comparing the actual content of echelon 1 with its stocknorm, the excess stock is treated as if it were redistributable over the N lower level products, which would cause the order to the central stockpoint to be less than the actual need of the system to achieve its service level.

The same reasoning can be applied if the inventory position of a lower level product is so large, that it contains the demand for $L+\ell+1$ periods as well as sufficient safety stock. Because it will have no influence on the orders, which are placed at the central stockpoint and at the supplier, this product could be totally left out of consideration for that period. Likewise all products with sufficiently large excess stock could be left out of the system.

Slowmovers typically have non-stationary demand (a little change in demand has relatively large impact) and relatively large batchsizes, so they are likely to have inventory large enough to leave them out of the divergent system. Since usually there is quite a percentage of the products slowmover, the reduction can be substantial. In this way a reduction of the number of items at the lower echelon is achieved, as well as a reduction of items with large coefficients of variation.

For this reduced system the heuristic of Section 4.2 can be applied together with the results of Section 2 as follows: In the CPC-situation L varies because of process-uncertainties and scheduling. To determine the variance of the total lower level products' demand during L periods (say var_L), $F_a(.)$ from Section 2.3 is used. $F_a(.)$ is approximately normally distributed, when p is close to 1. So, formula (4) with var_L

instaed of $L \cdot \Sigma \sigma_j^2$ can be used as an approximation of the system stock-out probability. For any desired stock-out probability β, α can be solved easily from (4). This α determines the echelon stocknorms.

Acknowledgements

We would like to thank Dr.Ir. F.J. Stommels and W.J.M. van der Linden of Philips Industries for their support.

Appendix

Theorem: The service level of a linear two-echelon inventory system as described in Section 2.1 is given by $\displaystyle\int_{-\infty}^{S_1} \psi^L(S_2-y) \cdot \psi^{\ell+1}(y)\,dy$.

Proof: Let x_t : the content of the first echelon at the beginning of period t

y_t : the order from the system to its supplier in period t

ξ_t : the demand in period t

C_{1t} : the content of the first echelon and stockpoint 2, just after demand occurred at the first echelon and an order has been placed at the supplier, whereas the order y_{t-L} has just arrived at stockpoint 2

C_{2t} : the content of the remaining system at the same time

Because of the "order every period up to"-policy, it is known, that y_t equals the demand of the last period. So $C_{2t} = \sum\limits_{i=0}^{L-1} y_{t-i} = \sum\limits_{i=0}^{L-1} \xi_{t-i}$.

Then $P(C_{2t} \leq c) = \psi^L(c)$, whereas $C_{1t} = S_2 - C_{2t}$.

Now, if $C_{1t} \geq S_1$, then x_{t+1} will be S_1, otherwise x_{t+1} will be C_{1t}.

Thus: $P(x_{t+1} = S_1) = P(C_{1t} \geq S_1) = P(S_2 - C_{2t} \geq S_1) = P(C_{2t} \leq S_2 - S_1) = \psi^L(S_2 - S_1)$

and $P(x_{t+1} \leq x) = P(C_{1t} \leq x) = P(S_2 - C_{2t} \leq x) = P(C_{2t} \geq S_2 - x) =$

$= 1 - \psi^L(S_2 - x)$ for $x < S_1$.

So $P(x_{t+1} \geq x) = \psi^L(S_2 - x)$ for $x \leq S_1$

$= 0$ for $x > S_1$

Service level $= 1 - \beta = P(x_{t+1} \geq \sum\limits_{i=1}^{\ell+1} \xi_{t+i}) = \displaystyle\int_{-\infty}^{S_1} P(x_{t+1} \geq y) \cdot \psi^{\ell+1}(y)\,dy$

$= \displaystyle\int_{-\infty}^{S_1} \psi^L(S_2 - y) \cdot \psi^{\ell+1}(y)\,dy$ 　　　　q.e.d.

References

[1]   Clark, A. and Scarf, H. (1960). Optimal Policies for a Multi-
      Echelon Inventory Problem. Management Science, Vol. 6, No. 4,
      pp. 475-490.

[2]   Deuermeyer, B.L. and Schwarz, L.B. (appeared in [10]). A Model
      for the Analysis of System Service Level in Warehouse-Retailer
      Distribution Systems: The Identical Retailer Case. pp. 163-194.

[3]   Eppen, G. and Schrage, L. (appeared in [10]). Centralized
      Ordering Policies in a Multi- Warehouse System with Lead Times
      and Random Demand. pp. 51-68.

[4]   Federgruen, A. and Zipkin, P. (1984). Approximations of Dynamic,
      Multilocation Production and Inventory Problems. Management
      Science, Vol. 30, No. 1, pp. 69-84.

[5]   Federgruen, A. and Zipkin, P. (1984). Computational Issues in an
      Infinite-Horizon, Multi-Echelon Inventory Model. Operations
      Research, Vol. 32, No. 4, pp. 818-836.

[6]   De Kok, A.G. (1985). Approximations for a Lost-Sales Production/
      Inventory Control Model with Service Level Constraints.
      Management Science, Vol. 31, No. 6, pp. 729-737.

[7]   Lawrence, M.J. (1977). An Integrated Inventory Control System.
      Interfaces, Vol. 7, No. 2, pp. 55-62.

[8]   Rosenbaum, B.A. (1981). Service-Level Relationships in a Multi-
      Echelon Inventory System. Management Science, Vol. 27, No. 8,
      pp. 926-945.

[9]   Rosenbaum, B.A. (appeared in [10]). Inventory Placement in a
      Two-Echelon Inventory System: An Application.
      pp. 195-208.

[10] Schwarz, L.B. (ed.) (1981). Multi-Level Production/Inventory
      Control Systems: Theory and Practice. North-Holland, Amsterdam.

[11] Simon, R.M. (1971). Stationary Properties of a Two Echelon
      Inventory Control Model for Low Demand Items. Operations
      Research, Vol. 19, No. 3, pp. 761-777.

[12] Wijngaard, J. (1982). On Aggregation in Production Planning.
      Engineering Costs and Production Economics, Vol. 6, pp. 259-
      265.

[13] Zipkin, P. (1984). On the Imbalance of Inventories in Multi-
      Echelon Systems. Mathematics of Operations Research, Vol. 9,
      No. 3, pp. 402-423.

HIERARCHICAL PRODUCTION PLANNING:

TUNING AGGREGATE PLANNING WITH
SEQUENCING AND SCHEDULING

Hartmut Stadtler
Universität Hamburg
Fachbereich Wirtschaftswissenschaften
Institut für Unternehmensforschung
Von-Melle-Park 5
D - 2000 Hamburg 13

Abstract

The first part of the paper describes the production planning problem
of a major German food manufacturer and the hierarchical production
planning system designed for solving it.

In the second part a major deficiency of Linear Programming models for
aggregate planning of batch production is worked out. To remedy the
defect the inclusion of 'effective lot size demand' within the Linear
Programming model is proposed. Numerical results conclude the paper.

1. Introduction

The aim of this paper is twofold. Firstly, it reports about an ongoing
project to devise a hierarchical production planning system (HPP-system)
for a major German food manufacturer. Secondly, it shows that aggregate
LP-models based on 'effective demand' data for product aggregates may
not allow adequate lot sizing and sequencing decisions. Instead the
calculation of 'effective lot size demand' is introduced. It will allow
a better fit between the decisions of the aggregate and the sequencing
and scheduling planning level.

We begin by describing the underlying production planning problem
(chapter 2) followed by a brief outline of the current status of the
two-level HPP-system (chapter 3).

The interface between the two planning levels in a rolling horizon environment is explained in chapter 4.

One of our research findings, the calculation of effective lot size demand for aggregate LP-models - is discussed in chapter 5 and supplemented by first numerical results comparing this new approach with a HPP-system based on effective demand (chapter 6).

The paper will end with some evaluations and an outline of future research.

2. Outline of the Production Planning Problem

A computerized production planning system had to be devised for a plant of a major Germand food manufacturer. The plant consists of seven departments, each producing a specific product line on its own manufacturing facilities. Interdependencies exist between departments due to exchange of personnel and to a minor extent to further processing of products in other departments.

Sales plans exist on a monthly basis for each "article" with a time horizon of five months. More accurate sales data are available for the next two months. Demand is seasonal with different patterns for different articles. The product lines consist of some hundred individual articles. As each department has its own specific production requirements, we will discuss the production process of the biggest department in greater detail.

Under normal conditions production operates on a two shift basis. Setup times are sequence dependent; if possible, larger setups are done before the beginning of the first shift of the day.

As products are perishable, lot size decisions have to take into account dates of expiration, while on the other hand production should not fall short of given minimum lot sizes.

Minimum lot sizes have to be taken into account in order to prevent too frequent setups of low demand products and not to lose production capacity due to extensive setup times.

There are five processing lines and nine packaging lines. For some products there is a choice of the processing line. The packaging line is always definite. Some products require an intermediate stage for cooling the processed material.

The flow of production of one lot between the two stages cannot be interrupted, because it is impossible to stock processed material without packaging. To run the production a product dependent number of workers is necessary.

3. Hierarchical production planning system

In compliance with current manual methods production planning is separated into two levels. The medium term aggregate plan covers a time span of five months and a short term production plan (sequencing and scheduling) covering five to nine weeks (see [14]). As a detailed production plan showing the sequence of lots on each line is required, none of the standard approaches to HPP [e.g. 2,3,4,8,10] is directly applicable.

Details of the submodels together with its objectives and methods of solution are now discussed.

Aggregate Production Planning (APP)

Given the sales plan for five months ahead, the aggregate plan should result in monthly production amounts for each article considering availble capacities and interdependencies between the departments of the plant.

The objective is to minimize inventory holding costs. Information about production amounts for each article are necessary for the purchase of raw material. Hiring and firing should not be part of the model.

The main measure to smooth production in case of capacity limitations should be to build up inventories. For some articles there maybe a choice of the machines involved. Extra capacity (like overtime) could only be made available in order to safeguard against an infeasible plan.

It was decided that a Linear Programming model is most suited for the aggregate planning level. The model has so far been constructed for the two biggest departments. By aggregating articles having the same production requirements (production rate, manpower, lines and share a common setup) into one article group, the number of different products within the model could be reduced from 146 to 100 for the biggest department. A further aggregation of variables did not seem appropriate due to the loss of accuracy.

The major portion of variables consists of the variable type
x_{ft} indicating the amount of production of article group f
produced in subperiod (month) t.

Constraints can roughly be grouped into

. inventory balance constraints for article groups
(simultaneously taking into account dates of expiration
and safety stock levels)

and constraints for

. production capacities and

. personnel availabilities and exchange between departments.

The size of the resulting LP-model for the two biggest departments comprises 1110 variables and 830 constraints.[1]

---

1) The issue of minimum lot sizes is tackled by iteratively altering
the LP-solution. This approach is not discussed in this paper. For
a similar application of the concept of 'repeated rounding' see
[12, p. 12].

Sequencing and Scheduling

The Sequencing and Scheduling planning will be performed separately
for each department. In order to study the effects of different designs
of the planning levels and its co-operation a slightly simplified
sequencing and scheduling model - compared to the real world system -
was created. Lot sizes are considered for article groups, which in
compliance with the well-known product aggregation scheme of Hax and
Meal and others [2,3,4,8,10] will further on be termed families, while
we will adopt the notion of items for articles. The assumptions
of the simplified model are as follows:

. Production takes place in continuous time
   (with no interruption by night shifts and weekends).

. Setup times last one hour (not sequence dependent)
   and reduce available production time.

. Manufacturing is of the open shop type.

. Backordering is a last resort in case other measures
   for timely production (e.g. production on stock) are
   unavailable.

. Minimum lot sizes are not considered.

. The only limiting production stage consists of the five
   parallel processing lines.

. Lot sizes of families will be disaggregated into items
   according to the objective of equal run out times
   [see 2, p. 36], explicitly considering the initial
   inventories of each item.

For the model a simple heuristic called 'progressive forward / back-
ward scheduling' has been devised. Its basic idea is the following:

. Find the processing line $\hat{m}$ which is the next to
  become idle.

. Determine that family $\hat{f}$ which could be produced on
  processing line $\hat{m}$ and is the next to fall below safety
  stock level.

. Try to load a lot of family $\hat{f}$, just before safety stock
  level is reached.

  - In case the lot cannot be loaded in time (backordering
    case) preceding lots on processing line $\hat{m}$ are shifted
    back as much as necessary or possible.

  - If backordering cannot be eliminated by shifting
    lots backwards, introduce an additional shift if
    still available (see: interface to the aggregate
    model, chapter 4).

  - Backordering will be allowed if all above mentioned
    measures are exhausted.

Further refinements of the heuristic are implemented but will not be
elaborated here.

As a lot sizing procedure well known heuristics - such as the
Silver / Meal heuristic [13] - could be applied, but in the absence
of accurate setup costs we derived lot sizes on the basis of the
practiced and aspired production 'cycle times', such that lot sizes
cover the demand within the next cycle. A heuristic to derive such
'cycle times' is known in the literature as 'Economic time supply'
[see 5, p. 1124].

The aim of the above heuristic is the generation of an acceptable
production plan with low stock holding costs and backordering
situations avoided. For different approaches to solve the scheduling
and sequencing problem see the excellent review of Graves [7]. To
illustrate the underlying idea of the heuristic an example schedule
covering one month (i.e. 4 weeks or 40 shifts) pertaining one machine
will be elaborated. Two families AB and C are considered, where family
AB consists of items A and B. For simplicity we assume no coupling

to the aggregate plan and no setup time. Table 1 depicts the required data:

Table 1: Data for families AB and C for scheduling and sequencing

family	item	initial inventory [t]	demand per month [t] 1	2	Production coefficient [$\frac{shifts}{t}$]	cycle time [shifts]
AB					.09	30
	A	40	100	120		
	B	9	60	80		
C					.09	20
	C	40	200	200		

Assuming a continuous demand rate, a lot of a family has to be started at the latest once the available stock of one of its items has expired. For family AB this first instance occurs at shift 6 (40 * min $\{\frac{40}{100}, \frac{9}{60}\}$) and for family C at shift 8.

Consequently, the first lot (L1) is for family AB starting at shift 6. As the machine is free at shift 6 it can be loaded. The lot size within the cycle time from shift 6 to shift 36 is the sum of the net demand of all its items within that cycle, i.e.

$$100 * \frac{36 - \max\{6, 40 \cdot \frac{40}{100}\}}{40} + 60 * \frac{36 - 6}{40} = 95 \text{ [t]}$$

Production of the first lot of family AB will take 8.55 shifts and thus will occupy the machine until shift 14.55.

The next family to run out of stock is family C at shift 8. As the machine is not available at shift 8 preceding lots are shifted backwards, preferable by 6.55 shifts. However, lot L1 can only be shifted by 6 shifts, resulting in a backlog of .55 shifts for lot L2. Accordingly, lot L2 is loaded at shift 8.55 covering demand over the cycle time from shift 8 to shift 28, assuming no lost sales in the backordering interval.

The loading of lots will continue in this manner until the demand of all families within the first month is covered.

Table 2 shows the relevant data of the resulting production plan for the first month.

Table 2: Data of the production plan for the first month

	L1	L2	L3	L4
family	AB	C	C	AB
actual starting time [shifts]	0	8.55	27	36
cycle interval [shifts]	[6,36]	[8,26]	[28,48]	[36,66]
shifts shifted backwards	6	-	1	0
shifts backlogged	0	0.55	-	-
production amount [t]	95	100	100	146
production time [shift]	8.55	9	9	13.14

The corresponding gantt chart provides a picture of the proposed
production plan.

Figure 1:   Gantt chart of the schedule

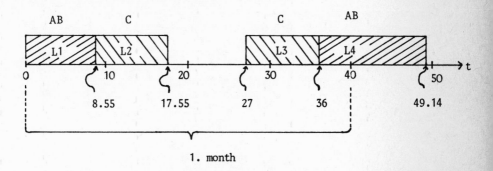

4. Conceptual Overview on the Design of the Hierarchical
   Production Planning System

The HPP-System designed consists of the APP-level and the subordinated
sequencing and scheduling level. It is assumed (for our experiments)
that the planning intervals of both planning levels are of equal
duration (e.g. one month).

The model components, data bases and interfaces to form a rolling
HPP-system are exhibited in flowchart 1 and described as follows:

At the outset each planning level will be provided with permanent
data like production coefficients (giving the number of time units
required to produce one unit of an item), holding cost coefficients etc..

As input of the APP-level information about the existing initial
inventory of items as well as the salesplan for T-periods ahead
is required. Ideally, a salesplan covering at least one seasonal cycle
is proposed. However, in the case described only shorter sales plans
covering 5-months ahead are obtainable (approx. a half of the seasonal
cycle). Furthermore, data on the availability of production facilities
for each subperiod of the planning period are needed as a basis for
the matrix generator to create the LP-model.

Flowchart: Conceptual Overview on the Rolling HPP-System

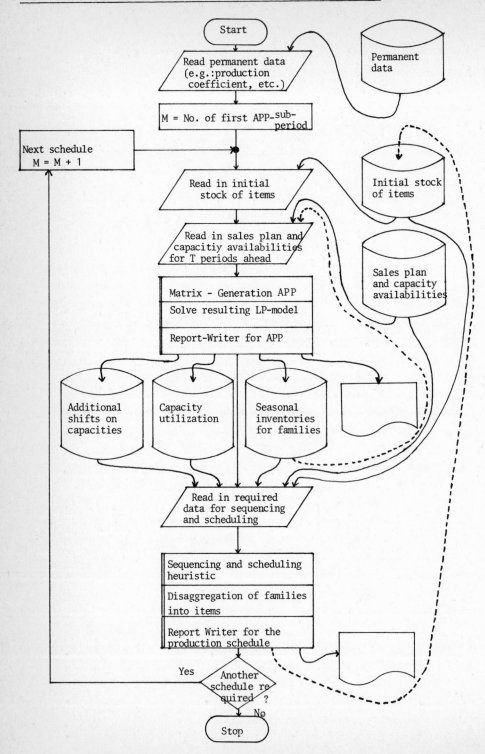

The resulting LP-model is solved by a standard LP-code (in our case MPS/X by Siemens Corp. [6]). The Report Writer serves three functions. It converts the MPS/X output into a representation of the aggregate production plan to be handed over to production management. Secondly, it provides the input for the purchasing of the required raw materials. Thirdly, it transfers data - via respective data bases - to the sequencing and scheduling planning level which enables the coordination of the two planning levels.

As coupling measures we have chosen end period inventories for families which act as targets, as well as additional shifts on processing lines (or other facilities or personnel) regarded as upper limits. Further information from the APP-level could be utilized advantageously due to its far-sightedness and be incorporated as a global guideline for decisions within the sequencing and scheduling heuristic (e.g. mean capacity utilizations in the first subperiod can guide the choice on which line a lot of a particular family should be loaded).

Similar to the APP-level the lower planning level needs the initial stock of items as well as the sales plan as input. The latter will normally be required only for a time interval covered by lot sizing decisions and will preferably be of a greater detail (due to fluctuations of demand within a subperiod). The sequencing and scheduling level will provide a detailed production plan (as a listing or on a data base) for the planning period (e.g. 1 month). Each lot of a particular family will have to be disaggregated into respective production amounts for the respective items.

A rolling schedule will be obtained, if the above procedure is executed again after the planning interval has passed. Of course, within each planning level, plans and data will be subject to management interactions. An explanation of the dotted lines in flowchart 1 is given in the next chapters.

5. Calculation of demand within the Aggregate LP-Model

Bitran / Hax [2] propose to use effective demand as demand data in an LP-model for APP. It is the actual demand of an item netted against the initial inventory. In contrast to Bitran / Hax, who propose effective demand for product types, our approach requires the incorporation of effective demand d_{ft} for family f in subperiod t which will be the sum of the effective demands of all its items. The reason not to aggregate families into product types is due to the fact that the latter would result in an unacceptable loss of accurarcy in the underlying case. An example of the demand for two items and the resulting effective demand of the corresponding family is shown in table 3.

Table 3:   Effective demand for a family AB, consisting
of items A and B

subperiod [month]	0	1	2	3	4	5
item A:						
initial stock minus safety stock	40					
gross demand		100	120	150	120	130
net demand		60	120	150	120	130
item B:						
initial stock minus safety stock	9					
gross demand		60	80	90	80	70
net demand		51	80	90	80	70
effective demand family AB	-	111	200	240	200	200

The above example serves to illustrate three deficiencies resulting from an aggregate LP-model based on effective demand.

Firstly, a typical solution of an aggregate LP-model - in the absence of binding capacity constraints - is to produce exactly the effective demand of family AB in each subperiod (see last row of table 3), resulting in end period inventories equal to safety stock level.

For the sequencing and scheduling decisions this means to start lots of each family at the beginning of each subperiod (2,3,4,5) which in the presence of many families, setup times and minimum lot sizes is impossible and will lead to backorders.

Secondly, such low inventories will often prevent the execution of desired low cost lot size decisions (see [7, p. 669]).

The reduction of end period inventories in the aggregate LP-model results from the objective to minimize inventory holding costs. It should be stressed that an LP-model only indicates the amount of stock -called seasonal stock - necessary to safeguard against future bottle-necks.[1] On the other hand the amount of lot size stock depends on decisions about the lot sizes (balancing stockholding and setup costs), decisions which are typically not part of an aggregate LP-model. None-theless, lot size stock plays a significant role in a batch production environment and should neither be neglected nor equated to seasonal stock in the planning process.

The third observation concerns the level of initial inventories. These are to a large extent due to the actual lot size production. However, in the standard model formulation initial inventories are treated as seasonal stock and can be used up in the first subperiods in the ab-sence of binding capacity constraints, thus underestimating capacity requirements necessary for adequate lot size production. Note, that in our example the proposed first period production (effective demand) is only a half of the following month's production.

---

[1] A similar reason to build up seasonal stock might be to make use of current low cost production opportunities.

We now want to present simple rules for a multiperiod APP-model
to overcome the above shortcomings, providing end period inventories,
which will allow consistent and acceptable sequencing and scheduling
decisions.

The only modification proposed in the APP-model is to substitute
effective demand by effective lot size demand for a family f in subperiod t, which is defined as the effective demand of all its items i
during that time interval which the lots produced in subperiod t have
to cover.

With effective lot size demand as an input to the aggregate LP-model,
the resulting production amounts will allow desired lot size decisions,
whereas the aggregate planning level is free to build up additional
seasonal stock if required. The underlying principle for harmonizing
hierarchical planning levels is based on the explicit consideration
and incorporation of the reasoning and logic inherent in lower level
decisions within the upper planning level.

The discourse will be based - although not limited - on the assertion
that a lot size rule with a fixed cycle time (e.g. Economic time
supply) is pursued (see chapter 3).

First Run of the Rolling Schedule

The calculation of effective lot size demand requires to find out what
lot sizing decisions will probably be taken at the sequencing and
scheduling planning level.

Thus, the first step consists of calculating the first cycle starting
time t_I of a lot of family f, which is that instant of time, when the
stock level of at least one of its items reaches zero (resp. safety
stock level).

Further lot cycle starting times for producing lots of family f
[t_{II}, t_{III}, t_{IV},..., see Fig. 2] are obtained by adding multiples
of the fixed cycle time to the first cycle starting time t_I.

From the example given above (see table 1) we obtain a cycle time of family AB of three quarters of a subperiod, which - knowing that item B reaches safety stock level first at time $\frac{9}{60}$ = 0.15 [time periods] - results in the following stream of lot production starting times:

$$t_I = 0.15, \ t_{II} = 0.90, \ t_{III} = 1.65, \ t_{IV} = 2.4$$
$$t_V = 3.15, \ t_{VI} = 3.9, \ t_{VII} = 4.65, \ t_{VIII} = 5.4$$

Note, that cycle starting times correspond with those of the preceding production plan (table 2).

Figure 2: Cycle starting times of lot production for family AB

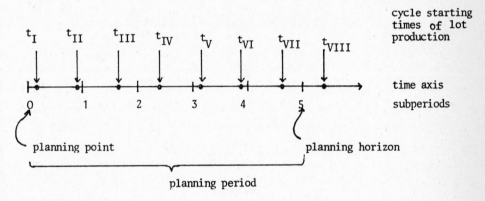

In a second step effective demand in the time interval marked by the first cycle starting time in subperiod t and the first cycle starting time beyond subperiod t is accumulated.

For our example effective lot size demand in subperiod 1 comprises the effective demand in the time interval $[t_I, \ t_{III}]$, effective lot size demand in subperiod 2 covers effective demand in the time interval $[t_{III}, \ t_{IV}]$ etc..[1]

---

1) A formal algorithm for the calculation of effective lot size demand is given in the appendix.

Table 4: Effective lot size demand for family AB

subperiod [month]	1	2	3	4	5
effective lot size demand					
item A	138	102	108	186.5	97.5
item B	103	64	66	113.5	52.5
family AB	241	166	174	300	150
lot size inventory at end of subperiod	130	96	30	130	80

The calculation of effective lot size demand of subperiod 5 has to be based on an assumption of the demand of future time periods, which is regarded to be the same as that of subperiod 5. A comparison with table 2 reveals that effective demand of family AB in subperiod 1 is equivalent to the planned production amount of the sequencing and scheduling level, as desired.

Given these expected production amounts for families per subperiod, the aggregate plan will check these figures with given capacity availabilities and can make decisions (like building up of seasonal inventories or transfer of personnel) accordingly.

Subsequent Runs of the Rolling Schedule
- Implications for the Aggregate Model

The preceding calculation of the first cycle starting time of a lot of family f was based on the assumption that the initial stock is made up of lot size stock only. However, in subsequent runs of the HPP-system we will know the extent of the seasonal inventory within the initial stock from the preceding run of the aggregate model.

In order not to alter the series of cycle starting times of lot production from one planning interval (run) to the next we will place the first cycle starting time at that instant of time when the initial lot size stock reaches zero. The initial lot size stock a_f^L is obtained by sub-tracting the planned endperiod seasonal stock of family f in subperiod 1 I_{f1}^{m-1} of the preceding run m-1 of the aggregate LP-model from the avail-able initial inventory, of all items belonging to family f ($i \in F_f$) i.e.

$$a_f^L = \sum_{i \in F_f} a_i - I_{f1}^{m-1}$$

To find out the seasonal stock level at the end of the first subperiod (I_{f1}^m) we have to adjust the initial seasonal stock level by the demand d_{i1} for all items i of family f in the first subperiod and the amount of additional seasonal stock at the end of subperiod 1 (S_{f1}^m) as proposed by the LP-model:

$$I_{f1}^m = \max (0, I_{f1}^{m-1} - \max \{0, \sum_{i \in F_f} d_{i1} - a_f^L\}) + S_{f1}^m$$

The series of cycle starting times for lot production will only change from one run to the next if there are deviations from forecasted demand to actual demand (in the preceding planning interval) or subsequent demand forecasts, as well as deviations from planned to actual productions.

However, it should be noted that in case the initial inventory of one item of a family reaches safety stock level earlier than the expiration of the initial lot size inventory would indicate, the earliest expiration date determines the first cycle starting time.

We will illustrate the modification again by family AB. Assume the first run of the aggregate model emphasized to build up a seasonal stock of 20 units at the end of subperiod 1 and that we are now planning for subperiod 2 (m = 2). Then supposing no forecast error in the first and subsequent subperiods, we will have an initial inventory of 150 units. Initial lot size inventory is calculated as

$$150 - 20 = 130 \text{ product units}$$

which expire at time unit

$$\frac{130}{120 + 80} = 1.65$$

There is a second reason and a very important one not to extend the
first cycle starting time until the overall initial inventory (excluding safety stock) has expired. Consider again the case of a
bottleneck in subperiod 2 which led to the preproduction of family AB
in subperiod 1 of 20 product units and demand forecasts unchanged
as given in table 1. If the new cycle in the next rolling schedule
(m = 2) starts at t_{III} = 1.75 instead of 1.65 it extends up to time
unit 2.5. Consequently the calculation of effective demand yields

$$0.25 \cdot (120 + 80) + 0.5 \cdot (150 + 90) = 170 \text{ product units}$$

which is even larger than the effective lot size demand of the preceding run, thus negating the desired effect of preproduction.

Conceptually, the planned seasonal stock at the end of the first
subperiod is saved on a data base and to be retrieved at the next
run (m + 1) by the matrix generator of the aggregate model (see inner
dotted line of flowchart 1).

- Implications for Sequencing and Scheduling

Given the aggregate plan has been established, the respective determination of lot sizes within the sequencing and scheduling planning
level for the first subperiod parallels that of the aggregate LP-model.
However, the first cycle starting time of a family (z_o)[1] does not
necessarily mark the latest feasible start of lot production. The
latter has to be chosen carefully in order to make adequate low cost
production decisions. Two aspects have to be considered:

- the extent of seasonal stock which should
  be used up before the first lot of a family
  should actually be started

and

- the timing of production of seasonal stock
  to be built up during the planning period
  of the sequencing and scheduling planning level.

---

1) See appendix

For the first aspect knowledge of the seasonal end period inventories of the preceding and actual run of the aggregate LP-model will provide information whether seasonal stock should be built up or used up. If the amount of seasonal stock at the beginning of the first subperiod (I_{f1}^{m-1}) is lower than that at the end of the first subperiod (I_{f1}^{m}), the difference indicates the amount of stock which maybe used up and vice versa.

Thus the minimum of both seasonal end period inventories

$$\min \{I_{f1}^{m-1}, I_{f1}^{m}\}$$

determines the seasonal stock that should be held throughout the planning period of the sequencing and scheduling planning level. Accordingly it is proposed to extend the latest feasible start of lot production until the level of the 'seasonal stock to be held' (plus safety stock) is reached.

The 'stock to be held in each item of a family' is excluded from meeting demand in the first month to make sure that it is still available at the end of the first month. Note that a strategy which contrary to the above proposals ignores the 'stock to be held', will - given there are two or more lots of a family within the schedule - result in an unbalanced schedule with low capacity utilizations at the beginning and heavy capacity utilizations at the end of the planning period.

An example will illustrate the point. Consider the sequencing and scheduling level in the planning point - at the beginning of month 2 - and assume that an initial seasonal stock of 20 units has been built up for familiy AB. However, now forecasted demand rate for item A has decreased to 110 units in subperiod 2 while all other demand rates remain unchanged. The actual run (m = 2) of the aggregate LP-model suggests a seasonal stock level of 17 units for family AB at the end of subperiod 2 as a target.

Then, as explained an amount of

$$\min \{20, 17\} = 17 \text{ product units}$$

should be held in stock from the initial inventory.

The initial inventory of item A (78 + 12 = 90 product units) and item B (52 + 8 = 60 product units) will expire at times $1 + \frac{90}{110} = 1.82$ and $1 + \frac{60}{80} = 1.75$ respectively.

Thus the latest feasible start of lot production is marked by the expiration of the initial stock of item B at 1.75 time units.

At this point there are still

$$(1.82 - 1.75) * 110 = 7.5$$

product units of item A in stock.

If 5 product units of family AB should be held in seasonal stock, the first starting time of a lot production for family AB remains unchanged at 1.75 time units. The five product units are excluded from the stock availabilities when determining the respective lot size. However, in case the stock to be held increases to 17 product units, the first starting time of lot production for family AB has to be

$$\frac{17 - 7.5}{110 + 80} = 0.05 \text{ time units}$$

earlier at time 1.70 at the latest. [1]

For the second aspect concerning the timing of production of seasonal stock to be built up by the end of the planning interval, we only have to consider the amount of stock which exceed the 'stock to be held'.

Although other strategies might be appropriate we chose to produce the remaining seasonal stock to be built up as part of the last lot of the respective family within the planning period.

6. Experiments and Numerical Results

The experiments are intended to reveal differences in the quality of production plans which are guided by aggregate LP-models based on 'effective demand' (ED) versus aggregate plans incorporating 'effective lot size demand' (ELSD).

---

[1] Note, that in case the latest feasible starting time of lot production precedes the planning point, the planned stock to be held is not available and should be adjusted accordingly.

Apart from the assumptions already mentioned in chapter 3 we assumed
a safety stock equivalent to one week's demand and an equal setup time
for each lot of $1/8^{th}$ of a shift. The planning period for aggregate
planning and sequencing and scheduling covered five months and one
month, respectively. The planning intervals of both planning levels
being one month. As endperiod inventories of the aggregate LP-model
an amount of half of the last (fifths) subperiod's demand was taken.
Proposed cycle times of lot production were specified by the company
for each family to be either one, two or four weeks.

The basis of our experiments were four consecutive actual salesplans
each indicating the demand for each item of one department for five
months ahead. The initial inventories at the beginning of the rolling
schedule were provided too. With no other information on sales given,
we assumed no forecast errors for the first month.

Designed as a purely linear model, the aggregate model cannot explicitly
tackle lot sizing decisions. Consequently, reasonable adjustments of
the available (net) capacity within the aggregate model have to be made,
reducing available gross capacity by the estimated amount lost due
to setup times. A few test runs indicated that a reduction by 10 p.c.
is appropriate [1] and will lead to feasible production plans.

The experimental design of the HPP-system resembles the concept depicted in flowchart 1 with the outer dotted line showing that the end
period inventories obtained as a result of the production plan of the
sequencing and scheduling level served as the initial inventory of
items in the next run of the rolling schedule. Furthermore, respective
capacity availabilities within each month were given by the company
as well as the necessary permanent data of the department modelled.

For both rolling schedules namely the ED-run and the ELSD-run the
aggregate LP-models were exactly the same except the respective demand
calculations. For the sequencing and scheduling level the same heuristics
were used, however, the lot size rule of 'fixed cycle times' was
modified for the ED-run in such a way that the last lot of a family
produced in a month had to end up with a stock level which equals the
seasonal stock provided by the aggregate LP-model (coupling measure)

---

1) The author is aware that further fine tuning might improve
   production costs of the resulting plans. However, for the
   comparison of the ED-HPP versus the ELSD-HPP the effect will be
   negligible.

plus safety stock. For the HPP-system based on ELSD, the target of
seasonal end period inventories as provided by the aggregate LP-model
was added to the last lot of a family to be produced in a month, while
the scheduling level was free to build up lot size stock to cover the
demand within the next cycle.

The capacity situation within the four months for which a production
plan was obtained on a rolling horizon basis can be described as
follows:

Out of the five processing lines, one line was a bottleneck in month 2,
3 and 4. Although seasonal stock was built up in month 1 additional
shifts were required too in the following months.

Furthermore, for the ELSD-run male personnel fell short in month 3
which led to additional seasonal stock in month 2.

A discrimination of the type of stocks held, depending on the causes
of their building up, provides insights into the importance of its
cost (see table 5).

The two major cost components of nearly equal size are the safety stocks
which range between 31 p.c. and 50 p.c. of the total stockholding cost
and the lot size stock (38 p.c. to 59 p.c.) irrespective of which
demand calculation scheme is used. The considerable extent of average
lot size stock also shows the rather artificial requirement of the
effective demand calculations which forces lot size stock down to zero
at the end of each subperiod.

Of less importance is the cost of seasonal stock, which has to be
considered as a cost factor in the first two months (3 p.c. to 12 p.c.).
The cost for stocks resulting from lots being shifted backwards due to
the unavailability of required machines (sequence dependent stock) is
rather small (0.4 p.c. to 6.7 p.c.). This supports our expectation
that the proposed 'progressive forward-backward' heuristic works
satisfactorily. However, it should be noted that with the reversal
of the simplifications for the sequencing and scheduling planning level,
namely by including all production capacities, this cost element is
expected to rise.

Table 5: Portion of costs of different stock types on overall
stockholding cost in a month

month	1		2		3		4	
	ED	ELSD	ED	ELSD	ED	ELSD	ED	ELSD
Safety stock [%]	50.1	45.7	40.0	40.4	36.5	31.4	43.1	44.4
Lot size stock [%]	37.5	48.0	46.9	50.2	57.7	59.2	56.2	51.7
Seasonal stock [%]	11.3	3.2	12.2	8.1	1.0	2.7	0.3	1.9
Sequence dependent stock [%]	1.1	3.0	0.9	1.4	4.8	6.7	0.4	2.0

One observation from the example provided (chapter 5) was that stocks
of an aggregate LP-model utilizing ED will - in the absence of seasonal
stocks - go down to safety stock level at the beginning of each subperiod. Consequently, each family will require the production of a lot
to be started at the beginning of each subperiod - or at least until
safety stock has expired. It was concluded that with the existence of
setup times and (minimum) lot sizes given [1] this will inevitably result
in backordering situations.

Table 6 shows that the above reasoning holds for our case.

Accepting the initial stock (month 1) for each family as given by the
company and assuming that it consists of lot size and safety stock only,
the number of backordering situations exceeding the safety reach of one
week is exactly the same for month 1 as expected irrespective of which
demand calculation is used in the aggregate model.

However, for the following months the consequences of the two demand
calculations become clear. In the production plans based on an aggregate
LP-model including ELSD backordering situations exceeding safety reach
were nearly totally avoided. This desirable effect occured despite the
fact that the reach of the initial stock fell from 2.7 weeks in the

---

[1] Note, that lot sizes had to cover demand within the next cycle time,
thus were not regarded as decision variables.

first month to less than 2.2 weeks in the following months. Assuming that safety stocks cannot be used to reconcile delayed production, the percentage of lots being late varies from 39 p.c. to 13 p.c..

On the other hand, backordering situations occured more often in production plans linked to an aggregate LP-model including ED. There are between 18 p.c. to 27 p.c. of the lots which were delayed more than one week, while even 54 p.c. to 77 p.c. of the lots had to be produced later than cycle time would suggest.

Accumulated backordering times (measured in shifts) further illuminate the superiority of aggregate LP-models based on ELSD.

Table 6: Performance of Production Plans resulting from ED-HPP-systems versus ELSD-HPP-systems

month	1		2		3		4	
	ED	ELSD	ED	ELSD	ED	ELSD	ED	ELSD
no. of lots produced	92	92	105	104	177	143	115	102
average reach of initial stock [weeks]	2.7	2.7	1.6	2.0	1.3	1.9	1.1	2.2
no. of lots delayed more than 1 week (safety reach)	5	5	26	2	31	1	31	0
no. of lots delayed	33	30	73	41	95	33	89	13
Accumulated backordering times beyond safety reach [shifts]	2.5	2.5	120.4	0.3	92.4	0.1	121.9	0.0
Accumulated backordering times of lots delayed [shifts]	137.4	120.5	618.3	109.8	583.1	68.9	630.9	34.6

Another observation from the experiments was that the overall stock-holding costs over 4 months were only 5.7 p.c. higher for the ELSD-HPP-system compared to the ED-HPP-system although ED forces lot size stock down to zero at the end of each subperiod. As a consequence of smaller lot sizes in the ED-runs the number of lots (and setup times) was 11 p.c. higher than the number of lots produced in the ELSD-runs.

7. Final Remarks

On the basis of the company's sales plans at hand, we were able to
support theoretical observations about the inappropriateness of aggregate
LP -models based on 'effective demand' in a batch production environment. The aggregate plans led to a considerable amount of backordering
situations at the beginning of the subperiods.

Aspired cycle times for lot sizes could in several cases not be executed
due to the need to reach given targets of end period inventories
provided by the aggregate model.

However, with the inclusion of 'effective lot size demand' within the
APP-model, backordering situations were nearly eliminated (in subperiods
at disposal i.e. subperiods 2,3 and 4). Adequate lot sizing decisions
covering the aspired cycle times were possible which resulted in less
frequent setups accompanied by a small increase in holding costs.

These first results from the rolling HPP-system will be extended by
further experiments which on the one hand will increase compliance
of the sequencing and scheduling level with reality by including e.g.

. minimum lot sizes

. more flexible decision rules
  e.g. reduction of lot sizes to prevent
  backordering situations.

On the other hand experiments can be conducted revealing the effects
of different structures of the HPP-system e.g.

. a variation of forecast errors
. capacity utilizations
. different planning horizons both for the
  aggregate and the sequencing and scheduling
  level

and

. the effect of the distribution of initial
  inventories and measures to maintain a
  favourable distribution of end period inventories.

Appendix: Calculation of Effective Lot Size Demand

List of symbols

Indices:

i	item
f	family
F_f	index set comprising of all items i (i $\in F_f$)
t,s	subperiod of the aggregate planning period (t= 1,...,T)

Constants / Variables:

a_i	initial inventory of item i minus safety stock
Δ_f	planned initial lot size stock of family f
c_f	cycle time for lots of family f
d_{it}	demand rate for item i in subperiod t
d_{ft}	effective lot size demand for family f in subperiod t
l	time variable
p_o	latest start of lot production in the planning period due to the expiration of a_i
$\lceil p_o \rceil$, $\lceil z_o \rceil$	smallest integer <u>greater than</u> p_o, z_o
rw_i	number of subperiods (real) the initial inventory of item i will cover
I_{f1}^{m-1}	seasonal stock built up for family f by the end of subperiod 1 in the preceding run of the aggregate LP-model (m-1)
z_t	first cycle starting time in subperiod t

A) Determination of cycle starting times within the planning period for a given product family f.

0) Initialization

$$p_0 = + \infty$$

1) Find the latest feasible starting time p_0 of the first lot production

For all $i \in F_f$:

1.1) $t = 0$, $d_{i,T+\lceil c_f \rceil + 1} = + \infty$

1.2) $t = t + 1$

1.3) If $d_{it} < a_i$, THEN $a_i = a_i - d_{it}$

$$\text{GO TO } 1.2$$

$$\text{ELSE} \quad rw_i = (t - 1) + \frac{a_i}{d_{it}}$$

$$p_0 = \min \{p_0 , rw_i\}$$

2) Find first lot cycle starting time z_0 in the planning period (Considering initial seasonal stock)

2.1) $t = 0$

2.2) $t = t + 1$

2.3) $\Delta_f = \max \{0, \sum_{i \in F_f} a_i - I_{f1}^{m-1}\}$

2.4) If $\sum_{i \in F_f} d_{it} < \Delta_f$, THEN $\Delta_f = \sum_{i \in F_f} a_i - \sum_{i \in F_f} d_{it}$

$$\text{GO TO } 2.2$$

$$\text{ELSE} \quad z_0 = \min \{p_0 , (t - 1) + \frac{\Delta_f}{\sum_{i \in F_f} d_{it}}\}$$

3) Find first lot cycle starting time z_t in subperiod t

3.1) $z_t = + \infty \ \forall \ t = 1, \ldots , T + 1$

3.2) $t = \lceil z_0 \rceil$, $z_t = z_0$, $1 = z_0$

3.3) $1 = 1 + c_f$

3.4) If $1 < t$: GO TO 3.3)

3.5) $t = \lceil 1 \rceil$

3.6) $z_t = 1$

3.7) If $t \leq T$: GO TO 3.3)

4) S T O P

B) Calculation of demand for that time interval which the lots
    started in subperiod t have to cover for a given product family f
    and all subperiods within the planning period

0)   Initialization

$$d_{ft} = o \qquad \forall \, t = 1, \ldots, T$$

IF $z_o \geq$ THEN

　　　　　　　GO TO 4)

　　　　ELSE
　　　　　　$s = \lceil z_o \rceil$

1)   Effective demand in subperiod t   (1. term):

 1.1) t = s

 1.2) For all i $\in F_f$:

　　IF $rw_i < t : d_{ft} = d_{ft} + (t - \max \{z_t, rw_i\} \cdot d_{it}$

2)   Effective demand in subsequent subperiods (2. term):

 2.1) s = s + 1

 2.2) IF $z_s < s$: GO TO 3)

 2.3) For all i $\in F_f$:

　　IF $rw_i < s : d_{ft} = d_{ft} + (s - \max \{s - 1, rw_i\}) \cdot d_{is}$

 2.4) GO TO 2.1)

3)   Effective demand in the last subperiod a lot started in
      subperiod t has to cover   (3. term):

 3.1) For all i $\in F_f$:

　　IF $rw_i < z_s : d_{ft} = d_{ft} + (z_s - \max \{s - 1, rw_i\}) \cdot d_{is}$

 3.2) IF $s \leq T$: GO TO 1)

4)   S T O P

References

1) Axsäter S., Jönsson H., Aggregation and Disaggregation in Hierarchical Production Planning, EJOR, Vol. 17, 1984, 338 - 350

2) Bitran, G.R., Hax A.C., On the Design of Hierarchical Production Planning Systems, Decision Science, Vol. 8, 1977, 28 - 55

3) Bitran G.R., Haas E.A., Hax A.C., Hierarchical Production Planning: A Single Stage System, Operations Research, Vol. 29, No. 4, 1981, 717 - 743

4) Bitran G.R., Haas E.A., Hax A.C., Hierarchical Production Planning: A Two-Stage System, Operations Research, Vol. 30, No. 2, 1982, 234 - 251

5) Bitran G.R., Magnanti Th.L., Yanasse H.H., Approximation Methods for the Uncapacitated Dynamic Lot Size Problem, Management Science, Vol. 30, No. 9, 1121 - 1140, 1984

6) Fujitzu Corp., Siemens AG: MPS/X-User's Guide, München, 1979

7) Graves S.C., A Review of Production Scheduling, Operations Research, Vol. 29, No. 4, 646 - 675, 1981

8) Graves S.C., Using Lagrangian Techniques to Solve Hierarchical Production Planning Problems, Management Science, Vol. 28, No. 3, 1982, 260 - 275

9) Günther, H.-O., Revidierende Produktionsplanung bei Sorten-fertigung, in: D. Ohse, A.C. Esprester, H.-U. Küpper, P. Stähly, H. Steckhan, (eds.), Operations Research Proceedings 1984, Berlin, Heidelberg, New York, 1985, 140 - 147

10) Hax A.C., Meal H., Hierarchical Integration of Production Planning and Scheduling, in :Geisler M.A. (ed.), Studies in Management Science, Vol. 1, Logistics, Amsterdam, New York, 1975, 53 - 69

11) Jaikumar R., An Operational Optimization Procedure for
    Production Scheduling, Comput. & Ops. Res., Vol. 1, 1974,
    191 - 200

12) Krajewski L., Multiple Criteria Optimization in Production
    Planning: An Application for a Large Industrial Goods
    Manufacturer, Research Paper, Academic Faculty of Management
    Science, The Ohio State University, without year

13) Peterson R., Silver E.A., Decision Systems for Inventory
    Management and Production Planning, New York, Chichester,
    Brisbane, Toronto, 1979

14) Stadtler, H., Critical Design Aspects of Hierarchical Production
    Planning Systems, Paper presented at the EURO VII Conference,
    Bologna, Italy, June 16 - 20, 1985

15) Zäpfel G., Tobisch H., Ein Model zur hierarchischen Produktions-
    plannung, Forschungsbericht des Instituts für Industrie und
    Fertigungswirtschaft an der Universität Linz, 1980

THE DESIGN OF AN HIERARCHICAL MODEL FOR PRODUCTION PLANNING AND SCHEDULING

H.O. Günther

Universität Mannheim
Lehrstuhl Unternehmensforschung
Schloß, D-6800 Mannheim (FRG)

In this paper, the design of an hierarchical model for production planning and scheduling is discussed in a real-life case study. The overall decision problem is partitioned into four levels: (1) aggregate production planning for product families, (2) detailed scheduling and sequencing, (3) determination of production orders for items, and (4) distribution and dispatching. Heuristic solution procedures are developed for all sub-problems. To respond to changes in input data, a rolling horizon procedure at the aggregate level and interactive replanning at all lower levels are suggested.

1. Introduction

Production planning and scheduling encompasses a large number of decisions and involves managers at various echelons within the organization. These decisions differ by complexity, scope, and time horizon. Moreover, relevant data differ by their degree of certainty and aggregation. Usually, it is not possible to consider every detail of the information available in the decision process. For practical reasons, the information being processed is aggregated depending on the nature and horizon of the planning problem, the particular production environment, and the organizational structure of the firm.

Theoretically, a monolithic model comprising all detailed decision problems over the entire planning horizon could be formulated. This approach, however, is not consistent with the nature of the managerial decision process. Essentially, production planning and scheduling is a complex process consisting of multiple tasks and requiring effective coordination throughout the organization. These aspects are recognized by structuring a planning system in an hierarchical fashion.

In the design of an **hierarchical planning system**, the partitioning of the planning process, the selection of adequate sub-models at each level and their coordination are the most essential aspects. (Design problems and industrial applications of two-level hierarchical production planning systems are extensively discussed by Gelders and van Wassenhove [40].) The different levels within the planning hierarchy have to fit appropriately in the organizational structure and the linking mechanisms must ensure feasible and consistent disaggregation at all lower levels. Finally, the hierarchical planning system must produce solutions sufficiently close to optimality.

Several hierarchical production planning systems have been developed in the literature (e.g. Hax and Meal [49], Bitran and Hax [17], Bitran et. al. [15,16], Gabbay [39], and Graves [43]). Other examples of work dealing with hierarchical planning systems are reported in Armstrong and Hax [4], Axsäter [5,7], Axsäter and Jönsson [9], Bitran and von Ellenrieder [19], Chen Chuan [28], Dempster et. al. [31], Gelders and Kleindorfer [41,42], Hax [47], Lasserre et. al. [58], Maxwell and Muckstadt [61], and Meal [63]. In a case study based on input data from industry Jönsson [50] investigates the performance of a hierarchical production planning system.

Very often, there are only two levels within an hierarchical production planning system. An **aggregate model** is used to assist a higher managerial level in deciding upon production quantities of product families and capacity and work force utilization. The problem of aggregating product data within an hierarchical production planning system is extensively studied by Axsäter [6,8]. Aggregation is for instance concerned with the consolidation of similar items into product families, a series of machines into a production centre, or a number of shifts into a planning period (e.g. Boskma [23]). The aggregate plan, then imposes constraints upon the subsequent planning level. With the aid of a **detailed model**, operations management develops the short term production schedules.

Also, material requirements planning systems (MRP) used within many component manufacturing systems can be looked upon as an hierarchical planning and scheduling system (e.g. Andersson et. al. [2] and Bahl and Ritzman [10]). Most standard software systems for MRP are based on the same sequential planning concept: they start with an aggregate production plan at the end-item level (usually denoted master production schedule), then explode it into detailed production and procurement schedules for all components and raw materials, and finally, release and control production orders for all items involved in the production process. Although this concept is far from optimal, an increasing number of implementations has been reported in the literature (Scheer [68]).

The design of an hierarchical planning system described in this paper resulted from the analysis of the production and distribution system of a major German producer of washing powder. Heuristic solution procedures for specific sub-problems are reported in more detail in Günther [45,46] and Feser et. al. [35]. For a general review of quantitative models for production planning and inventory control and their application within the planning system of a firm, the reader is referred to the excellent textbook of Silver and Peterson [71].

The paper is organized as follows: The following section analyses the particular planning problem. As a result, the overall decision problem is partitioned into four levels: (1) aggregate production planning for product families, (2) detailed scheduling and sequencing, (3) determination of production orders for items, and (4) distribution and dispatching. In Section 3, the design of the hierarchical production planning system is laid out. To deal with the adaptation to changes in input (especially demand uncertainty), rolling horizon and interactive replanning systems can be applied. These implementation schemes and the coordination of planning horizons are discussed in Section 4. In Section 5, simple heuristic procedures for each level of the hierarchical production planning system are presented. To conclude, some aspects of coordination within the hierarchical production planning system are discussed in the final section.

2. Analysis of a planning problem

2.1 The production and distribution process

As a case study, the production of washing powder by a major German company is considered. Three brands of washing powder are produced, basically using the same production process. Finished goods delivered to the customer vary according to the brand and the packaging format (5 shapes and sizes of boxes). Following the product structure suggested by Hax and Meal [49], the three brands of washing powder can be regarded as **product families** while the packaging formats correspond to specific **items** within a family (see Figure 1).

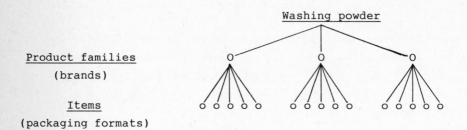

Fig. 1: <u>Product structure</u>

The production process and material flow are outlined in Figure 2. With some simplifications, production can be considered as a two-stage process. In the first stage, washing powder is continously produced in a single high-speed unit. The output, then is stored in a buffer storage in order to absorb fluctuations in the product flow. In the second stage, packaging is performed on a number of machines depending on the specific format. The capacity requirements for individual packaging lines vary according to the forecasted item demand.

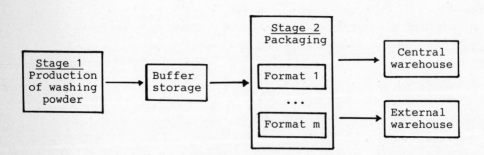

Fig. 2: <u>Production process and material flow</u>

At any one time, only a single product family can be produced. Whenever the production process is set up for another product family, a fixed changeover cost is incurred. Since items within a product family share a common manufacturing setup cost and each packaging line is fixed to a certain format, changeover costs are only associated with product families. Due to the capacity of the buffer storage, a changeover from one product family to another does not cause a shutdown of the whole production process. Thus, setup times do not affect production capacity.

Finally, finished goods are loaded on pallets and stored either in a central or in an external warehouse. In the central warehouse, storage costs are comparatively low, but capacity is limited. Costs are considerably higher in the external warehouse which offers practically unlimited capacity. It is obvious that storage in the central warehouse is preferred. Only when the central storage capacity is insufficient, excess output is stored in the external warehouse.

2.2 Planning hierarchy

An hierarchical planning system has implicitly been used by the company considered here. However, only little support by computerized information and planning systems has been provided yet. An aggregate production plan is released by the central planning department every 4 weeks and production managers in the local plants carry out the detailed scheduling on a trial and error basis. Decisions at various stages in the planning process are informally coordinated.

Company management believes that considerable cost savings can be achieved from more effective decision support systems for specific sub-problems and from a better coordination of interacting planning activities. The system design had to consider four criteria: (1) capability for interactive decision support, (2) ease of implementation, (3) an hierarchical planning procedure consistent with the organizational structure, and (4) coordination of different stages in the planning procedure. This paper deals with the design of the overall system concept. The proposed hierarchical planning and scheduling system consists of four levels (see Figure 3):

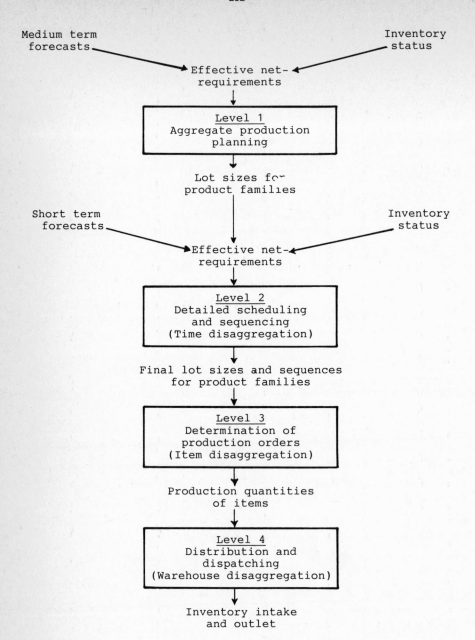

Fig. 3: <u>Hierarchical structure of the planning system</u>

(1) Aggregate production planning for product families

Let decisions on capacity and workforce be fixed, the aggregate production plan determines the timing and sizing of **lot sizes** for various **product families** over a medium term horizon with weekly planning periods. Forecast requirements must be met without backordering and without exceeding available production capacities.

(2) Detailed scheduling and sequencing (Time disaggregation)

Given lot sizes as an output from the aggregate planning level, a **detailed schedule** and **sequence** of production lots is determined and resources are allocated among product families over a short term horizon with fairly reliable demand forecasts. Contrary to the aggregate production plan, production operations within the detailed schedule are developed shift by shift (time disaggregation). If necessary, lot sizes are adjusted in order to assure consistency with the aggregate level.

(3) Determination of production orders (Item disaggregation)

In general, the distribution of a product family's demand among items is very difficult to forecast. Due to sales promotions and changes in customer order sizes, demand considered at the item level is highly stochastic even in the short run. Let the detailed production schedule be fixed at the product family level, lot sizes are disaggregated resulting in **final production quantities of items** to be produced on various packaging lines.

(4) Distribution and dispatching (Warehouse disaggregation)

Daily or even more frequently, **intake** and **outlet** for all items and the two warehouses have to be determined. Given production quantities in the packaging process and on-line information about inventories in both storage locations, output has to be directed to one of the two warehouses, and it is decided from where to dispatch customer orders (warehouse disaggregation).

3. An hierarchical production planning system

3.1 Aggregate production planning

In the hierarchical production planning system, laid out in the previous section, aggregate production planning is carried out at the
highest level. In particular, **aggregation** is concerned with **products,
time,** and **capacity:** similar items are consolidated into product families, the 10 shifts within a week are treated as a homogeneous planning period, and the two-stage production system with multiple machines is considered as a single unit. Furthermore, the existence of
two warehouses with different costs and storage capacities is ignored.
The purpose of aggregation within production planning is to reduce the
complexity of the decision problem and to obtain a problem formulation
which is easier to solve.

The main features of the physical system considered and the aggregate
planning level are compared in Figure 4. (Similar comparisons are
given in Figures 5, 6, and 7 for all lower planning levels.) Essentially, aggregate production planning corresponds to the first stage
in the production process. Both output from the first production stage
and lot sizes obtained from the aggregate planning level are expressed
in quantities of a particular product family. Disaggregation with respect to time, items, and storage locations is carried out in the subsequent planning levels.

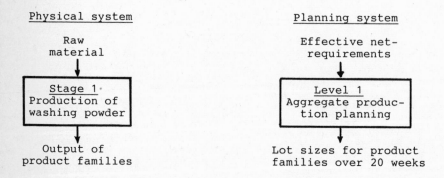

Fig. 4: <u>Physical and planning system considered at the aggregate
planning level</u>

In the case study considered here, the decision problem of aggregate production planning can be described as follows:

Since only a single product family can be produced at the same time and setup costs are incurred whenever production changes from one product family to another, the aggregate production plan states which product families are to be set up and which **lot sizes** should be produced over the planning horizon of 24 weeks. Requirements for all product families must be satisfied without backordering and without exceeding the available production capacities. Because of the buffer storage capacity, a changeover of product families does not cause a breakdown in the production process. Consequently, setup times need not to be considered. Carrying units of products in inventory from one period to another causes holding costs. Thus, the objective is to determine lot sizes which minimize the sum of costs incurred by setups and inventory holding.

This decision problem, addressed in the literature as the **capacitated lot size problem,** can be solved heuristically within reasonable computer time. A new heuristic based on marginal costs is outlined in Section 5.1. As a result, lot sizes for all product families, satisfying the production capacity constraints, are obtained over a medium term horizon. In the subsequent planning level, the aggregate production plan, which is based on weekly planning periods, is disaggregated into a shift-by-shift schedule.

3.2 Time disaggregation

In the literature, lot-sizing and sequencing are generally treated as independent sub-problems within a production planning system. Exceptions are for instance the approaches of Dorsey et. al. [34] and Aras and Swanson [3], who integrate lot-sizing and sequencing for the case of a single stage production system. Recently, Afentakis [1] made some propositions to transform the multi-stage lot-sizing problem into an equivalent job shop scheduling problem. Also Olhager and Rapp [67] consider issues of flow shop scheduling in the determination of lot-sizes.

In the hierarchical planning system discussed here, aggregate planning and detailed scheduling form subsequent levels of the planning system. Whereas lot-sizing is based on weekly time periods, much smaller periods are usually required for detailed scheduling and sequencing. For practical reasons, let us define a shift as a basic period. Throughout this period only a single product family is produced. A changeover to another family is always carried out at the beginning of a shift.

Given lot sizes for all product families from the aggregate production plan, the **sequence of batches** to be produced within a short term horizon has to be determined and actual **starting times** have to be assigned to each individual batch (see Figure 5). In the short run, more accurate demand forecasts are available and most customer order sizes are already fixed. The heuristic described in Section 5.2 tends to keep the aggregate plan unchanged and to **adjust lot sizes** only in order to prevent backorders and interferences in the production sequence.

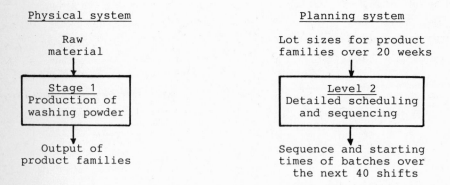

Fig. 5: <u>Physical and planning system considered at the time disaggregation level</u>

Lot sizes are determined such that processing times of batches comprise an an integer number of basic periods (shifts). Furthermore, the model is based on the assumption that demand is known per basic period. In fact, delivery dates of most customer orders are fixed in the short run. However, forecasting of future requirements is based on weekly time periods, and therefore, a plausible disaggregation rule must be applied in order to obtain forecast demand per shift.

The heuristic presented in Section 5.2 makes use of the fact that lot sizes are available from the aggregate planning level. These lot sizes have been determined with respect to medium term demand forecasts and can also be considered as near optimal solutions in the short run. The aggregate plan, however, only identifies production quantities per week without stating the sequence of batches in the production process. By means of the scheduling and sequencing heuristic a feasible time disaggregation is achieved.

In the single machine lot sequencing problem, to be solved here, the minimization of sequence dependent holding costs is often considered as a performance criterion. Provided that all items cause similar holding costs, the minimization of the total amount of stocks is an equivalent objective. The heuristic procedure presented in Section 5.2, schedules lots as late as possible in order to meet this objective. However, no explicit objective function is incorporated into the heuristic.

3.3 Item disaggregation

From the detailed scheduling sub-system a sequence of final lot sizes and their timing are obtained. Assuming that production capacity in the packaging process is sufficient, we now need to determine **production orders** for each item over a short term horizon. This is achieved by disaggregating the product family based lot sizes into production quantities of items per basic period (see Figure 6). The item disaggregation is **consistent** with the aggregate plan, if the production quantities of product families are completely allocated among items belonging to the corresponding product family and net-requirements for all items and periods are met without backordering (Gabbay[38]).

For the disaggregation of product family based lot sizes into production quantities of items we use a slightly modified version of a heuristic suggested by Hax and Meal [49]. The essence of their approach is to **equalize run out times** of items belonging to the same product family. It can be shown that the equalization of run out times leads to a consistent disaggregation (Fontan et. al. [37]) and is an optimal disaggregation rule under certain conditions (Karmarkar [51]). This heuristic, well known from the literature, is in brief explained in Section 5.3.

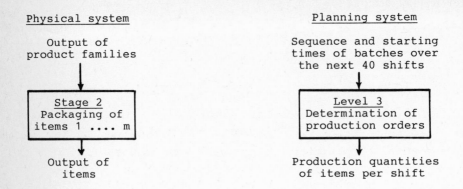

Physical system

Output of
product families

Stage 2
Packaging of
items 1 .... m

Output of
items

Planning system

Sequence and starting
times of batches over
the next 40 shifts

Level 3
Determination of
production orders

Production quantities
of items per shift

Fig. 6: <u>Physical and planning system considered at the item disaggregation level</u>

3.4 Warehouse disaggregation

Given production quantities per basic period, the **intake** and **outlet** for all items and warehouses have to be determined (see Figure 7). The two warehouses available differ significantly in their storage costs and capacity. The central warehouse with limited capacity is operated at low costs, while considerably higher costs are incurred in the external warehouse with practically unlimited capacity.

With respect to inventory holding and handling costs, it is desirable that total output is stored in the central warehouse and orders are dispatched from this location first. In the case of insufficient central storage capacity, output has to be allocated among the two warehouses. To solve this operational planning problem, a simple heuristic allocation rule, suggested by Feser [35] et.al., is presented in Section 5.4.

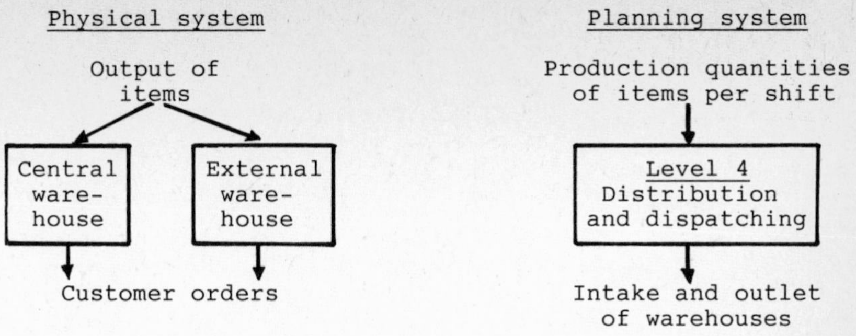

Physical system   Planning system

Output of   Production quantities
items   of items per shift

Central ware-house	External ware-house

Level 4 Distribution and dispatching

Customer orders   Intake and outlet
of warehouses

Fig. 7: <u>Physical and planning system considered at the warehouse disaggregation level</u>

4. Replanning

4.1 Planning horizon

The effect of planning horizons on aggregate production planning and
lot-sizing have been treated in several investigations (e.g.
Kunreuther and Morton [55,56], Lundin and Morton [59], Morton [65], Mc
Clain and Thomas [62], Miller [64], Nagasawa et. al. [66]). Very
little attention has been paid so far to the **coordination of planning
horizons** at different levels of an hierarchical production planning
system (an exception is the paper of Chung and Krajewski [29]).

The four planning levels described in Sections 2 and 3 require a significantly different horizon. Evidently, the planning horizon tends to
increase with a higher degree of aggregation. If setup costs need to
be considered in the aggregate planning, the entire planning horizon
should at least cover the required implementation lead time and the
expected time between several production orders. If possible, the
horizon should be extended to include even a full seasonal cycle of
external demand. With respect to the hierarchical structure of the
planning system, the entire planning horizon can be separated into 3
partitions as shown in Figure 8.

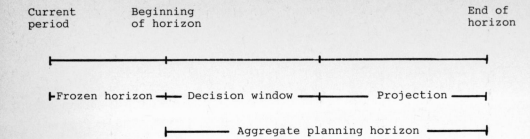

Fig. 8: <u>Partitions of the planning horizon</u>

Within a **frozen horizon**, the production schedule is fixed. No altera-
tions of existing schedules are normally allowed, because it is impossible to implement changes within the production lead time.

During the subsequent periods, however, production plans may be revised, if necessary. It is obvious that detailed schedules should only
be worked out for a short term period. This partition of the entire
planning horizon is denoted as a **decision window** in the following. Its
length is determined by the time period for which implementation of
production schedules is intended. The decision window also is the
maximum time interval between two successive planning runs.

The remainder of the horizon provides **projections** of future operations
and may serve as a basis for procurement decisions and manpower planning, for instance.

The **aggregate planning horizon** covers the decision window and the projection period.

Provided that lot sizes for product families are already determined,
detailed scheduling and item disaggregation, as the subsequent planning levels, are performed over the decision window. Thus, schedules
are implemented beginning with the first period of the decision window, until the schedule is revised (see the following section). In the
production planning system considered here, the aggregate planning
horizon comprises 24 weeks consisting of a 4-week decision window and
a 20-week projection period, while schedules are fixed over a frozen
horizon of 4 weeks. Distribution and dispatching, as the lowest plan-

ning level, are carried out daily or even more frequently using inter-active computerized decision support.

4.2 Implementation schemes

Due to the stochastic nature of the decision problem, demand forecasts and production schedules are frequently revised. Very often, stochastic fluctuations in external demand are the major source of nervousness in the production planning system of a firm. Although it is essential to replan from time to time, production control managers often prefer fixed production schedules for a considerable time period.

There are two basic implementation schemes for production planning: **rolling horizon** and **interactive systems** (see Figure 9). In the first system, the process of production planning is repeated periodically, typically once a week or once a month, and decisions are implemented only for the near future. Periodically, the model is updated to reflect the actual (usually more reliable) input data. New data are appended to the horizon and the model is re-solved. An interactive system, however, allows replanning to be carried out on a virtually continous time basis. In this system, replanning may be caused by a transaction or a significant change in input (e.g. a change in a customer order size, a loss in quality, a shortage of raw material, or a machine breakdown).

In the literature on production planning, most systems suggested for the implementation of production plans are of the rolling horizon type. Applications of such systems are investigated in many publications (e.g. Baker [11,12], Baker and Peterson [14], Blackburn and Millen [21,22], Carlson et. al. [24], Kropp et. al. [53,54], and Chand [27]). The effects of changing existing lot-schedules within a rolling horizon procedure are explicitly considered in Carlson et. al. [25], Kropp and Carlson [52], and Chand [26]. In the context of production planning, very little attention has been paid so far to interactive planning systems.

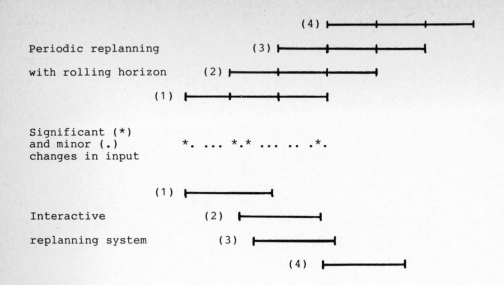

Fig. 9: <u>Rolling horizon and interactive replanning systems</u>

With respect to computerized information systems, a rolling horizon implementation scheme corresponds to a **batch processing system** while the interactive system is based on **real-time information processing** (see Scheer [68]). In a batch oriented system, all data to be processed are collected over some period of time. Periodically, the information system is run and the entire decision problem is resolved (**regeneration concept**). On the contrary, an interactive system processes data and updates files whenever a major transaction occurs. To adapt to changes in input data, modifications are limited to the affected activities (**net-change concept**). At present, many computer applications in business turn from batch oriented towards interactive systems. There is an increasing need to develop replanning concepts which extensively use the capabilities of modern business data processing systems.

In the production planning system considered in this study, it is suggested that replanning is carried out on a rolling horizon basis at the aggregate level and interactively at all lower levels (Günther [45]). Within this concept, an aggregate production plan over an horizon of 24 weeks is determined every 2 to 4 weeks in order to adapt to changes in external demand. Detailed production scheduling and sequencing are then carried out for a decision window of 4 weeks.

At any time, a single transaction can cause modifications in the production schedule at the detailed level. Consequently, the decision window is redefined as the next 4-week horizon. A change in a customer order size, for instance, will normally not affect the aggregate planning level. However, it may cause modifications in the starting times of batches and the production quantities of items.

Some judgement of the decision maker is used in deciding on how quickly to respond to changes and how often replan the schedule. Too frequent and too extensive changes of existing schedules are usually not desired, since they can create nervous reactions of the planning system. In general, only the affected sub-system is replanned without resolving the entire decision problem.

5. Heuristic solution to sub-problems

5.1 A marginal cost heuristic for the capacitated lot size problem

The decision problem of aggregate production planning (addressed as the capacitated lot size problem in Section 3.1) can mathematically be formulated as follows:

Minimize

$$\sum_{t \in T} [\sum_{i \in M} (S_i \ \delta(X_{it}) + h_i \ I_{it})]$$

subject to

$$I_{i,t-1} + X_{it} - d_{it} = I_{it} \qquad i \in M , \ t \in T$$

$$\sum_{i \in M} a_i \ X_{it} \leq C_t \qquad t \in T$$

$$X_{it}, I_{it} \geq 0 \qquad i \in M , \ t \in T$$

$$\delta(X_{it}) = 1, \text{ if } X_{it} > 0$$
$$= 0, \text{ otherwise} \qquad i \in M , \ t \in T$$

where

S_i	=	setup cost for product family i
h_i	=	holding cost per unit and period for product family i
d_{it}	=	effective net-requirement of product family i in period t
a_i	=	production time per unit for product family i
C_t	=	capacity available in period t

and the decision variables are

X_{it}	=	lot size of product i in period t
I_{it}	=	inventory of product i at the end of period t
$\delta(X_{it})$	=	binary decision variable indicating whether product i is set up in period t or not

For the aggregation of item demand into net-requirements of product families, the concept of effective net-requirements has been introduced by Hax and Meal [49]. This concept allows consistent disaggregation at the item level (see Section 5.3).

To predict the external demand of items over the aggregate planning horizon, the company uses an interactive forecasting approach. The **net-requirement** d_{jt} of an item $j \in J$ in period $t \in T$ is obtained by balancing the forecasted item demand f_{jt} and the desired safety stock ss_{jt} against inventories I_{j0} available at the beginning of the planning horizon.

$$d_{jt} = \min \left\{ \max \left\{ 0 ; - I_{j0} + ss_{jt} + \sum_{k \leq t} f_{jk} \right\} ; f_{jt} \right\}$$

$$j \in J, \ t \in T \qquad (1)$$

Finally, **effective net-requirements** d_{it} for all product families $i \in M$ are computed by summing the individual net-requirements over all items $j \in J(i)$ belonging to product family i.

$$d_{it} = \sum_{j \in J(i)} d_{jt} \qquad i \in M, \ t \in T \qquad (2)$$

Due to the numerical complexity of the capacitated lot size problem, an optimal solution within reasonable computer time is not available so far (see Bitran and Yanasse [20], Florian et. al. [36], and Schrage [69]) except for the case of a single item (Baker et. al. [13]). Various heuristic solution procedures for the multi-item capacitated lot size problem have been suggested in the literature (see de Bodt et. al. [30] and van Wassenhove and Maes [72] for a review and critique). Heuristics of the **period-by-period** type are proposed by Lambrecht and Vanderveken [57], Dixon and Silver [32], and Dogramaci et. al. [33] among others. These heuristics are easy to implement und quite effective as well. A numerical investigation by Maes and van Wassenhove [60] shows that these heuristics yield solutions with an average deviation of only 1% from optimality for a number of test problems.

It is common to all period-by-period heuristics that they develop production quantities for the current period using some basic lot size criterion, then proceed to the next period and repeat the process until the end of the horizon is reached. In a situation, where several products compete for a scarce resource, a **priority index** is applied in order to subsequently allocate capacity among products which need to be set up. The priority index, usually based on one of the well known unconstrained dynamic lot-sizing heuristics, indicates cost savings which can be gained by increasing the lot size of a particular product. In the current period, lot sizes are increased further, until no more capacity is available or no more potential cost savings can be achieved.

However, if total demand exceeds the available capacity in the remainder of the horizon, then some kind of **capacity balancing** must be performed in order to ensure feasibility. Again, products are arranged with respect to a priority index indicating additional costs incurred by the pre-production of future requirements. The lot size for the product with the least cost penalty is increased and the procedure is repeated until the capacity overload is balanced.

The logic of a period-by-period heuristic recently suggested by Günther [46] is explained in the following. (For a detailed description of the heuristic the reader is referred to the original publication.) The major steps consituting the heuristic are outlined in Figure 10.

For all periods k=1 to H-1, perform the following steps:

> Repeat the following steps,
>
> > Evaluate marginal cost savings associated with an increased lot size for all products which need to be set up in the current period according to (3).
> >
> > Select the product with the maximum positive marginal cost saving and increase the lot size.
>
> until no more cost savings can be achieved or the capacity available is insufficient to increase any lot size further.
>
> While capacity in the future periods is overloaded perform the following steps:
>
> > For all products, evaluate additional costs incurred by pre-production of future requirements according to (4).
> >
> > Select the product with the minimum cost penalty and in-crease the lot size.

Fig. 10: <u>Structogram of the lot-sizing heuristic</u>

Assume that a lot of some product i, scheduled in the current period k, already satisfies the demand of T_i periods. If the next requirement d_{ip} (from period p(i)) is included in the lot size, the expected **marginal cost savings per unit of capacity absorbed** can be expressed as

$$u_i = [\ 2\ s_i\ /\ h_i\ -\ d_{ip}\ T_i\ (p(i)-k+1)\ ]\ /\ (d_{ip}\ a_i) \tag{3}$$

This coefficient (based on Groff's [44] criterion for unconstrained single product lot-sizing) is computed for all products which need to be set up. Only for the product with the maximum positive value of the priority index u_i ist the lot size increased. This procedure is repeated, as long as cost savings can be achieved and capacity is available in the current period.

A solution to the capacitated lot size problem is feasible, if the cumulative capacity requirements do not exceed the cumulative capacity available with respect to any future period. Otherwise, future requirements must be satisfied by pre-production in the current period. Shifting some q_{ip} units of product i from a future period p(i) to the current period k causes additional holding and setup costs. The **cost increase per unit of capacity absorbed**

$$v_i = [(p(i)-k) q_{ip} h_i + S_i (1-\delta(X_{ik}))] / (q_{ip} a_i) \qquad (4)$$

serves as a priority index in capacity balancing. Only for the product with the minimum value of the priority index v_i is the current lot size X_{ik} increased in order to reduce the capacity overload in the remainder of the horizon. This procedure is repeated, until feasibility is ensured over the entire horizon. The lot-sizing procedure then continues with the next period until the end of the horizon is reached.

The heuristics of Lambrecht and Vanderveken [57], Dixon and Silver [32], and Günther [46] not only differ in their lot-sizing criteria, but also in the way in which they ensure feasibility. The first two approaches are based on the Silver and Meal [70] and the latter on Groff's [44] lot sizing criterion. Lambrecht/Vanderveken and Dixon/ Silver use a feedback and a lookahead procedure, respectively, while Günther derives upper and lower bounds for the pre-production of future requirements by reformulating the capacity constraints. These bounds are included in the lot-sizing procedure in order to prevent infeasibilities.

5.2 A scheduling and sequencing heuristic

The decision problem to solve in the detailed scheduling and sequencing sub-system (see Section 3.2) is assigning product families to basic periods. Mathematically, this problem can be stated as a mixed integer mathematical program.

Minimize

$$\sum_{p \in P} \sum_{i \in M} (z_{ip} S_i + I_{ip} h_i)$$

subject to

$$I_{i,p-1} + y_{ip} A_i - d_{ip} = I_{ip} \qquad i \in M, p \in P$$

$$\sum_{i \in M} y_{ip} \leq 1 \qquad p \in P$$

$$z_{ip} \geq y_{ip} - y_{i,p-1} \qquad i \in M, p \in P$$

$$I_{ip} \geq 0 \qquad i \in M, p \in P$$

$$y_{ip}, z_{ip} \in \{0,1\} \qquad i \in M, p \in P$$

In addition to the symbols already defined in the previous section, we use the following notation:

p = basic period ($p \in P$)

A_i = output of product family i per basic period

h_i = holding cost per unit and basic period for product family i

d_{ip} = effective net-requirement of product family i in basic period p

The decision variables are

y_{ip} = 1, if product family i is produced during period p

= 0, otherwise

z_{ip} = 1, if product family i is set up in period p

= 0, otherwise

I_{ip} = inventory of product family i at the end of period p

Instead of finding the mathematical optimum of the above decision problem, a simple heuristic procedure is suggested (see Günther [45]).

Assume that a total number of N lot sizes X_{it} for product families $i \in M$ to be scheduled in planning period (week) t have been determined in the aggregate production plan. For reasons of convenience, let us number the batches in **topological order** with the first N positive integers, such that n* < n indicates that batch n* is located in the same or in an earlier period in the aggregate plan as batch n (i.e. the N_1 batches from the first planning period occupy the first N_1 numbers, the N_2 batches from the second period occupy the next N_2 numbers, etc.). Henceforth, lot sizes are denoted by X_n without respect to the particular product family being manufactured and the original planning period.

In addition, an **index** $i(n)$ is defined so as to identify the particular product family to be manufactured with batch n. Accordingly, $N(i)$ is defined as the index set to include all batches of product family i.

For each batch $n \in N(i)$, an **immediate predecessor** $n* \in N(i)$ is defined as the last batch of the same product family $i(n)$ scheduled prior to n. If no immediate predecessor exists because batch n is the first one of product family i in the schedule, then $n* = 0$ is assumed.

A particular product must be scheduled whenever its stock is insufficient to meet the requirements in the particular period. Accordingly, for each batch $n \in N$ a **regeneration period** r_n can be determined as the latest period in which the batch must be scheduled in order to meet the customer service requirements. Assume that product family $i(n)$ under consideration was previously scheduled in batch $n*$ and let t_0 denote the beginning of the decision window. Consequently, the regeneration period can be obtained as the time supply of the immediate predecessor $n*$ (i.e. r_n is the period in which the cumulated net-requirements of product $i(n)$ equal the lot size X_{n*} of batch $n*$).

$$r_n = \min_{p \geq r_{n*}} \{ p : X_{n*} \leq \sum_{r=r_{n*}}^{p} d_{nr} \} \qquad n \in N \qquad (5)$$

with $X_0 = 0$ and $r_0 = t_0$

Subsequently, batches are **renumbered** such that $r_1 < r_2 < \ldots < r_N$ and earliest and latest start times can be calculated for all batches according to their sequence.

Each batch $n \in N$ requires a processing time of $X_n a_n$ units depending on the specific product family $i(n)$ to be manufactured. The first batch in the sequence (n=1) is started at the beginning of the decision window (period t_0). All other batches (n=2,...,N) can be scheduled after the preceding batch n-1 is completed. Thus, we obtain the **earliest start time** EST_n of the first batch as

$$EST_1 = t_0 \tag{6a}$$

and of all other batches $(n=2,\ldots,N)$ as

$$EST_n = EST_{n-1} + X_{n-1}\, a_{n-1} \tag{6b}$$

The **latest start time** LST_n of batch n depends on its regeneration period and the latest start times of all succeeding batches. Beginning with the last batch

$$LST_N = r_N \tag{7a}$$

we are able to calculate latest starting times recursively for all preceding batches $n=N-1,\ldots,1$

$$LST_n = \min\{\, r_n \,;\, LST_{n+1} - X_n\, a_n \,\} \tag{7b}$$

The slack time ST_n of a batch $n=1,\ldots,N$ is defined as the difference between the earliest and latest start time.

$$ST_n = LST_n - EST_n \tag{8}$$

If all slack times ST_n are greater than or equal to zero, then the given lot sizes lead to a feasible schedule and all batches may be scheduled at their latest start times. If interferences occur (indicated by negative slack times), then the size of the first batch n- with a negative slack time is reduced by $-(ST_{n-}\, a_{n-})$ units in order to meet the service requirements without backordering. As a consequence, the regeneration periods of all successive batches of the same product family are adjusted, all batches in the remainder of the horizon are renumbered according to their regeneration periods and the earliest and latest start times are re-calculated.

This procedure is repeated, until a feasible solution is obtained. The major steps constituting the proposed heuristic are outlined in Figure 11.

For all batches n∈N, perform the following steps:

> Determine the regeneration period r_n according to (5) and renumber the batches in increasing order of r_n.

> Calculate the earliest and latest start time and the slack time according to (6), (7), and (8).

> Schedule each batch at the latest start time.

While at least one batch with a negative slack time exists, perform the following steps:

> Determine the first batch n- with a negative slack time ST_{n-}.

> Reduce the size of batch n- by $-(ST_{n-}\ a_{n-})$ units.

> Update the regeneration period r_n according to (5) for all succeeding batches of product family i(n-) and renumber all batches in the remainder of the horizon in increasing order of r_n.

> Re-calculate the earliest and latest start time and the slack time for all batches in the remainder of the horizon according to (6), (7), and (8).

Fig. 11: <u>Structogram of the scheduling and sequencing heuristic</u>

5.3 Equalization of run out times

Given a sequence n=1,...,N of final lot sizes X_n and their timing, production quantities of items have to be determined. According to the consistency conditions, defined in Section 3.3, we need to determine item quantities x_{jn} such that the product flow between both production stages is balanced

$$\sum_{j \in J(n)} x_{jn} = X_n \qquad n \in N \tag{9}$$

and requirements of all items are satisfied until the particular product family is set up again

$$x_{jn} \geq \sum_{p=r_n}^{r_{n'}-1} d_{jp} \qquad n \in N, \; j \in J(n) \tag{10}$$

In expression (10), n' denotes the **immediate successor** of batch n, i.e. the next batch of the same product family $i(n)$ scheduled after batch n, and r_n and $r_{n'}$ are the regeneration periods according to (5). If no immediate successor exists because batch n is the last one of product family $i(n)$ in the schedule, then $r_{n'} = R+1$ is assumed, where R is the last period within the decision window.

In order to equalize run out times of items belonging to the same product family we disaggregate a product family based lot size X_n into production quantities x_{jn} of items by

$$x_{jn} = X_n \; [\; \sum_{p=r_n}^{r_{n'}-1} d_{jp} \; / \; \sum_{k \in J(n)} \sum_{p=r_n}^{r_{n'}-1} d_{kp} \qquad n \in N, \; j \in J(n) \tag{11}$$

This simple decision rule is easy to implement and promises to perform well in the production environment considered here. However, more sophisticated disaggregation procedures can be found in the literature (e.g. Bitran et. al. [15], Bitran and Hax [17,18], and Hax and Golovin [48]).

5.4 Allocation of inventory intake and outlet among warehouses

In the final disaggregation step, the output of items $j \in J$ in basic periods $p \in P$ has to be allocated among the warehouses $w \in W$ and it is decided from where to dispatch customer orders. The decision problem to solve can be formulated as a linear program.

Minimize

$$\sum_{j \in J} \sum_{p \in P} \sum_{w \in W} (I_{jpw} \, h_{jw} + u_{jpw} \, h^+_{jw} + v_{jpw} \, h^-_{jw})$$

subject to

$$I_{jpw} = I_{j,p-1,w} + u_{jpw} - v_{jpw} \qquad j \in J, \; p \in P, \; w \in W$$

$$\sum_{w \in W} v_{jpw} \geq f_{jp} \qquad j \in J, \; p \in P$$

$$\sum_{w \in W} I_{jpw} \geq ss_{jp} \qquad j \in J, \; p \in P$$

$$\sum_{w \in W} u_{jpw} \geq x_{jp} \qquad j \in J, \; p \in P$$

$$\sum_{j \in J} I_{jpw} \, b_j \leq B \qquad p \in P, \; w=1$$

where

u_{jpw} = production quantity of item j in basic period p, stored in warehouse w

v_{jpw} = quantity of item j dispatched in basic period p from warehouse w

I_{jpw} = inventory of item j at the end of basic period p in warehouse w (initial inventory given)

h_{jw} = holding cost per unit and basic period for item j in warehouse w

h^+_{jw} = handling cost per unit of item j, stored in warehouse w

h^-_{jw} = handling cost per unit of item j, dispatched from warehouse w

x_{jp} = output of item j in basic period p (given from the upper planning level)

f_{jp} = demand of item j in basic period p

ss_{jp} = safety stock of item j in basic period p

b_j = storage space per unit of item j in the central warehouse (in pallets per ton)

B = storage capacity in the central warehouse (in pallets)

Instead of solving the above linear programming model, a simple heuristic procedure, yielding solutions very close to optimality, can be applied (see Feser et. al. [35]). The essence of this approach is to maximize inventory turnover in the central warehouse. The proposed heuristic proceeds as follows:

In an initial solution step, total required storage space is calculated for all basic periods in the decision window without taking restrictions on storage capacity into account. If central storage capacity is sufficient, then a feasible solution is already achieved. Otherwise, some excess output must be directed to the external warehouse.

Let there be a basic period p* which is the first one within the decision window where central storage capacity runs short. It is clear that some output of those items produced in p* or prior to p* must be stored in the external warehouse. An index set J* is defined to include relevant items. For all items j∈J* the minimum inventory L_j in the central warehouse over the remainder of the decision window is calculated. The excess storage requirement of period p* (denoted by E_{p*}) is allocated among items j∈J* proportional to their minimum inventory L_j in the central warehouse. The quantity e_j of item j∈J* to be directed to the external warehouse is obtained by

$$e_j = (E_{p*} / b_j) (L_j / \sum_{k \in J*} L_k) \qquad j \in J* \qquad (12)$$

Assuming that orders are always dispatched from the central warehouse first, inventory balances are updated. The procedure is repeated until storage capacity requirements are balanced for all periods within the decision window.

6. Concluding remarks

This paper was concerned with the design of an hierarchical model for production planning and scheduling in a real-life case study. Instead of formulating a monolithic optimization model, the overall decision problem was partitioned into four sub-problems which are linked in an hierarchical fashion. Thus, the complexity of the decision problem could considerably be reduced. Heuristics were proposed for each of the sub-problems taking special care in computational efficiency with respect to interactive decision making.

Levels within the planning hierarchy were partitioned according to the organizational structure and the sequential planning process which has been implicitly applied by the company for many years. As stochastic fluctuations in external demand were identified as the major source of changes in input data, suggestions were made in order to decouple the aggregate and detailed planning level. Lot-sizing for product families was assigned to the aggregate level, whereas sequencing of batches and disaggregation of item based production quantities were assigned to the detailed level. Furthermore, the concept of a decision window was introduced for detailed scheduling and sequencing and the subsequent disaggregation task.

Aggregate decisions on lot sizes are made first using effective net-requirements for all product families as input and impose constraints upon the more detailed decisions. For a given aggregate plan, a feasible sequence in the production process does not necessarily exist. If interferences and/or backorders occur lot sizes are adjusted accordingly. In practice, lot sizes are rarely adjusted since a considerable amount of slack capacity is available in most periods. A lot sequence satisfying the effective demand of all product families over the decision window also ensures a feasible and consistent disaggregation for items and their allocation among storage locations.

In order to simplify the description of the hierarchical model, it has been purposely ignored in this paper that lot sizes may be affected by the different costs of the storage locations and that processing times of batches actually depend on the mix of items within the lot size of a product family. However, the suggested hierarchical model can easily be extended to consider these aspects.

Numerical investigations have shown that the proposed heuristics perform well compared with other applicable solution procedures. Clearly, linking the different sub-models in an hierarchical fashion can produce highly suboptimal solutions with respect to the overall decision problem. However, in the case study considered here results of a simulation study (Feser et. al. [27]) promise considerable cost savings to be gained from improved coordination of interacting planning activities.

7. References

[1]   **P. Afentakis,** Simultaneous lot sizing and sequencing for multi-stage production systems, Working paper #84-003, Department of Industrial Engineering and Operations Research, Syracuse University, 1985.

[2]   **H. Andersson, S. Axsäter, H. Jönsson,** Hierarchical material requirements planning, International Journal of Production Research 19 (1981) 45-57.

[3]   **Ö.A. Aras, L.A. Swanson,** A lot sizing and sequencing algorithm for dynamic demands upon a single facility, Journal of Operations Management 2 (1982) 177-185.

[4]   **R.J. Armstrong, A.C. Hax,** Design of a naval tender shop, Applied Mathematical Programming, St. Bradley et. al., editors, (Addison-Wesley, Reading, 1977) 425-452.

[5]   **S. Axsäter,** Coordinating control of production-inventory systems, International Journal of Production Research 14 (1976) 669-688.

[6]   **S. Axsäter,** Aggregation of product data for hierarchical production planning, Operations Research 29 (1981) 745-756.

[7]   **S. Axsäter,** Decentralized production planning and choice of organizational structure, International Journal of Production Research 20 (1982) 17-26.

[8]   **S. Axsäter,** Feasibility of aggregate production plans, Research Report No. 78, Linköping Institute of Technology, 1983.

[9]   **S. Axsäter, H. Jönsson,** Aggregation and disaggregation in hierarchical production planning, European Journal of Operational Research 17 (1984) 355-361.

[10] **H.C. Bahl, L.P. Ritzman,** An empirical investigation of different strategies for material requirements planning, Journal of Operations Management 3 (1983) 67-77.

[11] **K.R. Baker,** An experimental study of the effectiveness of rolling schedules in production planning, Decision Sciences 8 (1977) 19-27.

[12] **K.R. Baker,** An analysis of terminal conditions in rolling schedules, European Journal of Operational Research 7 (1981) 355-361.

[13] **K.R. Baker, P. Dixon, M.J. Magazine, E.A. Silver,** An algorithm for the dynamic lot-size problem with time varying production capacity constraints, Management Science 24 (1978) 1710-1720.

[14] **K.R. Baker, D.W. Peterson,** An analytical framework for evaluating rolling schedules, Management Science 25 (1979) 341-351.

[15] **G.R. Bitran, E.A. Haas, A.C. Hax,** Hierarchical production planning: a single stage system, Operations Research 29 (1981) 717-743.

[16] **G.R. Bitran, E.A. Haas, A.C. Hax,** Hierarchical production planning: a two-stage system, Operations Research 30 (1982) 232-251.

[17] **G.R. Bitran, A.C. Hax,** On the design of hierarchical production planning systems, Decision Sciences 8 (1977) 28-55.

[18] **G.R. Bitran, A.C. Hax,** Disaggregation and resource allocation using convex knapsack problems with bounded variables, Management Science 27 (1981) 431-441.

[19] **G.R. Bitran, A.R. von Ellenrieder,** A hierarchical approach for for the planning of a complex production system, Disaggregation problems in manufacturing and service organizations, L.P. Ritzman et. al., editors, (Martinus Nijhof, Boston, 1979) 107-125.

[20] **G.R. Bitran, H.H. Yanasse,** Conputational complexity of the capacitated lot size problem, Management Science 28 (1982) 1174-1186.

[21] **J.D. Blackburn, R.A. Millen,** Heuristic lot-sizing performance in in a rolling schedule environment, Decision Sciences 11 (1980) 691-701.

[22] **J.D. Blackburn, R.A. Millen,** The impact of a rolling schedule in a multi-level MRP system, Journal of Operations Management 2 (1982) 125-135.

[23] **K. Boskma,** Aggregation and the design of models for medium term planning of production, European Journal of Operational Research 10 (1982) 244-249.

[24] **R.C. Carlson, S.L. Beckman, D.H. Kropp,** The effectiveness of extending the horizon in rolling production scheduling, Decision Sciences 13 (1982) 129-146.

[25] **R.C. Carlson, J.V. Jucker, D.H. Kropp,** Less nervous MRP systems: a dynamic economic lot-sizing approach, Management Science 25 (1979) 754-761.

[26] **S. Chand,** A note on dynamic lot-sizing in rolling-horizon environment, Decision Sciences 13 (1982) 113-119.

[27] **S. Chand,** Rolling horizon procedures for the facilities in series inventory model with nested schedules, Management Science 29 (1983) 237-249.

[28] **J. Chen Chuan, J.B. Lasserre, F. Roubellat,** Hierarchical planning: a case study, Operational Research '81, J.P. Brans, editor, (Elsevier, Amsterdam, 1981) 539-552.

[29] **Ch.-H. Chung, L.J. Krajewski,** Planning horizons for master production scheduling, Journal of Operations Management 4 (1984) 389-406.

[30] **M.A. De Bodt, L.F. Gelders, L.N. Van Wassenhove,** Lot sizing under dynamic demand conditions, Engineering Costs and Pro duction Economics 8 (1984) 165-187.

[31] **H.A.H. Dempster, M.L. Fisher, L. Jansen, B.J. Lageweg, J.K. Lenstra, A.H.G. Rinnooy Kan,** Analytical evaluation of hierarchical planning systems, Operations Research 29 (1981) 707-716.

[32] **P.S. Dixon, E.A. Silver,** A heuristic solution procedure for the multi-item, single-level, limited capacity, lot-sizing problem, Journal of Operations Management 2 (1981) 23-39.

[33] **A. Dogramaci, J.C. Panayiotopoulos, N.R. Adam**, The dynamic lot-sizing problem for multiple items under limited capacity, AIIE-Transactions 13 (1981) 294-303.

[34] **R.C. Dorsey, T.J. Hodgson, H.D. Ratcliff**, A network approach to a multi-facility, multi-product production scheduling problem without backordering, Management Science 21 (1975) 813-822.

[35] **P. Feser, H.O. Günther, Ch. Schneeweiß**, Coordination of production schedules and distribution (a case study), Engineering Costs and Production Economics 9 (1985) 185-192.

[36] **M. Florian, J.K. Lenstra, A.M.G. Rinooy Kan**, Deterministic production planning: Algorithm and complexity, Management Science 26 (1980) 669-679.

[37] **G. Fontan, S. Imbert, C. Mercé**, Consistency analysis in a hierarchical production planning system, Engineering Costs and Production Economics 9 (1985) 193-199.

[38] **H. Gabbay**, Optimal aggregation and disaggregation in hierarchical planning, Disaggregation problems in manufacturing and service organizations, L.P. Ritzman et. al., editors, (Martinus Nijhof, Boston, 1979) 95-106.

[39] **H. Gabbay**, Multi-stage production planning, Management Science 25 (1979) 1138-1148.

[40] **L.F. Gelders, L.N. Van Wassenhove**, Hierarchical integration in production planning: theory and practice, Journal of Operations Management 3 (1982) 27-35.

[41] **L.F. Gelders, P.R. Kleindorfer**, Coordinating aggregate and detailed scheduling decisions in the one-machine job shop: Part I. Theory, Operations Research 22 (1974) 46-60.

[42] **L.F. Gelders, P.R. Kleindorfer**, Coordinating aggregate and detailed scheduling decisions in the one-machine job shop: Part II. Computation and structure, Operations Research 23 (1975) 312-324.

[43] **S.C. Graves**, Using lagrangian techniques to solve hierarchical production planning problems, Management Science 28 (1982) 260-275.

[44] **G.K. Groff**, A lot sizing rule for time phased component demand, Production and Inventory Management 20 (1979) 47-53.

[45] **H.O. Günther**, Revidierende Produktionsplanung bei Sortenfertigung Operations Research Proceedings 1984, Papers of the 13th annual meeting (Springer, Heidelberg, 1985) 140-147.

[46] **H.O. Günther**, Planning lot sizes and capacity requirements in a single stage production system, paper presented at EURO VII, Seventh European Congress on Operational Research, Bologna, Italy, June 16-19, 1985.

[47] **A.C. Hax**, Integration of strategic and tactical planning in the aluminum industry, Applied Mathematical Programming, St. Bradley et. al., editors, (Addison- Wesley, Reading, 1977) 269-290.

[48] **A.C. Hax, J.J. Golovin**, Hierarchical production planning systems, Studies in Operations Management, A.C. Hax, editor, (Elsevier, Amsterdam, 1978) 400-428.

[49] **A.C. Hax, H.C. Meal**, Hierarchical integration of production planning and scheduling, TIMS Studies in Management Science, Vol. 1, Logistics, M. Geisler, editor, (Elsevier, Amsterdam, 1975) 53-69.

[50] **H. Jönsson**, Simulation studies of hierarchical systems in production and inventory control, Ph.D. Thesis, Linköping Studies in Science and Technology, No. 91 (Linköping University, 1983).

[51] **U.S. Karmarkar**, Equalization of runout times, Operations Research 29 (1981) 757-762.

[52] **D.H. Kropp, R.C. Carlson**, A lot-sizing algorithm for reducing nervousness in MRP systems, Management Science 30 (1984) 240-244.

[53] **D.H. Kropp, R.C. Carlson, S.L. Beckman**, A note on stopping rules for rolling production scheduling, Journal of Operations Management 3 (1983) 113-119.

[54] **D.H. Kropp, R.C. Carlson, J.V. Jucker**, Use of dynamic lot-sizing to avoid nervousness in material requirement planning systems, Production and Inventory Management 20 (1979) 49-57.

[55] **H.C. Kunreuther, T.E. Morton**, Planning horizon for production smoothing with deterministic demands: I. all demand met from regular production, Management Science 20 (1973) 110-125.

[56] **H.C. Kunreuther, T.E. Morton**, Planning horizon for production smoothing with deterministic demands: II. extensions to overtime, undertime and backlogging, Management Science 20 (1974) 1037-1045.

[57] **M.R. Lambrecht, H. Vanderveken**, Heuristic procedures for the single operation, multi-item loading problem, AIIE-Transactions 11 (1979) 319-326.

[58] **J.B. Lasserre, J.P. Martin, F. Roubellat**, Aggregate model and decomposition method for mid-term production planning, International Journal of Production Research 21 (1983) 835-843.

[59] **R.A. Lundin, T.E. Morton**, Planning horizons for the dynamic lot size model: protective procedures and computational results, Operations Research 23 (1975) 711-734.

[60] **J. Maes, L.N. van Wassenhove**, Multi item single level capacitated dynamic lotsizing heuristic: a computational comparison (part I: static case), (part II: rolling horizon), to appear.

[61] **W.L. Maxwell, J.A. Muckstadt**, Coordination of production schedules with shipping schedules, TIMS Studies in the Management Sciences 16 (1981) 127-143.

[62] **J.O. Mc Clain, J. Thomas**, Horizon effects in aggregate production planning with seasonal demand, Management Science 23 (1977) 728-736.

[63] **H.C. Meal**, A study of multi-stage production planning, Studies in Operations Management, A.C. Hax, editor, (Elsevier, Amsterdam, 1978) 253-285.

[64] **L.W. Miller,** Using linear programming to derive planning horizons for a production smoothing problem, Management Science 25 (1979) 1232-1244.

[65] **T.E. Morton,** Universal planning horizons for generalized convex production scheduling, Operations Research 26 (1975) 1046-1058.

[66] **H. Nagasawa, N. Nishiyama, K. Hitomi,** Decision analysis for determining the optimum planning horizon in aggregate production planning, International Journal of Production Research 20 (1982) 243-254.

[67] **J. Olhager, B. Rapp,** Balancing capacity and lot sizes, European Journal of Operational Research (to appear).

[68] **A.-W. Scheer,** Interactive production planning and control, Advances in Production Management Systems, G. Doumeingts, W.A. Carter, editors, (Elsevier, Amsterdam, 1984) 337-348.

[69] **L. Schrage,** The multiproduct lot scheduling problem, Deterministic and stochastic scheduling, M.A. Dempster, J.K. Lenstra, editors, (Reidel, 1982) 233-244.

[70] **E.A. Silver, H.C. Meal,** A heuristic for selecting lot-size quantities for the case of a deterministic time-varying demand rate and discrete opportunities for replenishment, Production and Inventory Management 14 (1973) 64-74.

[71] **E.A. Silver, R. Peterson,** Decision systems for inventory management and production planning, Second edition, (Wiley, New York, 1985).

[72] **L.N. Van Wassenhove, J. Maes,** Multi-item single level capacitated lotsizing heuristics: a critique, Working paper 84-25, Katholieke Universiteit Leuven.

About authors

Sven Axsäter ("Aggregating Items in Multi-Level Lot-Sizing") is Professor of Transportation and Material Flow Systems at Lulea University of Technology. Dr. Axsäter obtained his degree at the Royal Institute of Technology in Stockholm in 1967. His main research interests are multi-stage production/distribution systems and hierarchical planning systems. He is chairman of the European Working Group for Production and Inventory Control. Dr. Axsäter is the author of many scientific papers on production and inventory control and of two text-books.

Siriam Dasu ("Two-Stage Production Planning in a Dynamic Environment") is a Ph.D. student at Sloan School of Management, MIT, Cambridge, Massachusetts, USA. From 1975-1980 he studied Mechanical Engineering at I.I.T. Bombay, and 1980-1982 at Calcutta. From 1982-1983 he was Management Consultant with S.B. Billimoria & Co.

Karel von Donselaar ("Practical Application of the Echelon Approach in a System with Divergent Product Structures") is a Ph.D. student at the Department of Industrial Engineering and Management Science, Eindhoven, University of Technology, Netherlands. He received a M.S. degree in Econometrics at Erasmus University Rotterdam. His research interests are in inventory control and information systems.

Ludo F. Gelders ("A Branch and Bound Algorithmn for the Multi Item Single Level Capacitated Dynamic Lotsizing Problem") is Professor in Industrial Management and Department chairman at the Katholieke Universiteit Leuven. He holds degrees in electromechanical and industrial management. After four years of activity in an industrial company, he started doctoral research. He spent the academic year (70-71) at the MIT Sloan School of Management and got his Ph.D. in industrial mamnagement at K.U. Leuven in 1973. His main research interest is in operations and logistics management. He pusblished several articles in professional journals and he is on the editorial board of international journals such as IEEE Transactions on Engineering Management, European Journal of Operations Research, Engineering Costs and Production Economics, O.R. Spektrum. He is a member of ORSA, TIMS, IIE and PICS. He represents the Belgian O.R. Society within IFORS.

Stephen C. Graves ("Two-Stage Production Planning in a Dynamic Environment") is an Associate Professor of Management Science at the Alfred P. Sloan School of Management, Massachusetts Institute of Technology. He received an A.B. and M.B.A. from Dartmouth College, and a Ph.D. from the University of Rochester. He has published several articles in the area of production and operations management. His current research interests include inventory management, production planning and scheduling.

Hans O. Günther ("The Design of an Hierarchical Model for Production Planning and Scheduling") is lecturer in Computer Science at the University of Mannheim, Fed. Rep. of Germany. He received his Masters degree in General Business Administration (Diplom-Kaufmann) from the University of Saarbrücken (FRG) and his Ph.D. degree in Operations Research from the Free University of Berlin (FRG). His research interests include medium term production planning, flexible labor patterns, material requirements planning, lot-sizing, decision support systems, personal computing.

Claus E. Heinrich ("Multi-Stage Lot-Sizing for General Production Systems") is assistant at the Department of Operations Research at the University of Mannheim (FRG). He holds a masters degree in General

Business Administration (Diplom-Kaufmann) and is currently preparing his doctoral dissertation. His research interests are hierachical production planning, material requirements planning and multi-level lot-sizing. He has co-authored several scientific papers and he is a member of ISIR and of the European Working Group for production and Inventory control.

Henrik Jönsson ("Overview of a Stock Allocation Model for a Two-Echelon Push System Having Identical Units at the Lower Echelon") holds a position as assistant professor in optimization within the Department of Mathematics, Linköping Institute of Technology. He was in November 1977 awarded the degree of Master of Science in Industrial Engineering at Linköping Institute of Technology, Sweden. In March 1983 he was awarded a Ph.D. in Production Economics at the same university. During one academic year beginning in September 1983 Dr. Jönsson worked as a postdoctoral fellow with Professor Silver at the University of Calgary, Canada. Since September 1984 Current research activities and interests concern, for example, coordination of transportation policies and inventory control in multi-echelon inventory systems, buffer dimensioning in public transportation systems and applications of decomposition methods.

Robert Luyten ("System-Based Heuristics for Multi-Echelon Distribution Systems") is assistant at the Department of Applied Economic Sciences of the Katholieke Universiteit Leuven. He holds masters degree in Applied Economics and Managerial Informatics and is currently preparing his doctoral dissertation on "Protective Stocks in Multi-Stage Production/Inventory and MRP-Systems". R. Luyten has co-authored several articles on this subject which appeared a.o. in Engineering Costs and Production Economics and in the International Journal of Production Research.

Johan Maes ("A Branch and Bound Algorithm for the Multi Item Single Level Capacitated Dynamic Lotsizing Problem") is a Ph.D. student at the Katholieke Universiteit Leuven, Division of Industrial Management. He spends the 1985-86 academic year at Cornell University. He holds degrees in mechanical engineering and in industrial management. His research deals with multilevel capacitated production systems.

Harlan C. Meal ("Two-Stage Production Planning in a Dynamic Environment"), currently Senior Lecturer in Operations Management at the Sloan School of Management at MIT. Educated at Harvard University, his doctoral research was in molecular structure. He entered the field of Operations Research in 1953 at the Operations Research Office of Johns Hopkins. He was a consultant in production and distribution planning at Arthur D. Little, Inc., in Cambridge, Brussels and Zurich for many years prior to joining the Sloan School. Primary research interests are in production planning and scheduling, especially the design and implementation of hierarchical planning systems.

John A. Muckstadt ("Planning Component Delivery Intervals in Constrained Assembly Systems") is Professor and director of the Cornell Manufacturing Engineering and Productivity Program (COMEPP). He studied at the University of Rochester for the A.B. degree in mathematics and at the University of Michigan for the M.S. in industrial administration, the M.A. in mathematics, and the Ph.D., granted in 1966, in industrial engineering. He joined the Cornell faculty in 1974 after twelve years of active military service as a faculty member of the Air Force Institute of Technology and an operations research analyst at the Air Force Logistics Command Headtquarters. Professor Muckstadt has served as a consultant to numerous industrial organizations, including the Chicago Pneumatic Tool Company, General Motors,

RAND, and Xerox, and he has been an associate editor of several professional journals. His teaching interests include applied operations research, production and inventory conrol, logistics, manufacturing control, and materials handling. Presently, Professor Muckstadt is conducting research related to manufacturing logistics and inventory control. He has written over 40 papers on these subjects. He is a member of ORSA and TIMS. He is also an Associate Editor of the Naval Research Logistics Quarterly and Operations Research Letters and Area Editor for IIE Transactions.

Henry L.W. Nuttle ("Aggregating Items in Multi-Level Lot-Sizing") is currently Associate Professor of Industrial Engineering at North Carolina State University, Raleigh, NC, USA. He received his B.S. in Mathematics from Dickinson College, Carlisle, Pennsylvania and his Ph.D. in Operations Research from John Hopkins University. Dr. Nuttle's research interests are in the application of operations research to production and logistics problems.

Yuping Qiu is Ph.D. student at Sloan School of Management, MIT, Cambridge, Massachusetts, USA. He got B.S. in mathematics 1982 from Fudan University Shanghai, China. From 1982-1983 he was Teaching Assistant at the Department of Mathematics at that University.

Kaj R. Rosling ("Optimal Lot-Sizing for Dynamic Assembly Systems") is Assistant Professor at Linköping Institute of Technology, Sweden. He received his MBA from the University of Lund, Sweden, and his M.Sc. in Operations Research from the University of California at Berkeley, U.S., and his Ph.D. in Production Economics from Linköping Institute and the University of Karlstadt, Sweden. Professor Rosling is currently doing research in production and inventory control and related financial problems.

Christoph Schneeweiss ("Multi-Stage Lot-Sizing for General Production Systems") is Professor for Operations Research at the University of Mannheim. He holds degrees in physical chemistry, theoretical physics and operations research of the univerities of Frankfurt and Bonn. In 1972 he became Professor for Operations Research at the Free University of Berlin and changed to Mannheim in 1981. Dr. Schneeweiss is author of four books and of many scientific publications on dynamic programming, stochastic control theory and inventory control. He is on the editor board of Engineering Costs and Production Economics and is former co-editor of OR-Spektrum, the official journal of the German OR-society. He is member of DGOR, TIMS and ISIR. Dr. Schneeweiss was President of the German OR-society for the election period 1979/80 and is now Vice President of EURO.

Edward A. Silver ("Overview of a Stock Allocation Model for a Two-Echelon Push System Having Identical Units at the Lower Echelon") is a Professor of management science in the Faculty of Management at the University of Calgary. He received a B.Eng. (Civil) from McGill University and Sc.D. (Operations Research) from the Massachusetts Institute of Technology. He is also a registered professional engineer. Prior to his appointments at Calgary he was a professor in the Department of Management Sciences (Faculty of Engineering) at the University of Waterloo. Other experience includes 4 years with Arthur D. Little, Inc. and sabbatical leaves as a Visiting Professor at the Ecole Polytechnique Federale de Lausanne, Switzerland and at Stanford University. Professor Silver has published over 60 articles in leading professional journals and has co-authored the book, Decision Systems for Inventory Management and Production Planning, John Wiley & Sons, First Edition (1979), Second Edition (1985). He has consulted for a number of industrial and government organizations throughout North

America and has conducted several executive development seminars. His research and consulting activities have centered on the analysis of both tactical and strategic problems arising in the management of operations. Specific areas of application have included capacity planning, inventory management, production planning, logistics management, facilities layout, maintenance management and distribution planning. Dr. Silver is a member of a number of professional societies. He has been particularly active in the Canadian Operational Research Society of which he was the President in 1980-81. During the same year he served as chairman of the Grant Selection Committee for Industrial Engineering of the Natural Sciences and Engineering Research Council of Canada.

Hartmut Stadtler ("Hierarchical Production Planning: Tuning Aggregate Planning with Sequencing and Scheduling") is an assistant at the Operations Research Department at the University of Hamburg. He received a M. Sc. Econ. from the London School of Economics and Political Science, a Diploma in Business Administration and a Ph.D. both from the University of Hamburg. His current research interests focus on production planning and the design of decision support systems.

Luk N. Van Wassenhove ("A Branch and Bound Algorithm for the Multi Item Single Level Capacitated Dynamic Lotsizing Problem") is Assistant Professor in Industrial Management at the Katholieke Universiteit Leuven. He received degrees in mechanical engineering and in industrial management from K.U. He spent the academic year 1977-78 at the Wharton School of the University of Pennsylvania and obtained his Ph.D. degree from K.U. Leuven in 1979. His teaching and research interests are in quantitative approaches to logistics.

Jacob Wijngaard ("Practical Application of the Echelon Approach in a System with Divergent Product Structures") is Professor of Operations Research at the Department of Industrial Engineering and Management Science, Eindhoven University of Technology, Netherlands. He received a M.S. degree in Mathematics at the Free University of Amsterdam and a Ph.D. in Operations Research at Eindhoven University of Technology. His research interests are production and inventory control, stochastic models and manpower planning.

Vol. 184: R. E. Burkard and U. Derigs, Assignment and Matching Problems: Solution Methods with FORTRAN-Programs. VIII, 148 pages. 1980.

Vol. 185: C. C. von Weizsäcker, Barriers to Entry. VI, 220 pages. 1980.

Vol. 186: Ch.-L. Hwang and K. Yoon, Multiple Attribute Decision Making – Methods and Applications. A State-of-the-Art-Survey. XI, 259 pages. 1981.

Vol. 187: W. Hock, K. Schittkowski, Test Examples for Nonlinear Programming Codes. V. 178 pages. 1981.

Vol. 188: D. Bös, Economic Theory of Public Enterprise. VII, 142 pages. 1981.

Vol. 189: A. P. Lüthi, Messung wirtschaftlicher Ungleichheit. IX, 287 pages. 1981.

Vol. 190: J. N. Morse, Organizations: Multiple Agents with Multiple Criteria. Proceedings, 1980. VI, 509 pages. 1981.

Vol. 191: H. R. Sneessens, Theory and Estimation of Macroeconomic Rationing Models. VII, 138 pages. 1981.

Vol. 192: H. J. Bierens: Robust Methods and Asymptotic Theory in Nonlinear Econometrics. IX, 198 pages. 1981.

Vol. 193: J. K. Sengupta, Optimal Decisions under Uncertainty. VII, 156 pages. 1981.

Vol. 194: R. W. Shephard, Cost and Production Functions. XI, 104 pages. 1981.

Vol. 195: H. W. Ursprung, Die elementare Katastrophentheorie. Eine Darstellung aus der Sicht der Ökonomie. VII, 332 pages. 1982.

Vol. 196: M. Nermuth, Information Structures in Economics. VIII, 236 pages. 1982.

Vol. 197: Integer Programming and Related Areas. A Classified Bibliography. 1978 – 1981. Edited by R. von Randow. XIV, 338 pages. 1982.

Vol. 198: P. Zweifel, Ein ökonomisches Modell des Arztverhaltens. XIX, 392 Seiten. 1982.

Vol. 199: Evaluating Mathematical Programming Techniques. Proceedings, 1981. Edited by J.M. Mulvey. XI, 379 pages. 1982.

Vol. 200: The Resource Sector in an Open Economy. Edited by H. Siebert. IX, 161 pages. 1984.

Vol. 201: P. M. C. de Boer, Price Effects in Input-Output-Relations: A Theoretical and Empirical Study for the Netherlands 1949–1967. X, 140 pages. 1982.

Vol. 202: U. Witt, J. Perske, SMS – A Program Package for Simulation and Gaming of Stochastic Market Processes and Learning Behavior. VII, 266 pages. 1982.

Vol. 203: Compilation of Input-Output Tables. Proceedings, 1981. Edited by J. V. Skolka. VII, 307 pages. 1982.

Vol. 204: K.C. Mosler, Entscheidungsregeln bei Risiko: Multivariate stochastische Dominanz. VII, 172 Seiten. 1982.

Vol. 205: R. Ramanathan, Introduction to the Theory of Economic Growth. IX, 347 pages. 1982.

Vol. 206: M.H. Karwan, V. Lotfi, J. Telgen, and S. Zionts, Redundancy in Mathematical Programming. VII, 286 pages. 1983.

Vol. 207: Y. Fujimori, Modern Analysis of Value Theory. X, 165 pages. 1982.

Vol. 208: Econometric Decision Models. Proceedings, 1981. Edited by J. Gruber. VI, 364 pages. 1983.

Vol. 209: Essays and Surveys on Multiple Criteria Decision Making. Proceedings, 1982. Edited by P. Hansen. VII, 441 pages. 1983.

Vol. 210: Technology, Organization and Economic Structure. Edited by R. Sato and M. J. Beckmann. VIII, 195 pages. 1983.

Vol. 211: P. van den Heuvel, The Stability of a Macroeconomic System with Quantity Constraints. VII, 169 pages. 1983.

Vol. 212: R. Sato and T. Nôno, Invariance Principles and the Structure of Technology. V, 94 pages. 1983.

Vol. 213: Aspiration Levels in Bargaining and Economic Decision Making. Proceedings, 1982. Edited by R. Tietz. VIII, 406 pages. 1983.

Vol. 214: M. Faber, H. Niemes und G. Stephan, Entropie, Umweltschutz und Rohstoffverbrauch. IX, 181 Seiten. 1983.

Vol. 215: Semi-Infinite Programming and Applications. Proceedings, 1981. Edited by A. V. Fiacco and K. O. Kortanek. XI, 322 pages. 1983.

Vol. 216: H. H. Müller, Fiscal Policies in a General Equilibrium Model with Persistent Unemployment. VI, 92 pages. 1983.

Vol. 217: Ch. Grootaert, The Relation Between Final Demand and Income Distribution. XIV, 105 pages. 1983.

Vol. 218: P. van Loon, A Dynamic Theory of the Firm: Production, Finance and Investment. VII, 191 pages. 1983.

Vol. 219: E. van Damme, Refinements of the Nash Equilibrium Concept. VI, 151 pages. 1983.

Vol. 220: M. Aoki, Notes on Economic Time Series Analysis: System Theoretic Perspectives. IX, 249 pages. 1983.

Vol. 221: S. Nakamura, An Inter-Industry Translog Model of Prices and Technical Change for the West German Economy. XIV, 290 pages. 1984.

Vol. 222: P. Meier, Energy Systems Analysis for Developing Countries. VI, 344 pages. 1984.

Vol. 223: W. Trockel, Market Demand. VIII, 205 pages. 1984.

Vol. 224: M. Kiy, Ein disaggregiertes Prognosesystem für die Bundesrepublik Deutschland. XVIII, 276 Seiten. 1984.

Vol. 225: T. R. von Ungern-Sternberg, Zur Analyse von Märkten mit unvollständiger Nachfragerinformation. IX, 125 Seiten. 1984

Vol. 226: Selected Topics in Operations Research and Mathematical Economics. Proceedings, 1983. Edited by G. Hammer and D. Pallaschke. IX, 478 pages. 1984.

Vol. 227: Risk and Capital. Proceedings, 1983. Edited by G. Bamberg and K. Spremann. VII, 306 pages. 1984.

Vol. 228: Nonlinear Models of Fluctuating Growth. Proceedings, 1983. Edited by R. M. Goodwin, M. Krüger and A. Vercelli. XVII, 277 pages. 1984.

Vol. 229: Interactive Decision Analysis. Proceedings, 1983. Edited by M. Grauer and A. P. Wierzbicki. VIII, 269 pages. 1984.

Vol. 230: Macro-Economic Planning with Conflicting Goals. Proceedings, 1982. Edited by M. Despontin, P. Nijkamp and J. Spronk. VI, 297 pages. 1984.

Vol. 231: G. F. Newell, The M/M/∞ Service System with Ranked Servers in Heavy Traffic. XI, 126 pages. 1984.

Vol. 232: L. Bauwens, Bayesian Full Information Analysis of Simultaneous Equation Models Using Integration by Monte Carlo. VI, 114 pages. 1984.

Vol. 233: G. Wagenhals, The World Copper Market. XI, 190 pages. 1984.

Vol. 234: B.C. Eaves, A Course in Triangulations for Solving Equations with Deformations. III, 302 pages. 1984.

Vol. 235: Stochastic Models in Reliability Theory. Proceedings, 1984. Edited by S. Osaki and Y. Hatoyama. VII, 212 pages. 1984.

Vol. 236: G. Gandolfo, P.C. Padoan, A Disequilibrium Model of Real and Financial Accumulation in an Open Economy. VI, 172 pages. 1984.

Vol. 237: Misspecification Analysis. Proceedings, 1983. Edited by T. K. Dijkstra. V, 129 pages. 1984.

Vol. 238: W. Domschke, A. Drexl, Location and Layout Planning. IV, 134 pages. 1985.

Vol. 239: Microeconomic Models of Housing Markets. Edited by K. Stahl. VII, 197 pages. 1985.

Vol. 240: Contributions to Operations Research. Proceedings, 1984. Edited by K. Neumann and D. Pallaschke. V, 190 pages. 1985.

Vol. 241: U. Wittmann, Das Konzept rationaler Preiserwartungen. XI, 310 Seiten. 1985.

Vol. 242: Decision Making with Multiple Objectives. Proceedings, 1984. Edited by Y. Y. Haimes and V. Chankong. XI, 571 pages. 1985.

Vol. 243: Integer Programming and Related Areas. A Classified Bibliography 1981–1984. Edited by R. von Randow. XX, 386 pages. 1985.

Vol. 244: Advances in Equilibrium Theory. Proceedings, 1984. Edited by C. D. Aliprantis, O. Burkinshaw and N. J. Rothman. II, 235 pages. 1985.

Vol. 245: J. E. M. Wilhelm, Arbitrage Theory. VII, 114 pages. 1985.

Vol. 246: P. W. Otter, Dynamic Feature Space Modelling, Filtering and Self-Tuning Control of Stochastic Systems. XIV, 177 pages. 1985.

Vol. 247: Optimization and Discrete Choice in Urban Systems. Proceedings, 1983. Edited by B. G. Hutchinson, P. Nijkamp and M. Batty. VI, 371 pages. 1985.

Vol. 248: Plural Rationality and Interactive Decision Processes. Proceedings, 1984. Edited by M. Grauer, M. Thompson and A. P. Wierzbicki. VI, 354 pages. 1985.

Vol. 249: Spatial Price Equilibrium: Advances in Theory, Computation and Application. Proceedings, 1984. Edited by P. T. Harker. VII, 277 pages. 1985.

Vol. 250: M. Roubens, Ph. Vincke, Preference Modelling. VIII, 94 pages. 1985.

Vol. 251: Input-Output Modeling. Proceedings, 1984. Edited by A. Smyshlyaev. VI, 261 pages. 1985.

Vol. 252: A. Birolini, On the Use of Stochastic Processes in Modeling Reliability Problems. VI, 105 pages. 1985.

Vol. 253: C. Withagen, Economic Theory and International Trade in Natural Exhaustible Resources. VI, 172 pages. 1985.

Vol. 254: S. Müller, Arbitrage Pricing of Contingent Claims. VIII, 151 pages. 1985.

Vol. 255: Nondifferentiable Optimization: Motivations and Applications. Proceedings, 1984. Edited by V. F. Demyanov and D. Pallaschke. VI, 350 pages. 1985.

Vol. 256: Convexity and Duality in Optimization. Proceedings, 1984. Edited by J. Ponstein. V, 142 pages. 1985.

Vol. 257: Dynamics of Macrosystems. Proceedings, 1984. Edited by J.-P. Aubin, D. Saari and K. Sigmund. VI, 280 pages. 1985.

Vol. 258: H. Funke, Eine allgemeine Theorie der Polypol- und Oligopolpreisbildung. III, 237 pages. 1985.

Vol. 259: Infinite Programming. Proceedings, 1984. Edited by E. J. Anderson and A. B. Philpott. XIV, 244 pages. 1985.

Vol. 260: H.-J. Kruse, Degeneracy Graphs and the Neighbourhood Problem. VIII, 128 pages. 1986.

Vol. 261: Th. R. Gulledge, Jr., N. K. Womer, The Economics of Made-to-Order Production. VI, 134 pages. 1986.

Vol. 262: H. U. Buhl, A Neo-Classical Theory of Distribution and Wealth. V, 146 pages. 1986.

Vol. 263: M. Schäfer, Resource Extraction and Market Structure. XI, 154 pages. 1986.

Vol. 264: Models of Economic Dynamics. Proceedings, 1983. Edited by H. F. Sonnenschein. VII, 212 pages. 1986.

Vol. 265: Dynamic Games and Applications in Economics. Edited by T. Başar. IX, 288 pages. 1986.

Vol. 266: Multi-Stage Production Planning and Inventory Control. Edited by S. Axsäter, Ch. Schneeweiss and E. Silver. V, 264 pages. 1986.